THE EXPANDED REILLY METHOD

ALSO BY MIKE MCCARDELL

Chasing the Story God
Back Alley Reporter
The Blue Flames that Keep Us Warm
Getting to the Bubble

THE
EXPANDED
REILLY METHOD

or

HAVE A GREAT DAY, FOREVER

Mike McCardell

HARBOUR PUBLISHING

1 2 3 4 5 — 13 12 11 10 09

Harbour Publishing Co. Ltd.
P.O. Box 219, Madeira Park, BC, V0N 2H0
www.harbourpublishing.com

THE CANADA COUNCIL | LE CONSEIL DES ARTS
FOR THE ARTS | DU CANADA
SINCE 1957 | DEPUIS 1957

Dust jacket photographs by Nick Didlick
Edited by Ian Whitelaw
Printed on 100% recycled stock using soy-based ink
Printed and bound in Canada

BRITISH
COLUMBIA
ARTS COUNCIL
Supported by the Province of British Columbia

Harbour Publishing acknowledges financial support from the Government of Canada through the Book Publishing Industry Development Program and the Canada Council for the Arts, and from the Province of British Columbia through the BC Arts Council and the Book Publishing Tax Credit.

Sales of this book help support Variety—the Children's Charity.

Library and Archives Canada Cataloguing in Publication

McCardell, Mike, 1944–
The expanded Reilly method / by Mike McCardell.

ISBN 978-1-55017-500-4

I. Title.

PN6231.J68M33 2009   C818'.602   C2009-904720-9

Dear Zoë—

Bless you, bright eyes.
Have a great day, forever.

CONTENTS

REILLY'S RULES

What do you want? I mean, really, what do you want? Health, happiness, success? The ability to hold your bladder when someone else gets to the bathroom before you at Starbucks?

Simple questions. Do you want to get along with your wife or kids? If the last of those wishes include a teenager you need immediate assistance. Check page 42. Living with teenagers is possible. Unbelievable, but possible. You just have to do what one Burnaby teacher did: tell them to save the world.

But before you see how teens can be turned into valuable human citizens, I should tell you I have found "The Secret," even though that title was taken a year or so ago. I have found "The Way," even though religions use that term.

Am I joking? No. I am just an ordinary schmuck kicking a can down the street of life, and yet along the way I have found the cure for depression and colds and flu, even though the drug companies say they have the same thing, but they will charge you big bucks with no guarantee. I guarantee this works. No cost, no DVDs to buy, no pills.

I have found the answer to enjoying an incredible life, no matter who you are or where you are or what you are doing or how much you weigh. It is all through the secret taught to me by a snot-nosed kid. You try it, and you'll say, "Holy mackerel, it works." Yes it works. Yes it is easy. Yes you can have what you want, no matter what, immediately.

And I am not kidding.

It started more than five years ago with a kid I mentioned in my last book. His name was Reilly and he was autistic and he was fishing in Trout Lake. His nose was running and a glob of green mucus kept sliding out of his right nostril while he talked.

It fell down in a sickly, sticky, slimy, slithering nose snake trying to escape but he kept sucking it back up inside his head with powerful nose-vacuuming pulls of air. I wanted to throw up.

All the while he was sniffing and sucking this glob back up he talked about believing that he would catch a fish. Sniff, ugh. He was using a branch as a pole. It still had twigs and leaves growing out of it. Sniff. Ugh, oh I feel sick.

And he had a string tied to the end with a paper clip as a hook.

He talked slowly because he was not good with words, or with his temper or with the ability to do much of anything. Sniff. Oh, God, that is sickening.

But he said he would catch a fish if he tried hard enough. And then the glob slid down again.

I wanted to say, "Hey, kid, blow your nose," but I am not allowed to do that in my profession. I just watch things happen and then report on what I think happened.

Then the glob came out again and I bit my tongue trying to hold my stomach down.

He sucked it back home into his head and again said he believed that whatever you want will happen, if you believe it.

My heart wanted more. The sickly, sweet fluid rising up through my throat said that was enough.

You know some of this already if you read the book *Getting to the Bubble*. I mentioned Reilly. I dedicated the book to him. But what you don't know, because I did not know it then, was that Reilly was right. Reilly had the secret. Reilly had the answers. Reilly had the key to the bathroom. He just did not have a tissue.

Later I started to think about what Reilly said. I know the Bible says you can move a mountain if you believe strongly enough. But I figured that was just Bible talk and you could only do it if you had a John Deere excavator and dynamite, so it didn't really count.

On the other hand, of course you need heavy equipment and big explosives and government permits to move a mountain. But, so what? Religions don't say you are going to do the work of mountain moving just by staring at it, and Reilly did not expect to catch a fish without his rod.

The trick is to get the job done after you have the tools, even if the tools are just in your head. That is where most of us fail. We get the books and pay the tuition, but say university is too hard.

We get a job but say the boss is mean. We get a cold and say I can't go to my class or job today, and I cannot enjoy life because I am not feeling well.

That is dumb. It is like getting into the shower without the soap. The solution to cleaning up in this world is so simple. Get the soap. Tell yourself you feel fine and today is going to be good and by gosh, the dirt goes away and you stop feeling miserable.

Basically, we cop out. We have sometimes been called a society of excuse-makers, quitters and losers. Sorry, fellow or lady, if Reilly can hold that pole while snot is running down his face you can go to school with a little bit of sneezing coming out of your nose.

The amazing thing is this is so simple and so true. You don't need anything else, not a new diet or exercise plan or prayer or meditation course. It is all in a stick and string and a paper clip and the faith that those are all you need to get what you want.

The rules of Reilly are not gentle, but follow them and you will have whatever you want, if you want it. And once again, I am not joking. In this book are stories that will not only make you feel good—they are stories that teach you that you can feel good every day. And you can have whatever you want.

Reilly was saying he would catch a fish and he had the rod and the bent paper clip to do it. He believed he would. That is different in only one way from the construction crew with a diesel-powered digger and a remote-controlled explosion who believe they will move a mountain. The difference is Reilly knew in his heart he would get a fish, while the construction workers had a backup plan in case they did not.

So, you think, what's the big deal about moving a mountain if you have the right equipment?

Then what is the big deal about Reilly, who is not smart enough to read past very simple sentences and has only a stick and string and a paper clip to believe he will catch a fish? The big deal is he has no doubt.

And what is the big deal about not having a sick day in five years, or learning that every encounter will be a good one or that you can hold your bladder? That's me since I met Reilly.

I know you think that last one is impossible. Ha. Just wait. You can have your bladder under control. You can. No kidding. It works.

I know there are countless books on positive thinking. But to me they were like exercise or diet books. You buy them. You think they will change your life. You bring them home and have a beer.

And then you have the weeds to pull out of the garden and the leak to fix under the sink and you have to finish your taxes because you only have two days to go and you can't find the receipts you need and that leak is still leaking and the taxman/woman is still waiting and the weeds are still growing.

I can't handle all this!

And on top of that you have to get along with your teenager, which is impossible and no one on earth knows what you are going through.

You don't have time or space in your head to do all that plus try to make your thoughts be positive.

"Anyone in my situation would be negative, so I am too. Besides, that positive thinking stuff is for wimps who can't face the real world."

I don't know who said that, but many have. They are wrong.

Unlike the self-help books, Reilly was not something I could put down. He believed he would catch a fish and he had never read any of those books.

Just for a joke I wondered if I applied the Reilly method to my desires what would happen.

LESSONS FROM A LEAK

This is really basic.

There is a leak under the kitchen sink, my wife tells me.

It is late at night and my first thought, like many people who are presented with a problem, is; No, there can't be a leak. Don't you know it's late at night? Can't problems start in the morning?

"Is it bad?" I ask. "Can it wait?"

"Well, just take a quick look."

I get on my knees because getting under a kitchen sink is a job for a well-paid plumber or a small child. It may be a small leak, but it has caused a soggy flood of everything that could absorb water, which was basically everything that had cardboard or paper wrapped around it, which was nearly everything under the sink.

A half hour later all the soggy stuff was out and the space under the sink was mopped up enough to try to take a quick look.

I don't need positive thinking at this point, I really need a plumber. But do you know what plumbers cost?

I can see drips coming out right under the downspout from the sink. That should be easy, just tighten the pipe.

I see it by bending down, but how do I get there with a wrench? My body does not bend that way. If I lie on my side I can get the wrench up around the pipe with one hand but my other arm is holding myself up so the edge of the bottom of the cabinet under the sink does not dig into my ribs.

But if I only have one hand I can't tighten the wrench. Okay, plumbers are worth every penny, but I should be able to do this myself. Maybe I can just wrap my hand around the pipe and see if it is loose. I squeeze it.

Crunch. The chrome pipe, which is as old as the house, which is old, collapses under my fingers like an eggshell.

"Darn," I shout very loudly, using a different word.

"I found the leak." I added that to try to turn the disaster into a joke.

"I can't hear you while you're under the sink," said my wife. "But did you find the leak?"

That sort of takes the punch out of the punchline. I try to pull myself out from under the sink with the crunched pipe still in my hand and bang, my head hits the overhang at the top.

"Oww."

"Be careful," she says.

"Could you warn me earlier next time," I say while trying to put my hand back where my head hurts, but the pain is so demanding for attention that I forget that I have the piece of pipe in that same hand.

"Darn," I say again, but worse this time.

"That was dumb," she says.

A master of the obvious, I am thinking.

I show her the pipe.

"Why'd you break it?"

This is where the "for better or worse" part comes in. This is a test, I know, and I am about to fail.

But here is the problem. What do Reilly and positive thinking and belief that things will work out have to do with a crumbled pipe, a banged head and a sink that can't be used and, worse, the full knowledge that I have no idea how to fix it? Plus, it's late and I had been planning to go to bed right before someone mentioned that there was a small leak that somehow we had been living happily unaware of for some time.

I stare at it for a while. In the pre-Reilly days I did a lot of staring when I had a problem. It never worked but at least I felt like I was doing something. I put a sign in the sink saying Don't Use This Sink and I go to bed.

In the morning I walk to the kitchen and out of habit turn on the faucet.

"Darn."

I mop out under the sink again and put a pail under the pipe that isn't there.

So where does positive thinking come into play with the real things in life, like sinks and leaks? Reilly, where are you?

Okay, step one. Reilly's Basic Rule: Believe you will.

I will get the sink fixed. I will. I believe I will. On the other hand, that is stupid to say because I have never successfully fixed anything in my life.

No father in my life and my mother could not fix things, so broken things stayed broken.

"I wish I had a hammer," my mother once said.

"Why?"

"So I could hit this toaster before I throw it out."

I managed to get into trouble as a teen, which is what some teens do, and go through a hitch in the air force and become a reporter and get married and have children without ever being able to fix anything.

I am actually terrified of trying to fix things.

So how is a leaking sink going to teach me anything about Reilly's Rules?

This is a small example, but it is the way life works—endless small things that often get the better of us because we let them control us instead of believing we can do the same to them, and ourselves, and fix the problem on top of that.

I will fix the sink. I believe I can fix the sink.

That was easy, but useless. It is still broken. But I said again, I believe I can fix this and I will fix it and it will work. I just don't know how. Now, say it again and again until I believe it, even if I don't know how.

The truth is, it is not too hard to fool yourself. Keep saying you believe something and you will believe it. Those who write propaganda know that. Advertisers know that.

On the truly negative side, those suffering anorexia know that. They see one thing in the mirror, but believe, truly believe, the opposite.

Hitler believed it. So be careful of what you believe you want to do. You have to believe in good things because if you believe in hurting others, someone else will believe more in stopping you. And they will believe it more strongly than you. That is what has always happened.

So very simply, believe in things that will make the world a better place, and you a better person. You will get what you want without someone else trying to save the world from you and put you behind bars.

That is heavy duty stuff. On the positive side I believe I will get the sink fixed. I don't know how, but I will.

One thing was different when I said that. In the old days I would have said, "I have no idea what I am doing," and I would worry about it and I would try to figure out how I could afford a plumber and would have had a bad day even before I went to the bathroom sink to fill the kettle, which did not fit under the bathroom faucet. This is not going to be a good day.

This time I said, "Fixing the pipe is a mystery, but it will be fixed and I will do it." And I used a cup to fill the kettle in the bathroom sink, which I laughed at. Actually, I laughed more at the thought that I wasn't annoyed. That was one step.

Another thing for sure, I wasn't worried. Just believing made me feel good. I knew that sink would be fixed, so I could go out and find a story for the news that night and then visit a hardware store on the way home and fix the leak tonight.

I can't impress enough, on you or me, the truth that I wasn't worried about it. That was amazing. I had worried my way through a lifetime of projects until quitting and begging or hiring someone to help, which meant doing it for me.

After work I brought the broken pieces to a hardware store. Most people who work in those places love looking at crushed pipes. They are the doctors of ailing sinks and lighting fixtures.

A friendly fellow who has learned English as a second language showed me the pipes to buy, showed me how to put them together and I went home a happy bird. I did what he said, and it still leaked.

Another darn. But I will fix the pipe. I will. The next evening I was back under the sink with the edge digging into my ribs and a flashlight shining up, but not pointing at the big nut I have to tighten.

I struggle. I think positive thoughts. It still leaks.

I crawl out from underneath and my wife asks, "Can I use it now?"

"Not tonight. Maybe tomorrow."

What does this have to do with Reilly? Is it a fraud? Is this positive belief thing all wrong? I believe I will fix the leak and it is still leaking.

The next day when someone asks "How are you?" I tell them how bad off I am. A few guys I work with ask if I used plumber's putty.

No. But now I remember the ESL man telling me to do that and me not understanding, but nodding.

Under the sink again. Edge of cabinet cutting into my ribs. I will do this. I will. And it will work.

Take it all apart, put on the putty, put it all together. Crawl out from under. Turn on the faucet. Crawl back under to watch. No leak. Remember not to jump up and bang my head.

I did it. I can't believe I did it.

Of course you could have done it the first time. Of course you don't need Reilly to help you fix a leak. Of course. But on the other hand, I did and I believed I could do it. I secretly knew I could not do it, but my belief and plumber's putty stopped the leak.

⋘●⋙

This is too ridiculously small an example for you to take seriously, right? You want the big ticket solutions.

Try this yourself, just for a test. You have a problem, anything, but pick something that you can see the results of in less than a day, because we all want instant gratification. Try some small-time problem.

Your garden is a mess, your homework isn't done, your mother, father, son, daughter, wife, husband doesn't understand you, and on top of that, before the test tomorrow you need to understand the theory of relativity.

Easy. And I am serious. Right now say you will get this done, whatever it is, you will learn this, you will solve that, and believe you will. You know you will and there is no way you won't do it. And you will do it now, and you will be successful.

"I believe I will catch a fish."

You have no idea how to do it, but you believe you will. If Reilly can believe in what most of us would think is impossible, you can certainly believe in something as easy as getting along with someone in your family.

Impossible? We don't know that member of your family? That one is impossible to get along with?

Not impossible. Not if you believe you can.

You don't even have to tell them you believe you will get along with them, you just have to believe you will. Of course you could make yourself clear to those who don't understand you and do it in a way you would like to be spoken to yourself; that would help.

But you might wind up arguing again.

Easier to just believe you will get along. Don't doubt. Don't snicker. Believe it. Say you will not be upset with those who are upsetting you. Say you will smile, no matter what. Say you will be happy, and believe it.

Don't worry about all the classes on family relations and the books and the theories that you have paid for and forgotten about. Just believe you will get along.

Try it. Check back with me at the end of the day. You are not going to

17

change them. No one changes someone else. But you are going to change the way you see them.

On the matter of that garden you haven't had any time to work on. Try the same thing. To some people a messy garden is as big a problem as a messy family, and as unsolvable.

I believe I will pull up those weeds. I will have them out before lunch, or dark, or whenever. I am in charge of that plot of ground and I will do it.

"I believe I will get whatever I want, if I want it."

It is irrelevant how hard you will have to work. It doesn't matter how impossible that yard is to clean up. You believe you can do it.

You will probably miss lunch, but check back later. Start with some weeds, the weeds you have been meaning to get to for weeks, or months, or years and you have been promising yourself you will do but you can't get to them because there are so many other problems.

Reilly says just believe you will get it cleaned up.

"My goodness, it's all clean." Of course you have aching arms. This is the magic of reality, not hocus pocus make-believe. The weeds are gone.

But really, weeding is such a simple thing, you are thinking. You want the big problems in life taken care of. That is coming. First give your small problems a test.

Homework? The same thing. You will do it. You believe you will get it done. And when you believe that it will be done, you are basically half done even before your start. Homework on a brain that doesn't fight against it is a lot easier than a brain that is groaning and worried. Try it—but you got to believe it. Then check back.

And that old theory of relativity, that is the easiest. Getting along with the relatives who don't understand you, or doing your homework or pulling weeds is all a matter of everything being different when you look at it in a different way—which is the theory of relativity.

Everything in the universe relates to everything else depending on how everything else relates to it. That means you are the centre of your own universe. You don't have to be Einstein to understand that when you pull up a weed it comes out and if you don't pull it up it doesn't come out.

You don't have to be Einstein to realize that when you get along with others in your family, life is a lot better. Shouting causes headaches. Getting along helps digestion. And you can get along if you believe it, even if they don't get along with you.

You think that's too simple to bother trying or too obvious to think about? Relatively speaking, it's the biggest thing in the world. You believe you will get your homework done and get along with your brother/sister and will weed the garden. You believe it and it will be done.

Little Reilly, the Einstein of Trout Lake.

COME ON, DOES IT REALLY WORK?

What I did have a wish for, a desire for, a longing for, was to find a story, something interesting and odd with maybe a touch of humour or a tear. I wanted that because that is my profession and also because the stories make me feel good.

The tough part is I want to find such a story every day. And the story has to be good enough to share with almost half a million people. And it has to be good enough for those people to talk about it after it's over and say to someone in the room "That was a cool kid" or "She was a sweet lady to do all that for someone else."

There are also the other problems of a travel budget that keeps me generally within a kilometre of Main Street, and a time restriction of a few hours. Six fifty-five p.m. comes at the same time every day no matter how much I plead with the digital numbers on my cellphone, which was now vibrating because the office was calling saying they needed the cameraman I was working with to cover yet another shooting.

"But I want to bring you good news," I said on the phone.

"Well, get your good news quick because bad news is breaking out all over."

I didn't have a fishing pole with a piece of bread for bait. I had a tight stomach and a street in front of me that was empty and a cameraman alongside me who knew the longer we took to find something, the faster he would have to work to catch up to the other photographers who were already on their way to where bullets had been flying, and that is certainly more exciting to a hard-nosed news picture taker than looking at the old man over there in the community garden who looks like Santa Claus.

"We could try him," I said.

"You try him," said the cameraman. "I've got to put the flack jacket over the camera for the real news."

He did not really say that, but he might have been thinking it.

I walked into the garden and thought, "Reilly, do your magic."

Then I did the magic that Reilly taught me. "This will work. I don't know how, but I know it will."

I was worried that just another gardening story really would not work. It would be a story about a man with a white beard showing us that he was hoeing in mid-March, which would not be strong enough to survive any strength test of TV news.

But think of Reilly. It will be good, I hear myself saying. It will be good. It will be incredible, amazing. It will be so good even I will not believe it is happening but it will be happening right in front of me. And it will be happening right here, right now, so the cameraman can go off and take pictures of someone who thought life as a drug dealer was exciting before he became the bull's-eye of another exciting drug dealer.

I had been looking for stories for more than forty years. I had been hoping I would find them. Often I did, but sometimes the clock would say six and the show was going on and no matter how much I wished I could find something interesting I found nothing. Those were terrible days. Enter Reilly.

Reilly believed he would catch a fish. He did not say he was wishing or expecting or hoping or praying he would catch a fish. He said he believed he would catch a fish.

So, because of Reilly, I believe this guy with a white beard will have something wonderful to tell me. I believe it. I am tempted to say I don't really believe it and will only pretend I believe it, but I know that will not work. So, I believe it.

"Hello, hate to bother you, but how's your garden?"

"Fine, great," he says. "I have some radishes already up."

"Wonderful," I say. "Terrible," I think.

Radishes? In mid-March. I could say, "It is amazing that radishes are growing in mid-March," except I can hear thousands of viewing gardeners saying, "So, big deal. You could grow radishes in the dirt in your socks." Radishes are very exciting, for a five-year-old.

The cameraman is taking pictures of the radishes. I am dying.

"I didn't see a car outside the garden," I say. "Do you live nearby?"

"No, I live by Granville Street. I walked here."

Oh, Reilly. Thank you.

"Do you do much walking?"

He smiled. His name was Stephen Heiley, and he had me in the palm of his hand and he knew it. He was the guy with the royal flush in a poker game. He could not lose.

"He wants to know if I do much walking? Ha." That's what he was thinking. I know that because he said: "Sunday I walked for eight hours. Monday and Tuesday and Wednesday I walked 130 kilometres."

Thank you.

"I walked from Chinatown to UBC to Clark Drive and then here. That was Monday."

"Here" was Strathcona Gardens, a short drive from Clark Drive.

Thank you.

I whispered to the cameraman that we had a walking machine and the story was not about his radishes but about him walking, obviously.

"So what do I do with the pictures of his radishes?" he asked.

"Save them for dinner. But please take pictures of his feet."

Luckily cameramen are forgiving. He started filming the feet of the gardener who was hoeing his radishes.

This was good enough. A marathon radish grower. Not one person in the province could relate to that, but still, a long-distance gardener is amazing.

Then I remembered the number one question that has saved me through ten thousand interviews. The question that everyone should ask when the topic does not make sense: "Why?"

"Why do you walk so much?"

"Because the doctors told me I would never walk again, or at least not walk without pain and a limp, unless I had reconstructive surgery."

Is this really happening? Is Reilly right? From Santa Claus with radishes I now have in front of me a man who got his legs back through walking. How did this happen? I stopped. I asked. I believed. It worked.

An accident had shredded Stephen's Achilles tendon. "It was hanging by a thread. The doctors said I needed an operation or it would never heal."

"What did you say to them?" I asked.

"I said, 'No, I could fix it myself.'"

"Why?"

"Because I believe in doing things for myself."

He said even though it hurt he started walking, which was really limping on a cane. He walked and rested and walked and rested and walked, then walked some more. Time passed. He was walking everywhere. He sold his car. He kept walking.

"Watch this," he said.

Then, on a bare spot on his garden plot next to his radishes, he jogged in place.

"Not bad for someone who's sixty-four and wasn't supposed to walk," he said.

Not bad for someone—me—who saw someone with a white beard leaning over his radishes.

Stephen told me that he believed he would get better because of his father. His father had a broken back when Stephen was a kid. His father was told he would never walk.

"He got up and walked," said Stephen.

His grandmother had taught Stephen to plant seeds and care for his garden. "Work on it, and have faith," she told him, "And everything will grow."

Call it whatever you want—faith, believing, whatever. There is no secret to this. Stephen said he knew he would walk and he knew his radishes would grow. So, his radishes were sprouting and he was walking. Life can be just as simple and predictable as that.

I am not saying that you can cure anything with belief. I am not saying that if your spinal cord is broken you can believe yourself into getting up. But I am saying that Rick Hansen believed he could go anywhere with a severed spinal cord, and he did.

I am not saying don't go to your doctor. But I am saying believe you will get better and your odds improve. I am not saying that cancer can be cured with belief. But I have heard many stories, including the famous one of a guy named Norman Cousins who was told he had terminal cancer.

He got a hotel room and rented every funny movie he could find. He got Laurel and Hardy and the Marx Brothers and modern funny movies and began watching them in his room. He laughed and howled and giggled and his cancer went into remission. He lived many years and wrote books about his cure. It was all in the attitude, he said.

What was as important as finding the story about Stephen and his radishes was sharing the reality that one man who was told something would never happen changed that. That was the miracle of belief in himself and what he could do.

Finding that story and putting it on TV may have given the idea to someone else who was watching that they could believe in themselves. Not bad for a few minutes in a community garden.

Was it just luck? I believed I would find a story and the long-distance gardener appeared. So strange. But in the more than five years since I met Reilly I have not missed one day of finding a story. That is more than one thousand consecutive days of looking for something uplifting and hopefully funny and finding it.

One thousand days without missing, because of the belief that I will find something. I no longer hope I will find something. I no longer wish for something. I no longer pray and twist my fingers in anguish and say "I've got to find something, got to, or I will fail and the show will end with just 'Good night.'"

I no longer do that hoping and wishing because I believe I will find something. And to my total surprise, I do.

And suddenly there is Stephen who walks to his garden, plants his radishes and believes they will come up. He does not hope for it or wish for it, he believes it.

And you say, of course radishes grow. They are a fail-safe crop. Growing radishes is not like making yourself walk.

But radishes will not grow if you do not put the seeds in the ground. And they will not grow, or at least you will not find them again, if you let weeds choke them. And they will not grow unless they get some water and unless they are in a spot where the sun warms and feeds them.

If you do all that, you have the right to say radishes are foolproof.

If you force yourself to walk after the doctor says you can't, you have the right to say your belief works.

Radishes also have a lot of vitamin C, which helps ligaments. Who knows?

One thing for sure, Stephen walked to his garden and his story was an inspiration to others.

One other thing: Reilly was right.

IF IT WORKS FOR ONE THING, MAYBE . . . ???

Then I expanded Reilly's method. I had many good days before I met him and some bad days. You have bad days. Days when the traffic lights turn against you and your boss gets mad and your coffee is cold and you lose that five dollars you know you had in your pocket and now it is gone and you get a notice from the tax department that you owe more money. Kill me right now.

I decided that I would have a good day, no matter what. I woke up one morning and said, "This will be the best day of my life." I believed it. If Reilly can believe he will catch a fish I can believe I will have a good day, and my odds are higher because I don't really know if there are any fish in Trout Lake.

Then the traffic light turned red just when I was ready to go.

But I believe this will be a good day. It turned green.

Okay, that always happens. All traffic lights turn green, you just have to wait. But I did not get upset at the red light, not even slightly, not even for an instant. That was different than the way I was in the past and that was a good feeling.

Then someone I love got mad at me for something I did that I didn't mean to do. I waited and said nothing because I was having a good day. She cooled down and the day was fine. There was no argument. How did that happen?

In time almost everyone cools down. But while waiting for that, I did not get upset. How can you argue with that? This was turning out to be a good day, just like I believed it would be.

My coffee got cold. Darn. It hit my lips and it was chilly. Cold coffee can ruin a good moment.

I warmed it up. The moment returned.

The five dollars was not there. I know I had it when I started out but now I don't.

I swallowed hard and thought of the time, a long time ago, when I found ten dollars. That was just once in my life, but things like that you don't forget. And when you remember them they make you feel better.

The tax people sent me a bad letter.

I will have a good day. I will.

If I divide the amount I owe them over a year, it's only ten dollars a week. I still hate the tax people. You don't have to love everyone to have a good day, but I can come up with ten dollars a week, and take it as an expensive lesson to be more careful in my calculating next time.

In five years I have not had a bad day.

Now here is a big test. I expanded Reilly's method to my health.

I still get colds. I still have a headache on New Year's morning because I am not mature enough to foresee effects in the immediate future. And I still hit my finger with a hammer because I am too dumb to pull it away.

"I will not feel bad despite this cold. I do not feel bad. I will not. I feel fine. I believe I feel good."

I don't feel so bad.

"My head does not hurt. Of course my head hurts. I have wine poisoning. I do not have a headache. I do not."

Coffee helps.

"I feel fine. I do. Honest to God, I do."

More coffee.

"I am feeling better."

My gosh. I don't feel so bad. The sun is shining, or the rain is falling, and I feel much better and it is still morning. Is this possible? Can you convince yourself you feel better?

"I do feel good, much better, even fine," I say out loud, because I am slightly shocked that I feel good. In the past I did not feel better after waking with a cold or, on New Year's morning, after waking with leftover stupidity until most of the day had been wasted. And then, after numerous little white extra strength pills I slowly became me again.

But then came Reilly, and I have not bought any Tylenol in the past five years. I have not missed a day of work. Of course I feel achy. Of course some days have started out with a pain. But by mid-morning, with a little coffee, I feel fine, because I believe I will. Is it the coffee or the faith? My answer is, "Don't mess with success, no matter where it comes from."

Does it work without coffee? I tried.

Yes. But I like the taste of coffee.

This may sound like preaching, but it is true. It is good to feel good. And I feel good because one autistic nine-year-old told me I would get what I believed I would get. And what I want to get is a good feeling.

My mouth was dry last night and the night before. My throat was sore this morning. I am getting a cold.

I do not feel so well. My head has an ache and thoughts are not clear, and I have had no wine. This is the classic cold, or flu, or virus. I am not sure which. But I am sure that my nose is stuffed up and when I blow it it sounds like a tug in Burrard Inlet in the fog.

"I will feel better."

This is insane. I have a cold.

"I will feel better."

Reilly says you get what you believe.

On the other hand I am crazy as a lunatic, which is politically incorrect to say. But I am crazy anyway because I have a cold and you cannot get rid of a cold by believing it will go away. Try anyway.

"I will feel better."

Stop. Blow my nose. Ugh. That is a lot of stuff that came out of my nose. Of course it is, I have a cold.

"I will feel better."

I feel rotten. Maybe I am doing this wrong. I do feel better. Right now I feel better. Right this second I feel better. I do, I do.

You are a nutcase.

NO! I feel better. I feel much better. I do not have a cold.

Sniff.

Okay, I have a cold, but it is not going to get me down. I am better than my cold, which I do not have. I feel fine. I feel good.

I am trying to read the newspaper. My gosh, I do feel better. The print that I could not focus on a half-hour ago I can now read and the letters make sense, sort of. What doesn't make sense is the news I am reading that says everything is bad and getting worse.

But not me. I am getting better.

When did that happen? And did it really happen?

All I can tell myself is I feel good. I don't feel better, I feel good.

Is this the power of mind over colds? Is this all it takes?

"I feel good." And I do feel good. And I cannot believe it. My head is clear. My nose is still running, but I do not care. I feel fine.

This has happened countless times since I met Reilly. I realize I cannot stop germs and bacteria and viruses from slipping into my body and ugly stuff coming out of my nose. I cannot change the world. I have no effect on reality. But I can change myself, if I believe it, and I believe it after I tell myself I do.

My head is clear, my aches are gone, my tissue is still wet from blowing my nose. I still have a cold, but it is not bothering me. I go to work and in an hour I forget about my sniffles.

My nose is no longer running and I feel fine. How the heck did that happen? But it did.

The short prescription: Decide you will feel good. It even works if you lie to yourself because eventually, as all advertisers know, you will believe it. So tell yourself you will feel good, and have a good day.

Compare that to telling yourself today will be bad and you are afraid and nothing good will happen.

Which do you think has more of a chance of happening?

I know you may be saying your life is miserable and no one understands how bad it is. But so many people I have met have truly had miserable lives and no one did understand them. But then they decided that simply thinking better thoughts would make things better.

In every case it worked. You will meet those people in the following pages.

Try it, take one capsule of belief that you will feel better. No, actually overdose on it (you can't take too many beliefs), and call me in the morning if it didn't work.

I don't expect the phone to ring.

BUT THIS IS STUPID

She sneezed. Then she blew her nose. Then blew again.

"Better wipe everything down with alcohol," said Jacquie, an editor at the TV station.

"I don't get sick," I said.

"Well, don't breathe around me and you can stay healthy."

She sneezed again.

I was tempted to tell her my secret, but I couldn't. It sounds so stupid: Just believe you will be okay and you will be.

She sneezed again.

"I have to tell you. You are going to think this is stupid, but just say you will get better."

She looked at me suspiciously, like I was someone who has just found religion and wants everyone else to experience the wonders of it.

She moved away, which is not easy in a tiny edit room.

"Honest. Just try it."

And at the moment of saying it I felt like someone who has just found religion and wants everyone to experience the wonders of it.

She looked at me again and said, "What pictures would you like next?"

Then she sneezed.

"Oh, God, I feel awful," she said between sniffs.

"I'm just trying to help you with your cold."

"You want me to put my hand on the radio and say, 'I feel BETTER. I FEEL GOOD?!'"

She is a funny woman, even when she feels like she is dying.

Sneeze.

"Just say it."

"I feel better. I feel good." Sneeze. "I feel wonderful. And I want my Nyquil."

Here is the ridiculousness of what I am saying. It does sound stupid. It does sound like the TV evangelists and the old travelling medicine men.

"Take this medicine and you WILL be cured."

"Send ten dollars to our cause and your sins WILL be erased."

"Put your hand on the radio and FEEL the power. Plus send money."

The weird part is, they all worked. And they did so because those who were listening believed it, and when they believed they had the cure.

But as soon as the medicine wagon was gone or the radio was off the sniffles came back.

All Reilly said was you get what you believe. All I did was believe my colds would go away quicker than a night of sleep, and it worked, even without a preacher or advertisement and without sending money.

"Okay, I feel better," said Jacquie. "I feel much better."

"Let's get back to work," I said sensing a touch of doubt in her eyes rolling over the ceiling.

"I do feel better," she said.

I looked at the monitor with the pictures from that day's work.

"Honest, I feel better," she said.

"Do you like the wide shot or the medium one?" I asked.

"I feel better," she said.

"Wide or medium?"

"Medium. I feel better."

"Cut it out," I said. No, I begged. "Please stop."

"But I think I feel better."

"Oh, stop it," I said. "I know what I'm telling you sounds stupid so I won't ask you to say it again."

"But I really feel better."

"You can't! It doesn't work that quick."

"But I do feel better."

"That's impossible and please stop rubbing it in."

"I'm not joking. I feel better."

I picked up the microphone, which is attached to a long cable, and swung it back and forth in front of her face like a watch on a chain.

"Watch the swinging mike. You are cured." We both laughed.

Then she sneezed and used the last tissue in the box.

"Are you kidding me?" I asked. "You cannot feel better in three minutes. You only feel better because you don't have any more tissues."

"Do you want the medium shot or the tight one over here?" she asked.

We both laughed again. Then we finished the story.

She didn't sneeze again.

Three days later I saw her again.

"How's your cold?"

I expected a sneeze.

"Fine, I'm all better. But in truth, it's thanks to Nyquil."

She looked sheepish.

At that moment I knew this could not be taught. You cannot just get someone to say the magic words and expect them to work. There is one ingredient missing.

"You get what you believe you will get," said Reilly.

You can believe in Nyquil. That is what many medicines count on. It's just that Reilly's method is cheaper.

And it works even if you don't have a spoon to measure out the doses. And Jacquie's cold was gone. Something had worked.

And a month later something happened that had not happened in five years. I woke up with my nose clogged like an unattended drain tile under a very old house. Water was oozing out, but no air was getting in. My throat was so hot and burning it could have been used for grilling a steak. It would have come out well done, but then I could not have swallowed it.

I was sick. Me. Sick. Impossible. I believe in positive wellness. I believe you will not be sick if you believe you will not be sick.

Then I tried to blow my nose and open my eyes. The nose became a hydrant. I was turning a box of tissues into a soggy mess. My eyes were tight. My throat was painful.

I cannot be sick. I will not be sick. I went to work.

I was sick.

I was trying to write in my little corner of the newsroom when Sandra, the accountant for all money matters in covering local news, passed by.

"You look terrible," she said.

"I feel fine."

"No you don't. Take one of these," she said.

It was a cold pill. I could not tell the brand. My eyes were too wet and blurry.

"I can't," I said. "I believe in positive thinking."

"And I believe in not suffering," she said.

I was weak. I took the pill.

In half an hour I was bright and pain free and dry and happy. Not bad for one little pill.

Thank you, Sandra, for the pill, and for teaching me that you can take anything, even good things, to an extreme. The next time I get a cold, hopefully in five years, I will believe I will get better, I will get to bed early, I will drink plenty of water, and I will take a pill. Darn it, I will be positive, but I am not going to be dumb.

HERE'S SOMETHING AMAZING

I have not had a disagreement with my wife in five years. And that is because I have not wanted to. We have had many wonderful times together, because we have had no disagreements. Also, in truth, she has had some disagreements with me, but I have not had any with her. I believe I won't, and I don't.

And if I don't, we don't.

This would seem like a simple truth to anyone who gives it even a passing thought. But before Reilly I never did. One harsh word leads to another and then, well you know, all reasons for loving have been replaced by all plans for never talking again and sulking on top of that.

But if you say you will get along you will, you really, honest to heaven will. Not you will try, not you will give it your best shot once again, or you will be quiet no matter what, but you will get along. That is positive. You will be friendly. That is positive. You will catch a smile and smile back.

There is no room for trying in there. Reilly is not trying to catch a fish. Reilly believes he will catch a fish. You will get along. Believe it.

Check it out. Call me in a week.

THE BIGGEST TEST,
THIS IS THE ACID TEST,
THE ONE YOU WON'T BELIEVE

And most pressing of all, if you have problems with your bladder you know how utterly unbearable and screamingly urgent that organ can be. If you don't have this problem you are young and lucky. But you will grow older so pay attention.

I know this is a private matter but if you are going to find a new way of living then thinking positively should take care of all the basic problems. Five years ago I would almost die trying to get to a bathroom. There was pain combined with the problem of imminent humiliation. There was gripping with clenched fingers, which can be embarrassing, and praying. "Please, God, help me to hold my pee and I will do anything for you."

I am not alone in knowing every bathroom in the city. Many of you plot out your day by the bathrooms along the way. Because I have used them so many times I have done stories on some of Vancouver's most famous toilets. The underground one at Main and Hastings is immaculately clean and drug free. It is safe and in the winter, warm. It has very attentive custodians.

The same with the one at Victory Square.

But if you are not near a bathroom it gets worse. You bite though your tongue. You wear black pants, all summer. You eventually consider the adult diaper and as much as the advertising says it takes the worry out of life, it also puts the humility into it.

And it gets even worse, but enough. If you suffer you know. The doctor says maybe pills, maybe an operation.

Or Reilly. You can have whatever you want, if you want it and if you believe it.

I have to go.

I will not go, I will not go, I will not go.

I have to.

I do not, I do not, I do not.

Yes you do.

I have no pain. I have no pain. I have no pain.

I think it's going away. Nope, coming back.

I have no discomfort. None. Nada. Nothing. I don't. I don't, I don't, I don't.

I can think the pressurized liquid back up to wherever it came from. Up. Up higher. Higher.

My gosh. Twenty years of pain and embarrassment and leaving the lunch table and the dinner table in the middle of a meal and suddenly, my gosh, with a kid with a fishing pole on my mind I don't have to go.

I know it is simply mind over matter, and the matter has a lot of pressure behind it, but it works. No drugs, no operation. It works.

The hard part is you have to believe it works, but when you do, it does. All this learned from a kid with a twig-covered fishing rod, who had a lot of other problems, but not this one.

Thanks again, Reilly.

But to be honest, as soon as you see a bathroom it is impossible to keep the faith for more than a minute longer. The sight of an available toilet is stronger than any belief that you don't need it. But at least it got you there.

WHAT'S BEHIND THE BLADDER, AND HOW YOU CAN MAKE IT WORK FOR YOU

I had to go. You know the feeling. Without getting too graphic it is right at the edge and you have only one centimetre of safety between you and something you don't even want to think about. You can't hold it and there is no place to go.

I was sitting in a parking lot in Mission waiting for the cameraman, Mike Timbrell, who has survived Siberia with me. If you have read the earlier books you know about him—young, energetic and swearing he will never eat hard-boiled eggs again, which we lived on in Russia, or drink vodka, which he almost died from in Russia.

Now I am waiting in Mission because a replacement for the camera co-ordinator told me Mike would be working in Mission and if I wanted a camera I should go there.

I have to go to the bathroom. I am in a public parking lot. My needs have nothing to do with reality. The woman driver of a school bus is sitting on the other side of the lot texting on her phone.

I bite my tongue.

Time passes. I have driven around Mission and cannot find anything to take pictures of. I think if I had a cameraman with me I might find something and that cameraman is somewhere in Mission doing a story. But as soon as he finishes we can get right into action.

My phone rings. Mike tells me he is in Maple Ridge and is finished with his early morning assignment in Ruskin.

"Maple Ridge? I thought you were in Mission."

"No, Maple Ridge. I needed to get something for my cough, which is killing me."

Maybe there is a bathroom near to where he got his medicine.

I start driving to Maple Ridge and call the substitute camera coordinator who sent me to Mission.

"He is in Maple Ridge, because you sent him to Ruskin and Maple Ridge is closer to Ruskin than Mission and much closer to Vancouver."

"Really? I should get a map."

He is young. He will learn. And then I will kill him.

In Maple Ridge I meet Mike.

He is drinking from a medicine bottle.

"Buckley's. It taste terrible," he gags.

I did not add, "but it works" because he coughed again, and again.

"You look terrible," I say.

"I feel worse and this tastes even worse than I feel."

But I am happy he is working because without him there is no one to take pictures no matter where I am.

What does this line by line typical daily account have to do with Reilly and getting what you want?

Everything.

We will find an interesting story and I will find a bathroom before it is too late. I believe that.

"Coffee?" he asks.

He has also bought me a coffee. That is a good friend, dying with a cold and getting me something warm, but this is not going to help my bladder.

"We'd better get going, it's getting late," he says.

"Let's go to Golden Ears Park, there might be something up there."

I get in because I am telling myself "I do not have to go to the bathroom. I do not. We will find a story. We will."

I am in pain, and putting more pressure on that is the fact that we can see nothing interesting in front of us.

We drive to Golden Ears campground, a long bumpy road, and Mike says we will find something there. I am hoping we find a bathroom. We cannot stop along the way because there is other traffic on the road.

"I don't have to go."

Repeat the words: "I believe I don't have to go."

There are a few tents, just enough so that I cannot get out and relieve myself behind a tree. You do not want to be seen doing that and then try to interview someone. Credibility is hard to recoup after being seen standing behind a tree peeing.

We see a woman cleaning up the empty camp sites.

"Anything new?" I ask.

"Toilets clogged," she says. "But that's nothing new."

We drive around again. Nothing new. Everything old. It looks like it looked when I first came to Canada and camped here: beautiful, natural, rustic, and the campground cleared enough so that there is not quite enough privacy anywhere to answer nature's call.

"Let's go back to Maple Ridge, maybe we will find something there," he says.

The long bumpy road again. I would like to say stop, but there are cars coming the other way. Why are there cars coming into a park on a Monday afternoon when I have to go to the bathroom?

"I do not have to go. We will find something interesting. I don't. We will."

We get back to town and there is construction up ahead.

"I do not have to go. I do not." I am quietly shouting this to myself. A woman holds a stop sign in front of us.

"I am going to die. I will not die."

We detour down a back alley off 220th Street.

"Use the lucky rocks," says Mike.

He keeps rocks for me in his glove box. They have worked in the past. All you have to do is believe.

I dig them out and roll them in my hands.

"Stop," I say.

Almost immediately in the back alley that we have been detoured into by the construction is a man with a backyard filled with lawn mowers. He is fixing one of them. What more could I ask for?

"The rocks worked!"

Mike makes a U-turn and I jump out and walk to the man and his mowers. There is no fence or gate or wall. His backyard is open to the lane.

I am polite and meek, as always. I stop twenty steps away from him.

"Excuse me, I hate to bother you, we are from Global TV and I was wondering if . . ."

He picks up a large pair of scissors, opens them slightly and walks toward me. This does not look good.

"I don't mean to intrude . . ."

He walks right past me. I think that maybe he is deaf, but then I am wondering why he does not see me. He takes five more steps and stops in the back lane then turns to me. I follow him.

"What do you want?" he says.

"I thought you didn't see me," I said.

"You were on my property. Now you are off it. Now we can talk."

"I didn't know I was on your property, I apologize."

"What do you want?"

This is not a good way to start a warm and fuzzy relationship. "Nothing, but have a good day," I say.

Mike is by his truck getting his camera out.

"What happened?"

"The rocks did not work."

Then I remember a fellow on Dewdney Trunk Road who has old cars in his front yard and we did a story about him a few years ago. Maybe we could try him again.

"No. You can't repeat that story," says Mike.

"Maybe there is something new."

But what I am thinking is, "I don't have to go. I don't have to go, at least not to the bathroom. I don't."

We drove to the house of the old cars. The fellow's wife was there and told us he wasn't home.

Darn, I thought.

"But he bought me a new car yesterday because he didn't think my old car could pass AirCare."

That's nice, I thought.

But you know what I am really thinking. "I don't have a pressing need. I am fine. I DON'T have to go."

"My new car is a '31 Studebaker."

"What!? Really?"

She nods.

"What's your old car?"

"A '41 Ford. He bought that for me ten years ago for Mother's Day after I had gone two years with my cancer in remission."

"What!? Really?"

She nods. "That was my 'thanks for not dying' present."

"He is a sweetheart."

And so are you, I think.

She said that her old Ford was her one and only car so she could not get collector plates on it and it had to go through AirCare. With collector licence plates you are exempt, but you cannot get them for your main car.

And just the day before we stepped into her yard, her husband bought her a gift, an antique Studebaker with spoke wheels.

"A car with those does not have to be tested," she said.

She had named her old Ford "Bunny," which was her name as a child. Her real name is Beatrice. She did not know what to name her new old car.

I suggested "My Sweet Hubby."

I asked how her health was now and she said she was determined to live to one hundred, just so she could drive her new old car. She said she believed she would do that. She was positive, optimistic and funny. She had a smile that did not fade.

Suddenly it was not her cars that were wonderful but her. She made me feel good. She could make anyone feel good. She spread sunshine. She was happy. That attitude was probably not the only thing that helped her with her cancer, but it did not hurt.

"What do you think of your husband?" I asked.

"I could have done worse." She laughed.

We left and I could not have been more full of story contentment and plain old joy. We had met a woman with heart and soul and two old cars.

I got back to the TV station, walked in the back door that we all use, and thought, "Oh, golly. I am going to die. I have ten steps to go. If I squeeze my teeth tightly enough and run I can make it to the bathroom."

I made it.

What does that all prove? I have taken you through a tedious account of a daily adventure ending in the bathroom. What does it have to do with getting what you want and positive thinking and being who you want to be?

EVERYTHING!

It wasn't until I was washing my hands in the men's room that I realized that mind over matter truly works. And getting what you believe you will get is true. And being the kind of person you want to be is equally true.

How?

When I forgot about me, my problems ceased. I forgot about me when I met Beatrice. She took over my mind.

Hypnotists know this. When they get your mind focused on something that is not you they can make you do anything. You can be concentrating so strongly on the swinging keys in front of your face that you do not know where you are, and when you are scratching like a monkey because you have been told to do that and everyone is laughing at you, you have no idea that is happening.

Some mystical oriental doctors do the same thing. I have seen the documentaries on the government station so they must be true. The doctors can get your mind so totally connected to something outside of yourself that they can operate on you without anaesthetic and you feel no pain.

Can you do this to yourself? Of course.

"I feel no pain. I have no need to go."

And then something came into and took over my life for a few minutes.

With the hypnotists it is the keys. With me it was finding someone fascinating, someone happy—Beatrice.

She took me away from my problems.

I was without pain for the three-quarters of an hour we were with her and her cars and for the three-quarters of an hour drive back while I was thinking about how to write the story so that the new old car comes as a surprise near the end of the story.

No pain. I was concentrating on something else.

If it worked once, it will work again.

The next time the pain came I said "I do not have to go. I believe I do not have to go. And I know it is possible to overcome this because I have done it."

I do not have the need. The mountain was moved.

Your bladder does not have to run your life.

And I apologize for talking so much about a private matter. But if you suffer, it can be done without pills or scalpel. You've just got to believe.

HOW TO FIX YOUR TEENAGER

Pull your teen down from whatever planet he or she is circling, tell them to leave their cellphone and iPod behind and lock yourselves in a room.

"We will stay here until we have found the secret to getting along," you say.

Your teen will be thinking of the text messages being missed.

"We will stay until we both promise to believe that life can be better and we can get along without wanting to murder each other."

Your teen will want to know where the music is that is not going into his or her plugged-in ears. Your teen will want to die.

"There is a way to enjoy being part of a family," you say. "And I will tell you how."

Your teen will be in desperation mode. Two minutes have passed without a text. Your teen will ignore you. Your teen will want to murder you. You will want to murder your teen.

Your teen is thinking, "This is longer than humanly possible to go without twittering to someone else to tell them what a hard life is being had at this moment."

"We will start now," you say.

Your teen will give you look of horror. He/she thought the session was over.

"Start? Now? But we've been going over this forever."

"Forever" takes nine agonizing seconds to say.

Tell your teen this story.

YOUR TEENAGE PAIN IN THE
(WE CAN'T SAY IT)

Your teenager can hurt your heart, and your head and your wallet. But most of all when teen years are mixed with hormones they are a pain the rear. There, we had to say it.

"I want you to do something to make the world a better place," David Ruzycki said to his students. He is a grade ten teacher at St. Thomas Moore Collegiate School in Burnaby.

The kids looked at each other with smirks, disdain and basic "Oh no, not another airy-fairy assignment" looks.

"We can't do anything with the world. It's the way it is," said one hulking boy.

When Dave the teacher spoke to me he said he got so angry at that answer he simply did not know what to do. He did not show his anger. He has been a teacher for a long time and knows better than that. But he thought he had failed them because after a year in the classroom teaching social studies to these kids he had not gotten through to them that we are the social part of the studies.

He said he went home determined to analyze the problem and go through his teaching manuals and prepare an outline on what the students could do to investigate the problems and solutions of society.

Then he went to bed and did not sleep.

In the morning he knew the answer. They were teenagers he was dealing with, mostly fourteen- and fifteen-year-olds, the hardest years of life outside of every other year.

Teens are not into subtleties. New styles are new styles, in or out, no discussion, no shades. New friends are the same. School work likewise. Airy-fairy academic assignments are the worst.

David shortened it to a do-or-die ultimatum. They would understand that.

"Go out and change the world and you get fifty points toward your grade, which will mean some of you who would not pass will pass," said teacher David. "Don't, and you get nothing. Any questions?"

After the shock wore off, the questions began about who and why and what was he talking about and what were they supposed to do?

"Any way you want. Anything you think of. Anywhere you see something wrong, fix it."

Pretty fundamental. Try it on your own kid.

By the time I met them, half of them had been to Main and Hastings. Half had been to homeless shelters. Half had been to trash-covered parks. Half had been to homes for battered women.

I know the math is bad. This is a class about life, not counting.

All of them had their lives changed, and all of them said they thought they had changed the lives of others.

"I never met anyone homeless before. I was scared," said a young, tiny girl with less eyeliner than she'd worn a few months previously.

"I was scared. They were shooting drugs right in front of us."

They were smart enough to tell the police what they were doing and some cops went along with them. Dave was not trying to get them killed, only to kill the apathy in them.

The kids shot a video on drugs and wasted lives. Teenagers may not like instruction, but they can teach each other how to work cameras. The videos are as good as any from any local TV station.

They showed the videos to the lower grades in their school. The younger kids watching did not blink.

The last image on one of the videos was of a destroyed youth in a filthy back lane. He has no hope, no future, no past, no name. He is the same age as the kids who are taking his picture.

"Don't do drugs, or you will wind up like me," he says.

No kid watching that will take drugs. Ever.

They also cleaned up parks.

"We got lots of condoms," said a boy and the class laughed. We all laugh over condoms.

"But I felt so good when we were done because that's where little kids play," he said.

And some girls collected cosmetics for battered women. It was not the lipstick that was so memorable, but the face-to-face encounter of a bruised face with a teenage face when there were almost no years separating them.

"I'm going back to help them," said a girl.

They also cooked at homeless shelters and helped count bottles for vagrants bringing them to bottle depots. It does not have to be big to be a gigantic help.

"In twenty-seven years of teaching I have never been so proud of any class," said Dave.

No one pooped out. No one said "That's not my bag, I'm going to hang out and skip that dumb assignment."

The bottom line: The problem with teenagers is they believe the world owes them everything, that they are more special than anyone else and they don't have to clean up their room because it is theirs and every one of the opposite sex is hungry for them or hates them.

That makes them pretty much like the rest of us, except they are still living at home, which makes it miserable for all of us.

What Dave did was say, "Fix it—not your world but someone else's world." What he did was tell them to help someone else. Not their parents. Teenagers don't help their parents. Parents are the cause of all their problems. So get away from that. Go fix the world.

"I will never be the same," said a girl in Dave's class. "I used to think it was all about me. Now I know there are so many who need help. I'm trying to do something for them."

What does this have to do with Reilly and positive thinking and you get what you want?

Really, nothing, or everything. I was looking for stories that would support Reilly's proposition that you get what you want if you believe in what you want.

Dave was taking a chance. He never said he believed the kids would do what he wanted. But what he did want was to make the kids in his class get in touch with the world and get away from themselves.

When he woke in the morning with the idea of how to do that he was bubbling. He believed it would work.

My God. If Reilly and Dave got together they could restore the salmon runs. You've just got to believe.

YOU DO GET WHAT YOU WANT

This is how things happen to people I have met. None of them has ever met Reilly. I don't think any of them has ever read a self-help book. Some are religious, some aren't. Those who are have had a variety of faiths.

The one thing they have in common is that somewhere deep inside themselves they feel things are okay, that smiling makes things better, and they expect good things will happen.

They expect it, so they get it.

They all want to be happy and help others and have a life that they enjoy, so that is what happens.

And without saying it, they know they are who they want to be, like all of us, which is wonderful and terrible. Who you are is who you want to be, no matter how much you may deny that.

You can say that those on skid row are not who they want to be.

Wrong.

It may be the most miserable life in the world and they are living it, and you see it and say it is horrible, but talk to them.

"Why are you here?"

"I can't get out. I have nowhere else to go."

"Do you want to be here?"

"No."

"Then why don't you leave?"

"You don't understand. This is where my friends are. This is where I get my drugs. This is my home."

"Do you want to clean up and get off drugs?"

"Of course, but you don't understand how hard that is."

"What are you going to do after we talk?"

"Buy some drugs, and I can't do that anywhere else but here."

"So you want to stay here."

"No, but I have to stay here. You don't understand. I have to stay. These are my people."

That is a verbatim conversation recorded on tape, with a woman who is what she wants to be.

"No," you say. She doesn't want to be that. You say she wants to be off drugs and that she is a product of her upbringing and environment, which have left her no other route than here.

But in truth, it is you who don't want her to be here. You want her to have a good life, and that is wonderful. But she weighs the cost of that life—giving up drugs—with the benefits of this life—friends, chemical highs and a familiar setting.

As for her upbringing, yes, it directed her here. But many have come down the same route and made a U-turn.

There will be examples later of those suffering from mental illness who could have ended up here, but didn't because they didn't want to, even with severe schizophrenia.

A TALE OF TWO DRUG ADDICTS

I f you just rewrite the lyrics a bit you can use that old song: "Standing on the Corner, Watching All the Girls Go By."

Standing at the corner of Main and Hastings you change that to "Watching All the Druggies Go By." Where Main Street meets Hastings there is music and there is hope—and there is hell.

The music was the sound of a trumpet playing "La Cucaracha." The notes happy, but soulful. The music flooded over the corner.

What the heck is someone doing playing the trumpet here?

"I was beaten up in the alley so badly and I was beaten up in jail," said Terry Haub, who had lowered his horn and was standing near the drug dealers.

It would be hard to beat up Terry. He is built like a bulldog with his shoulders pushing out on his jacket.

"I woke up one morning in stink and vomit and blood, all of it mine, and thought I can't spend the rest of my life like this."

That was all it took. That and more strength than you can possibly imagine and more determination and more faith in what he was doing than most of us can believe.

That was two years ago and he's now clean-shaven and smiling and healthy and the owner of an old trumpet that someone gave him. He learned to play as a kid, then gave it up for cocaine and crack and heroin. You get such beautiful music in your head when you load your brain up with chemicals.

The only problem is you can't stand or see straight and someone tries to take some money from you or some drugs and hits you and stomps on you and leaves you broken in the rain in a back alley.

But the music feels so good with those chemicals playing on your brain. The other trouble is your face is bleeding and your pants are torn and when you wake up you are hungry but you can't stand and you fall over.

Then the police come and put you in jail for something or other, which you can't figure out, and someone else in your cell doesn't like the way you look at him and hits you again.

But that music feels so good that when you get back on the street you try to rip off someone else so you can buy some more chemicals.

"Wait a minute," said Terry. "Hang on a second." In a moment of clarity when the heavens opened up he said he had this conversation with himself. "Hey, dummy, you want this for the rest of your life, which will not be very long?"

And Terry pushed himself off the ground and pulled himself up against a wall and somehow built up the courage to say, "No, I don't want your rotten drugs." He said that even though his insides were screaming that they did want that drug, or any drug, just so he could have the music again.

He held on. It takes courage, a lot of it. Then he washed and shaved and got a cup of coffee and a meal and got through the day.

And then he got through the next day. Two years passed and he brings his horn to his AA meetings to help others get through the day.

"I feel good," he said, and he picked up his horn and blew some more.

He was standing at Main and Hastings. Just a few steps away, around the corner, was Stephan. He was leaning on a litter can. His hair was ratty and matted and he needed a shave.

"The music's good," he said to me.

I agreed.

"You look a little tired," I said.

He stared at me with eyes that were ready to bleed.

"I was clean for five months, then I went back."

It is hard to say anything when you hear that except, you are a dummy. But I have never been there so I cannot say that. So I said, "This is trite, but do you wish you hadn't?"

"No, it's the right question. I wish more than anything I'd stayed clean. But it's insanity," he said.

We both watched Terry blow his horn.

"Insanity is doing the same thing over and over and hoping it will turn out different," said Stephan.

Then he said he had to go. We both knew where he was going. He headed for the alley behind the Carnegie Centre.

Terry finished his song and I told him about Stephan.

"You can't do anything for him," said Terry. "He has to want to come this way and he has to believe he wants it. Meanwhile, he is doing what he wants to do and being who he wants to be."

Those words were from someone who was there, who was one of them, and now is so much more. He knows.

You have to believe in what you want to be.

Everyone who deals with addictions knows that.

Then Terry headed up the steps of the centre for his meeting.

And that song, that same song that I made up at the beginning, I now added one other slight change:

"Standing on the Corner, Watching All the Heroes Go By."

PHILOSOPHER BRAKE MECHANIC

Y ou don't have to be on Main and Hastings to have a hard life. And you don't have to overcome drugs to find joy in life.

How about an ordinary guy with a much harder than hard job who is what he wants to be: happy. In fact, he is more than happy. He made me happy because I met him on a day when I had to find the most wonderful guy you could imagine. I had to.

That was the day the President of Global BC asked if he could go for a ride with me and see how I find these stories.

When the president asks to go for a ride you clean out the back seat, and you sit in it. He got the front seat.

This is an amazing guy. He rose up though the ranks, starting as a salesman, and got to the top. His name is Brett Manlove and probably the neatest thing about him is when he walks down the dark hallway where the editors work he knows their names. Some other presidents have not even known that the hallway existed.

And he went skiing with an editor and a cameraman who are outstanding skiers. This pair, Jamie Forsythe and Karl Casselman, ski down mountainsides that you really should not put a human being on, and sometimes they are taking pictures while doing it.

"Brett is crazy," said Jamie. "There was this ledge we looked over. It was like this." He held his hand pointing straight down.

"No way are we going to try that. Then Manlove goes right over it. I couldn't even watch."

When you have someone leading a company, that's the kind of guy you pray for.

But he wants to see how these stories are found and I want to find something that will be like a downhill ski race.

Don't fail me, Reilly. I know we will find something. I believe it.

We go to Main and Hastings and I take him to the bathroom underground on the corner. He is the first president of any television station in Canada to see that place.

"It's clean."

"Always," I say. "Meet the guy who keeps it drug free."

The keeper of the toilet under the toughest street in the city is reading a book. He and Brett hit it off.

But no story.

We walk East Hastings and some of the people I know want to talk and tell us their latest problems. Brett listens. He asks their names. No one from any corporate office in Vancouver has ever asked the name of anyone on East Hastings.

I see a construction site and out front is Steve Reno, whom I met a year earlier. He is Mike Reno's brother. Mike was the lead singer of Loverboy and Steve was a mainspring in his band. Now Steve is a construction safety foreman and much happier than travelling the rock and roll circuit.

"There's Steve Reno," I say to Brett, trying not to brag. "He's Mike Reno's brother. You've heard of Loverboy, right?"

Brett bolts across the street. He puts his hand out.

"Is your brother around by any chance?"

"He just left," said Steve.

"Shame. We were the best of friends."

It turns out Brett was a rock band promoter before being a television salesman. Finding a story that will impress him is not going to be easy.

But I believe. I am putting my full faith in that believing stuff. We will find something and it will be good. I hope.

No. Don't say you hope. You WILL find something. And it WILL be good.

We go to Queen Elizabeth Park. The famous statue of the love affair is still missing, stolen for its metal content. I tell him the story behind the statue, of two couples with the husband of one and the wife of the other having a secret, behind the scenes, fanny rub. He nods. But no story.

Reilly. Where are you?

We go to Northern Building Supply on the Fraser River. The cameraman for this excursion is John McCarron. He and I have been there many times. We always find something good. We will find something this time.

We take Brett to the incredibly tiny diner on top of the lumberyard and meet Bert the ninety-four-year-old who still runs the yard and eats grilled cheese and fries every day.

It is a greasy spoon with characters: Bert who started with nothing and now has one of the largest lumberyards in BC and the cook who failed as a writer in Los Angles and now fries eggs in a lumberyard. Both got what they wanted, both are at the top of their worlds. But both stories have been done.

Reilly. Honest, I do believe. But sometimes.

We stand by the river and I tell him about the Wall Street Journal writer from New York who lost his job after 9/11 and came here. Now he has a small boat and salvages logs on the river. He said it was the best thing he had ever done.

I tell Brett about the woman and her husband who live in a sailboat tied up behind the lumberyard. The man was in construction, but all his tools were stolen with his van one sad day.

She said that they could start a new business making fancy gift boxes out of that useless and basically free pine-beetle-destroyed lumber. When the beetles were finished with it the wood had turned blue, ugly for housing but beautiful for boxes.

They are now working overtime to keep up with the demand.

Brett was intrigued. He loves stories about people who succeed in business, especially when they start from the bottom.

But I have already done that story.

We walk up Borden Street just outside the lumberyard and meet Walter, who fixes cars and has been in five stories because he is such a character.

He started with nothing. Now he tries to squeeze in his business between vacations.

But no new story.

We walk past the barn where a fellow spent years trying to make a new kind of skateboard but lost part of his mind, temporarily, though breathing epoxy fumes.

Life has its ups and downs, sometimes so deep you crash. He is now a roofer and happy.

The day is getting late. I am worried. No, that is wrong. I believe, absolutely in my heart and soul that I will see something and Brett will say in admiration, "So that's how you do it."

"What's that?" asks Brett. "That sign. Naked Printer."

What sign? I did not see it.

"That one." He is pointing at it.

Reilly! What are you doing?

We follow the arrow that points that way to the Naked Printer. It goes past rusty tin shacks that are used for tiny manufacturing plants.

Another sign saying Naked Printer is in front of a worn out, greasy door at the end of a gasoline alley. This is at the foot of Borden near Kent Street if you want to visit.

We open the door and there is a mechanic in soiled coveralls.

"Are you the Naked Printer?" I ask.

"The Naked Printer left a year ago. He didn't do well. But he left me his signs." He laughed.

Anyone who laughs is ahead of the game, I think.

"Do you laugh a lot?"

It's a question. It's a starting point. And it seems to be at odds with the place he is standing in, which is filled, totally filled, with stuff that looks like junk.

There are stacks of brake parts and wheels and drill presses and compressors and it is gloomy. If he ever had any windows they were behind shelves of dusty boxes.

"Always," he said. "When you are happy you feel good."

"How's business?" I ask.

"Great, I can't keep up." His name is Chandra. He is from Fiji.

Brett is listening and looking around the shop. He seems fascinated with a business that appears to be running without overhead problems, without union and management conflicts, without advertising and with profit.

He sees a sign on a back wall: "DON'T WAIT FOR OTHERS TO BE HAPPY, SHOW THEM HOW."

"Why do you have that?" he asks.

"Because it's good advice," says Chandra with a smile.

He works alone in this shop. The smell, the dust, the grinding of brakes would be enough to drive many out of their minds.

"I try to think of things that make me feel good," he said.

"Do you really do that?" Brett asks.

"Life is full of pain, but don't think about it," he said. "You think of good things. Nobody cares about your problems, so forget them. Problems just make you feel bad and that makes you sick."

Suddenly we were in a seminar of positive thinking. In front of us should be someone with a sports jacket, ironed shirt and a scrubbed face.

Chandra was wearing a welder's cap and his oil-stained sweater under his coveralls came up to his neck. It was chilly in his shop.

I asked him about his health.

"I have not taken a day off sick in twenty-six years," he said. "I get the flu and colds, the same things everyone gets, but I don't think about it. I come to work and fix some things and I forget I'm sick."

We had found the Dr. Phil of Gasoline Alley. He has no audience but himself. He gets no praise for having a positive outlook, he gets no book royalties, but so what? It works. Not sick, smiling, happy while grinding brakes all his life. This guy should be hosting a network self-help television show.

"All of life has pain and happiness," he went on. "You just have to keep trying to be happy and the pain will hurt less."

My Lord, he did not say the pain would go away. He is a realist. He knows that pain is part of reality. But he also knows reality can be made better.

I remembered something I had heard a year earlier that sounded just like this. But it was not from a mechanic. It was from the greatest writer of all time: Shakespeare.

"There is nothing either good or bad but thinking makes it so."

Hamlet says that. Hamlet said a lot of things that make sense, but here he was basically quoting a brake mechanic. Or was it the other way around?

There were no books of Shakespeare in Chandra's shop, just greasy brake manuals.

"How did you learn your philosophy?" I asked.

"It's not philosophy. It's common sense," he said.

We left the shop in which the Naked Printer had been replaced by the Wise Brake Mechanic. Brett had found a man who refuses to get sick or sad, who just plain says no to those intrusions.

Chandra the brake doctor does it just by saying yes to what he wants and no to what he does not want and knowing he will get what he does want. Very simple. You get what you want, no matter where or who you are.

We went back to the office, me into an edit room and Mr. Manlove, company president, into a board meeting.

"Things will be good," he told the people at the meeting. "Believe it, try it, don't give in to negative thought, it won't do you any good. Believe sales and ratings will go up, and they will."

"How do you know?" someone asked.

"A brake mechanic told me."

That is taking him a hair out of context. He did say he met some wonderful people during the day and one of them advised him to believe things will be good and they will be.

Coincidently, the ratings and advertising sales for his station continue to increase.

FOR GOODNESS SAKE,
DON'T LOOK BACK

There is a rule for most professional photographers: Anywhere you are is a good place for taking pictures. There is another rule: Be somewhere, otherwise you will be in a bad place.

But no matter how hard you work and believe and try and have the right camera settings, sometimes you just know this is simply not the right spot.

"If I was there everything would be good. But I am here."

What do you do?

You make that spot the perfect place.

It happened in Vancouver at a place that no longer exists.

Now you can watch a couple of soccer games there on Sundays from the same vantage point where Queen Elizabeth viewed a race that changed the sporting world. Now you stand on a dirty bank next to some weeds and cheer your kids down on the field.

It is impossible to imagine that half a century ago this field was pulsating with cheers and screaming and yelling as the most exciting racing event in the history of the world was happening, right there, right where your little girl has almost scored a goal.

The stadium was built for the Commonwealth Games. The new, young, beautiful Queen Elizabeth would sit where she could see the mountains and the runners. It was called Empire Stadium, of course, because Elizabeth had an empire.

The stadium was at the edge of the Pacific National Exhibition, right on East Hastings and Cassiar Street, at the corner where Jerry the panhandler stands every day and waves at cars.

Bang. A gunshot started the race and eight men took off, four laps around for a mile. Quickly in front were Roger Bannister and John Landy. Everyone expected them to lead the pack. They were the fastest runners in the world. That was incredible enough. But this time they were up against each other. It would be hard for the Queen to root for one or the other. She cheered for both.

Landy from New Zealand and Bannister from England were flying around the track. History could be made here on August 7, 1954.

But the most important story of that day was not what the runners did, although they did make history and got all the headlines.

The story that kept their story alive was in the hands of a young photographer for the *Vancouver Sun*. Charlie Warner was twenty-five years old and supposed to be on a day off. I briefly worked with Charlie at the *Sun* but only learned about his day at the race from a book called *Instant Replay* by Len Corben.

"No, sir," Charlie said to his boss. "I do not want the day off."

What good is a day off when you work at a job that you love and that love might have a climaxing moment just waiting for your touch?

He might get a great picture of a great race.

But Charlie had to get credentials, which made him late for the games. And he had to push his way through the crowds because he was late, which made him later.

And he went to the finish line, but photographers from around the world had already staked out their spots.

And like another famous story, there was no room at the inn called the finish line.

At least a hundred cameras were pointed at the tape strung across the dirt, all aiming for a different angle of the same incredible moment.

It was called the Race of the Century. Both Landy and Bannister had each recently broken the four-minute mile, which many had said was impossible for the human body to do.

Roger Bannister, a doctor from England, was the first to do it. Three months earlier he had run the mile in 3:59.4.

A month later John Landy from Australia broke Bannister's record with 3:57.9.

Now they were together and a hundred million people around the world were listening on radio with millions more on early television.

It was heaven on the field for a photographer, but Charlie looked at the camera crowd at the finish line and sadly said, "Forget it." He would get nothing but elbows from that group. They were older, more experienced and in many cases famous.

He could have quit. He could have walked away and said his big chance had been ruined by the older guys. He could have felt sorry for himself.

He walked down the track alone. No one else was where he was standing because this was not the place you would get a good picture. You cannot photograph runners in a race before the race is over and expect to get anything worth looking at.

The big news would be at the finish line if both runners crossed it in less than four minutes.

He stood about seventy yards from the finish line, and took a shot as they ran by on the second lap. It was not exciting.

Then on the third lap Charlie saw Landy turn his head and look back. Well, that's strange. Runners don't look back. Or at least they should not look back. That is against common sense. You look back after the finish line.

But Landy was so far ahead it was a one-man race. Bannister was second, but more than two seconds behind. The other runners were in a race of their own picking up after Landy and Bannister's dust had settled.

For Landy to turn his head to see how much of a lead he had was silly, but when you have incredible wealth or an unbelievable lead over others you sometimes are tempted to measure it.

Suddenly Charlie had an idea—a one-shot idea. A shot that would look different—if Landy did it again, if he looked back when he passed roughly on the same spot on the track on the final lap, if he was close enough when he did it, and if he could push the shutter just at that infinitely short moment.

He raised his four by five Speed Graphic, the most common camera used by news photographers back then. It weighed about eight pounds. It had no zoom lens. It had a film holder in the back. You could take one picture, then you had to replace a sliding metal cover that went over the film.

This was not an easy process. After you had the film protected by the black metal cover you pulled the thick film holder out of the back of the camera. Then you flipped the film holder over and replaced it into the back of the camera. Then you pulled out the sliding black metal cover over the film on that side of the holder and then hooked the metal plate into a snap on the back of the camera. If you lost that plate you could take no more pictures.

In short, don't hope for a quick second shot.

Next you cock the shutter and then figure out what you are going to take your next picture of. A fast, experienced photographer could do all that in about ten seconds.

The stands were alive. The final lap. Bannister was closing in. He was one second behind. He was half a second behind. The crowd was screaming. The Queen was cheering.

It happened in less time than you can blink twice. Landy, pumping away, just as he was nearing the spot where Charlie was standing, looked back to his left. Bannister passed him on his right.

Charlie hit the shutter.

The runners were further away than the previous lap when Landy had turned his head. They were so small in the view finder in a field that was so large he was not sure he got them.

Charlie put the protective black metal plate over the film and shook. Maybe, just maybe.

The stands exploded. Yelling, cheering. Bannister had won and, more importantly, two Commonwealth men had broken the four-minute mile in one race.

Elizabeth was pleased.

Hundreds of photos were taken with Bannister breaking the tape and Landy on his heels. Thousands more pictures of exhaustion and raised arms and smiles and dejection were snapped after the race.

Charlie went back to the darkroom.

Under a red bulb you can watch an image appear while the film is in the developing solution. Charlie watched. It was there.

The head turned, the passing. He got it. And he was the only one who got it. It was the picture that was in the *Times of London* the next day, and on page one of most Canadian papers and on the sports pages of most papers around the world.

It was also chosen as the best sports picture of the year by the prestigious National Headliners Club in Atlanta, the first Canadian picture to get the honour.

Denny Boyd, the beloved columnist of the *Vancouver Sun*, suggested a statue be made from the picture and a local sculptor did it. It is now at the corner of Hastings and Renfrew; the look back, the passing, the moment just as Charlie got it. It is a philosophic lesson in living.

Later Charlie was using the same camera at a hockey game when a puck smashed into the lens. Its days were over, but it had one heck of a life.

A moral, if you want one: Charlie did not quit. He did not look at the crowd of photographers who had the best positions at the finish line and say he was out of luck.

He did not look back.

THE WAY IT WAS . . .
CLIMBING ABOARD A
STEAM ENGINE IN MOTION

In the last book and on TV you met Harold Wolverton, the retired dentist who was ninety and still riding a motorcycle.

When he was ninety-one he broke his hip tripping over his walker. When he got out of the hospital his daughter said he would have to give up his motorbike.

"I don't see why," he said. "I didn't fall off my motorcycle. I should give up my walker."

This is one tough dude. Last time he told us how he wanted to be a dentist but did not have enough money. So he and his brother used the thousand dollars he'd saved while in the air force during the war and they bought the wood to build a house. Neither of them had ever built anything before that.

They got instructions from a friend who told them while sitting around his kitchen table how to lay the foundation and put up the walls. They built the house in east Vancouver, and four more after it. All the profit went to Harold's education. His brother took nothing. His friend took nothing for telling them how to do it.

Harold became a dentist.

What kind of person becomes a dentist? If you have the idea of someone from a sheltered life that goes into a sheltered occupation, wrong.

When Harold got out of the hospital we met for coffee in Tim Horton's. He had to drive there in a car.

"It's not the same without the wind in my face."

He told me that in the old days he got around by train.

"I was staying at the home of the mother of a friend, but she had no money and I had no money to give her. I had to do something," he said.

He said he and his friend drank endless cups of coffee and smoked twists, tiny homemade cigarettes, while trying to figure out how to make something so they could contribute to the household.

Times were in a depressed state and many men were out of work. A name had to be given to this state and they called it the Great Depression. Many went to unemployment camps where they built roads for a dollar a day.

"I got a job at a cannery in Chase in the Shuswaps. Unfortunately in the middle of the summer the cannery caught fire and burned to the ground. It was a old wooden building," he said. "So I had to find something else."

Then he heard that he could sell trees to the telephone company to be used as poles. The trees had to be a certain height and straight as, well, straight as telephone poles.

"I told my friend I would go out and find some poles," he said.

Can you imagine someone twenty years old today who had never cut down a tree deciding he would go logging on his own?

He was told there might be some suitable trees north of Kamloops. He was in Vancouver with no money.

This is way beyond positive thinking. This is positive living.

There were only two ways of getting around without cash—hitching a ride on the road or riding the rails.

"I had spoken to someone who told me the best way of catching a train was to prowl around Water Street near the CPR yards. You could get the cross-Canada train there. And the only time to do it was at night."

The only problem was you had to get on after it was moving but before it was going too fast. If you boarded before it moved you could get arrested. If you waited too long you could get killed.

"I packed a bag with sandwiches and coffee and walked to the yards."

We have to understand that walking to the yards from where he was staying at Twentieth Avenue on the east side of Vancouver would take more than an hour.

Most of us now would say if the car is broken and the bus doesn't go direct we are not travelling that far.

"I watched a couple of trains pass by. I did not think I had the nerve."

He found a hiding place behind a telephone pole. Someone told him that was the best place to wait.

"I tried to visualize how I would have to stand so the engineer would not see me.

"I crouched. In a few minutes a gigantic steam locomotive was coming down the tracks straight for me. The idea was to run alongside the train and grab on to a ladder at the back of the locomotive."

In Tim Horton's he took a sip of coffee. He was remembering hiding in the dark with a train coming at him. Everyone remembers their first time, but not everyone remembers their first time grabbing onto a passing locomotive.

"I had been told that once you grabbed the handhold that it was fatal to let go because you would surely fall under the wheels of the engine and be mutilated.

"I girded my loins as they say." He laughed. "The headlight was shining right at me. It was gigantic. It was blinding. I couldn't see anything else. In half a minute it was dark, the light had passed and the steel monster was right alongside me moving at ten or fifteen miles an hour. I had to get ready to run on the stones and ties and I couldn't trip."

He held the cup in front of his lips but he was no longer drinking his coffee. He was in the rail yard running.

"The wheels were intimidating. They were bigger than me and they had the driving arms on the outside moving around and up and down. The noise was overwhelming. I was terrified."

He took a sip.

"I just took a look at the handles, then damned if the engineer didn't let go with a blast of steam from the pistons. He had probably spotted me."

Harold eyes were wide, but they were looking into the past. He saw the end of the engine passing by.

"The steam completely covered me. I knew I had to make my move. The wheels were clanking. I ran with my packsack bouncing on my back.

"But I couldn't see the ladder. I could only guess."

His speech was getting faster now while sitting at the coffee table.

"I made a frantic lunge and didn't have time to even think of what would happen if I missed. I grabbed something and held on. Instantly I was off the ground. I pulled with all my strength and my feet were flying."

He looked down and saw the wooden ties racing by.

"I didn't need to run any more, I just had to make sure that I did not hit any poles before I got myself between the cars."

Every word of Harold's was recorded. I cannot believe that I am listening to someone who actually grabbed onto a moving steam engine. "Riding the rails" is just an old saying, but it has no meaning, unless you are listening to someone who did it.

"The engineer and fireman were busy with this belching monster. I could see them with the fire and the steam surrounding them both. But I had heard that the railway police would be waiting at Barnett looking for hobos trying to get a free ride."

The steam engines had a coal compartment at the rear of the locomotive. Harold crouched down at the back of the coal car.

"When we got to the Barnett yard and stopped I snuggled up to the steel wall. I could see the policeman climbing up the ladder but I covered myself with a filthy canvas tarp that I had strapped to my knapsack.

"He probably would have seen me except he used both hands to scale the ladder and he didn't have his flashlight out. He looked around and went down.

"I did not move until the telephone poles alongside of the tracks were flying by."

He said he got out his squashed sandwich and flask of coffee and ate while curled up between the cars watching the blackness fly by. He had to get off in Hope.

"Jumping off was as scary as getting on."

If you waited too long you would pull into the station and the police were waiting. After all that work you would be in jail for stealing services, and you'd be shipped back to Vancouver to serve your time.

"But if you jumped off too far out the train was still going fast and you risked breaking your leg or your head."

He did get off, because he had to change trains. The one he was riding was going east and he had to go north. He found the Kettle Valley Line and got on and off another train the same way.

Somewhere north of Kamloops he went into the woods looking for trees. He walked all day, because most of the trees had already been cut, he said. Then he wrapped himself up in his canvas and slept.

He walked all the next day, and still found no grove of suitable trees.

"What did you eat?" I asked.

"Just raisins and nuts and coffee. If you brought any food the bears would smell it."

Water he drank from creeks. After three days he wandered into Chase and ordered ham and eggs to get his strength back. Then he was back in the woods.

Almost a week later he found the trees, and walked back to Kamloops to register them with the Forestry Department. Then, after negotiating what the stumpage fee would be, he rode the train back to Hope and then another to Vancouver the same way he went up there.

In Vancouver he hoped to borrow one hundred dollars to buy saws and axes. He went to his uncle who was in the financial business and who had some money.

"He said no," said Harold. "He said get a real job, not cutting down trees."

And then the twenty-one-year-old, who had jumped on moving steam engines and walked for days to find a way to make some money, cried.

He said his aunt saw him, asked what was wrong and gave him twenty-four dollars. His brother gave him all he had, twenty dollars, and Harold had fifteen that he had been saving for years.

Back on the trains to Kamloops, buy the axes and saws, and meet his friend, the son of the woman whose home he had been staying at.

"He was half native so I thought he would know about cutting down trees. But he had never cut a tree in his life. They were supposed to fall that way if we cut them here. They didn't."

By the end of the first day they had a jumble of trees half touching the ground. By the end of a week of non-stop working they had about eighty trees cut.

They rented a horse to pull them to a road. "But we did not know the horse was half blind and when he walked over this little bridge we had made over a creek he kept falling in."

So they built a wall of small logs for the horse to slide against.

Then they hired a truck to take the logs to Kamloops.

Then they tried to sell the logs. "For the best ones we got three and a half dollars. For the others, two dollars."

In the end, after paying their bills and loans, they made two hundred dollars profit. "My friend was hoping for a thousand dollars."

"What did you do with the money you made?" I asked.

"Well, we gave it to the woman we were staying with. We owed her for the room and board," he said.

That was it. That was the entire reason for risking his life and cutting trees and walking halfway across a forest.

Different time. Different way of going about living. But that was typical of the people of British Columbia, in fact much of the world, just two generations ago.

Most of the people of Harold's generation did not need to be told that to get what they wanted they had to go out and get it.

And they did not need to be told why they should do it.

ONE SAVED POINSETTIA

There was someone else who did not walk away from what she knew she had to do. She could have. A lot of others did, and it would not have mattered one tiny bit if she had too.

We saw her on Thurlow Street near Beach Avenue standing still and looking down.

Stop. Maybe she lost something and we could help. Or maybe she sees something and we can tell a story about whatever it is that she has found. In either case, a woman looking down means things for us are looking up.

"Hello, hello." The usual greetings, plus "what and why?" But we could see that before we even asked.

She was looking at one broken-off branch of a poinsettia plant lying on the sidewalk. It was big enough for everyone to notice and small enough not to care about.

"I was thinking of taking it home, but then I thought 'Don't be a silly old woman,'" she said.

"Why?"

"Well, I just cleaned out my apartment after Christmas and now I am looking at something that will start cluttering it up again." She laughed.

She laughed a lot. I asked where she was from because of her accent and she said, "I escaped from Toronto." Then more laughter.

This is a neat woman. Little old lady did not fit her even though she was

68

little and old and a lady. In truth she was wiry and alive and happy. Her name was Ingrid and before Toronto she was from Hungary.

She escaped after the revolution in 1956.

What I know about the revolt against Russia and communism was that America had promised the people aid if they stood up to the Russians, and then at the last minute backed out leaving the Hungarian people to fight alone.

The US backing down was done probably to prevent nuclear war, the same as Russia backed down over Cuba six years later. If no one blinks over a street fight with missiles there will be nothing to look at when the fight is over.

But the Hungarians were left with only their hands and a few rifles against the Russian tanks. The first girlfriend I had in my life also escaped. She told me about standing in the street with gunfire around her and throwing Molotov cocktails at tanks.

The bombs were bottles filled with gasoline with a burning rag sticking out of the top. You had to get close to the tanks. You had to hope the rag was tightly stuck in the neck of the bottle so it would not burst into flames in your hand. It took a lot more courage than planting a roadside bomb. My friend was twelve when she did that.

The woman we met over the poinsettia was about ten years older during the fighting. She probably would have done the same or even more daring things.

You could hardly tell that from someone looking at a small branch with red leaves on the sidewalk and laughing over a question of what to do with it.

"Well, I can't leave it here," she said.

Of course not. She knows what it is like to be abandoned. But she cannot take it home; small apartment all tidied up now.

She reached down and picked up the slender branch, walked over to some shrubbery alongside an apartment building and placed it in the tightly packed green leaves of a bush. It truly looked pretty.

"There. It will be happier now and I feel better," she said.

She left us and her walk was almost jaunty. This veteran of street battles had saved a lost branch with red leaves from being stepped on.

What we got out of that brief encounter was a story that said Thurlow Street looked better because one woman did something. Almost everyone who commented on it later said they got a warm feeling from her.

Sometimes it takes so little to do so much.

THE POT GARDENER

The picture on television was so touching; a plastic hook struggling to grab onto an old chain hanging from somewhere above. The hook reached for a link, but could not slip into it. The edge of the hook pushed away the chain.

It was an extreme close-up picture. Only the hook and the chain were visible. The struggle went on, the hook almost getting it, then missing. It was one of those little trials of life.

Then there was a groan. You know the sound—it is the one you make when you try to do something and you try again and again and you just can't get it.

Groan again.

Ron Eikenberry lowered the hanging basket to rest his arm. He had been holding it over his head, reaching as high as possible. He was a big, tall man, but the chain was just out of reach.

It was one of those inexpensive hanging baskets where the hook and the plastic struts holding it up and the basket are all one piece. And if you hold the basket from underneath by one hand it is almost impossible to move the hook where you want it.

He tried again, but no one can hold something in that position for very long. Once more. Missed again.

He laughed and put it down. "Later," he said.

People who laugh when they have a problem have much less of a problem than most of us.

"Time to water the garden," he said to his sister, who was standing around the side of the building, waiting.

"She wanted a garden, so I made her a garden," said Ron.

The problem was that they lived in social housing and there was no room for a garden.

So Ron got some plastic pails, the five-gallon white pails that cooking oil comes in. They are used by restaurants. Ron got them from a recycling plant and put them around the two-storey building where there was no garden.

He did not skimp on the pails. He had more than fifty of them.

"I didn't want her to think she just had a little corner. She deserves more."

His sister came from around the corner. His sister needed a garden. She needed many things.

"She only got to grade two," Ron said. "She's deaf, and partially crippled."

His sister's face was not fully formed on one side, making her looked squished. Even standing straight she only came up to her brother's elbow.

"You've been caring for her?"

"All her life," he said.

Ron's one job for more than thirty years was selling ice cream from a truck in the summer. In the winter he hunted for cans and bottles. Welfare was the main income.

He has done everything for his sister: cook, clean, entertain and have patience.

"She's my girl," he said and gave her a hug. Then he turned on the hose and handed it to her, and with it in her hand he aimed it in the direction of one row of pails.

"They call me the pot man around here," he said. "But I only grow flowers and vegetables. Then we give them away."

He was wonderful and warm, but this was not fitting with my interpretation of the basic rules: you get what you want. I figured that meant you get something for yourself. You believe you will get it and you get it. Profound and simple.

But the only thing Ron was getting was giving. Every moment of every day was consumed by care for his sister. Despite that, he was still smiling, still hugging and not complaining. You could tell that by looking at him. A person who complains about things does not have a happy face. A person who feels sorry for himself does not smile.

I did not ask, but when I met him he probably could not tell what he believed in or what he wanted. He probably would have said he wanted nothing other than his sister's flowers to bloom.

But what he got for himself was a pure joy that was plainly there. You could see it, you could feel it and it infected those around him. You stand by Ron and you feel good.

Then his son came out through the door. He was in his forties and leaning heavily on a cane. He had advanced, crippling arthritis.

"I can't really move much," he said. "But my father takes good care of me."

"He's a good boy," said Ron.

Then Ron picked up the hanging basket again.

He held it on the bottom so the whole pot and plastic wires and hook were above his head. A slight movement of his hand became a large movement of the hook.

"Almost," he said.

His sister was still watering her garden. His son was watching, but unable to take another step, much less to help.

"Almost," Ron said again.

We watched the hook hit the chain sideways and the chain moved, then came back and hit the back of the hook.

"Go on," I said to the hook. I shouted at it inside my head. "He is trying so hard."

"It will be a good summer," said Ron, "Lots of vegetables and flowers, thanks to my sister."

He said that while still looking up past the bottom of the pot trying to see the hook.

"He's always like that," said his son. "He has more energy than anyone I know."

His father was seventy-seven, and by energy I think he meant love, although he would not say it.

"Got it," shouted Ron.

The hook slipped into a link on the chain and the pot swung free.

"Looks good, doesn't it, sweetie?" he said to his sister as he pointed up to the pot.

She smiled, half a smile on half a face, and then she looked back at the nozzle of the hose.

Five years later I still remember her crooked smile and Ron's. But more than that I remember a guy who got nothing and gave everything because he wanted to, because he knew in his heart he wanted nothing else.

When I think of him now, I know what he got. You know people in hard situations who are worn out from caring for others and depressed and angry and exhausted and at the verge of throwing in the towel and shooting themselves or running away and drinking and in short having an unpleasant life.

All I remember is Ron's smile, and that he kept trying until he got that hook through the chain. There was no other life for him, but with the one he had he got the basket to hang.

THE COFFEE CUP

A research study I heard about on the radio, so it must be true, said that coffee tastes better when you drink it from your favourite cup.

Well, duh, who needed a study for that? Just ask anyone who has a favourite cup, which is basically everyone. That is why there are favourite cups.

CJ, who earns a living fixing things at Playland at the PNE, has a favourite cup. Buzz Lightyear, with a smiling face is his cup, and CJ is happiest when Buzz's innards are filled with steaming dark roast.

When I met him more than a year earlier he was walking around with his cup in his hand. He fixed the roller coaster and the merry-go-round and everything that was greasy on the insides.

Because of that his cup was greasy.

"I have never washed it," he said. "That's why the coffee tastes so good."

He had rinsed out the inside, but never cleaned Buzz Lightyear's face. Buzz's big, smiling, bulging cheeks were black with grease and soot.

His daughter bought Buzz for him when she was six. She was now sixteen. That was the story when we first met him.

A year later I was looking for something to show on TV. As always, I had no idea what I was looking for, but I knew that when I found it I would love it, whatever it was. Reilly's rule. I believe I will find it, I believe I will love what I find.

We started looking at the PNE. It was a month before the opening of the fair and maybe someone was fixing something and we could see the inner workings of a ride or something.

Nothing. Nothing anywhere except some guys working on the towering Hellevator, putting in new cables. The Hellevator is the hugely tall tower that shoots brave souls up two hundred feet, then drops them like a stone before shooting them up again and dropping them again. Somewhere their stomachs are left behind.

"Anything interesting or funny or amazing or anything?" I asked the guys at the base of the ride.

"Nope, just putting in new cables."

Nothing.

We looked around the rest of the fair. Nothing. But I do believe, plus it is early in the day and belief is easy when it is early.

We drove downtown. We looked. We looked for three hours. That is tedious. That includes the time when the eyelids are closing because driving around in circles looking for something when you don't know what you are looking for is exciting for just so long. Then you get sleepy. Then you need coffee.

Then you wake up and feel a touch of concern. I will find something, but I am starting to get worried. That is the feeling of dejection followed by determination. The determination is the Reilly factor. We will find something.

It all sounds crazy. Am I brainwashing myself? But on the other hand if I think we will not find anything, if I give up, then all is lost. You cannot find something or get something or be something if you don't believe in it. Then even if it does happen you might miss seeing it.

We tour Queen Elizabeth Park, which is a good place. There have been so many stories there, like the man walking around the grass lifting a dumbbell because he wanted to be strong enough to carry his wife across the threshold of their home on their fortieth anniversary, like he did on their first, and the woman who was repairing a knitted sweater that her grandmother had given to her because it was their link to each other.

Parks have many stories outside of the trees and grass. But Queen Elizabeth Park had none that day, at least none that I could find.

Then we went to Stanley Park, where someone once asked me to count the number of stories we have done there. I asked the library at the TV station: almost one thousand. Stanley Park is my treasure chest.

But today, nothing. Had we seen someone a few minutes before or after, they might have been doing something, but today, nothing.

On the other hand, I believe.

But how can you believe if every gold mine has been searched and nothing has been found? There comes a time, doesn't there, when things don't work.

No. I believe. I am doing this seriously. If I cannot believe in a snot-nosed kid, who can I believe in? This is not just a case of finding a story, this is a matter of proving to myself that belief does work.

But there is nowhere else to go and hope is disappearing because it is almost four-thirty and the cameraman is off in half an hour and, in reasonable terms, all is lost.

But if Reilly is right, even with his sniffing, then I believe we will find something. I do. Totally.

"We will find something, and we will find it quickly and you will get off on time and it will be wonderful," I say to the cameraman, who is Roger Hope, who is married to Debra Hope who is the anchor that night and whom Roger hopes will introduce the story and say after it is over, "That was great, especially the pictures."

But what Roger says is, "How?"

"Don't know, but go back to the PNE, please. At least we will be close to my car and at five o'clock you can say good night."

We went through the open gate, which had no attendant because there was no one inside except the workers, and they were getting ready to leave.

There must be something here. There must be. There had to be, because we were here and there was nowhere else to go. There is some logic to that, isn't there? We were back in Playland where the rides were still in pieces. We passed the Hellevator again.

The same guys were still working on it.

"Anything happen since the last time we were here?" I asked.

They laughed, shook their heads and went on working. They have real jobs, they are thinking. They use wrenches and gloves and muscles. I am just hanging around asking idiotic questions.

"Anything at all?" I asked.

"No. Absolutely nothing," said the one who had said the same thing earlier.

"Nothing?"

"Nothing," he repeated.

I believe, but it was almost five o'clock, quitting time for them and story dying time for me. It is not a good feeling to work hard for something and believe you will get it and then not get it.

But you must believe you will get it.

My car is right out there, outside the open gate. When I am in it the cameraman will leave and I will call the office and say, "Sorry."

But try the other approach. Try thinking of Reilly with his string in the water knowing he will catch a fish. "I will find something of interest. I will. Impossible, I know, but I will. I believe it will happen. That's what Reilly says."

We passed the maintenance office for Playland and remembered the guy with the coffee cup. Who knows? He might still be around and still have his cup and who knows?

Inside I asked two women who had piles of paperwork in front of each of them if they knew about the guy with the coffee cup and might he be still around by any chance? I did not remember his name or the name of the face on the cup.

"Yes, amazing you asked," said one of them. "That's CJ. His cup broke last week and he just got a new one today. He showed it to me this morning."

The zing of the unbelievable is melting the ice of disbelief in the middle of my chest.

"Where? Are you serious?" And again, "Where is he??!!"

"On the Hellevator," she said.

We were back at the bottom of the two-hundred-foot tower in one minute.

"The guy with the coffee cup?" I asked, almost trembling with excitement.

"CJ's up there," said the man who said there is nothing here.

He pointed at the top.

How do you interview someone two hundred feet up? Easy. Shout. Few interviews are better than those where you can just see an arm waving and hear, "Yes, it broke," followed by, "Yes, I got a new one."

Oh, bless me. The sound was clear. When there is no one on the rides you can hear forever at Playland, or anywhere where there are no crowds screaming and making other unnatural noises.

"Where's your cup?"

The question travelled two hundred feet up. The answer came down. If the cup is with him the story will not be so good because how do you say he has a new cup and not see it?

I say to Roger, "Almost."

He smiles and shakes his head. He understands what is needed. The cup is needed. "Almost," he repeats.

So close.

"It's down there," CJ shouted. "I can't bring it up here."

Where? Here? Oh goodness. Oh unbelievable. The cup is down here!!?? Where?

You may now be asking is all this believing and positive thought stuff just about a plastic cup with Buzz Lightyear's face on it?

Yes! Because that is what I believed in.

Think about the time you lost your keys, or your cellphone, or let's get onto really important things: your way, your meaning in life.

This is serious. This is dangerous to write about. Do you give up? No. Of course not. Not ever. A cup and a meaning in life have nothing to do with each other, except when you lose them. Belief has everything to do with everything. And believing you will find what you want has everything to do with it.

You cannot change reality. A lost child is the saddest thing in this life. Some children are lost forever and your heart breaks forever. But there was Abby Drover. She was in the last book and, after most of my life in this business, she is the most amazing case of a missing child that has ever been known.

A twelve-year-old girl, she survived six months handcuffed in a bomb shelter deep underground and was discovered by a fluke. Her parents never stopped believing.

Some others still have not been found. But the belief never dies.

Is it sacrilege to talk about finding a plastic coffee cup and lost children in the same breath? No. There is just the faith, the belief, the unshakeable belief that all will turn out good before the deadline. Sometimes that is 6:55 on the clock. Sometimes it is the end of life.

When you believe something, you don't quit.

But on the trite side of belief there was the cup and at the bottom of the ride they told me CJ would end his shift soon, but it would take many minutes before he climbed down here.

I held my breath the whole way. CJ was climbing two hundred feet straight down a metal ladder. He had a safety harness but that did not stop me from feeling a fear of falling even with both my feet on the ground.

At the bottom I remembered his face. He looked like Buzz Lightyear. It may be true that we get to look like our coffee mugs.

"I picked up the old cup one day and the handle broke off."

He said he had to get a new one because his daughter had given it to him, so what else could he do?

He found the replacement on the Internet. It was only slightly used. "Ten dollars for the cup, forty dollars for shipping."

But he was right. When your child gives you something it has a meaning that only a parent can know. A plastic cup becomes a gold cup. It had been his companion at work for a decade and now a new one that looked like the old one would take him close to retirement.

So simple a story, the cup that replaced a cup, not because a man loves a cup, but because a father loves a daughter.

The moral, if you need one: Just because you don't see something doesn't mean it's not there. Reilly keeps fishing in the same spot, and he knows what he is doing.

And CJ keeps drinking from the same cup.

And I keep believing.

LITTLE MISS RED STOCKINGS

Sometimes it happens in an instant. A moment that you see, then feel, then smile at, then for the rest of your life when you drive through a certain town or place you think of it and smile again. It was all about Little Miss Red Stockings.

And then you remember the woman who did not understand the story at all and you feel sad.

A bunch of kids on an outing with their teachers and parents were visiting the Port Moody museum at Rocky Point.

Port Moody was once going to be the terminus of the railway that would unite Canada, that would make the town internationally known like Montreal and Toronto.

Port Moody was going to be huge, with booming industry and crowds and businesses and money flowing in with the trains.

Then the head of the Canadian Pacific Railway said, "Nope. I changed my mind." Vancouver would be the end of the line, partly, or to tell the truth, largely, because the rail company owned more land around Vancouver than it did around Port Moody.

Greed and undercutting business moves are not limited to the stock market and hedge funds of our time. The old railway barons knew how to buy cheap and then inflate the value before they sold at the top end of the scale.

But that was then, and now a few freight trains and the West Coast

Express pass through Port Moody, which is happy being a pretty community far enough away from the big city to have peace and quiet.

Port Moody has a wonderful museum, just down by Rocky Point Beach. In front of it is a short stretch of railway track on which no trains pass. It is one of the exhibits they use to explain the history of the city.

I was watching as the group of kids and adults were coming out of the museum and then the kids did what kids do: they were balancing on the rails. First a couple of ten-year-olds, doing very well. Then other kids joined them.

But Little Miss Red Stockings, who was about two years old, was trying to walk between the rails. She had been brought by one of the parent volunteers, who could not leave her behind. It was a great place to be two.

But it is not easy for a two-year-old to walk on a flat floor. When you add stones and old wooden ties it is a monumental challenge.

She stumbled, then she got up, then fell again, then up again, but never with a cry or complaint.

She looked at the other kids on the rails, but kept trying to stay up on her own feet. That was a bigger challenge.

Then one of the older girls took her by the hands and guided her up to one of the rails. The little one stepped on it and walked. Her hands were held safely and she walked and the older girl held her and on the face of Little Miss Red Stockings was a moment of pure joy.

We put all that on television.

The next day I got an angry email. How dare I entice children to walk where they could be killed, even though it was clear the tracks only ran for twenty feet and no train could leap over the grass to get to them.

The complaint went on: you are encouraging children to walk on active train tracks where they could be hit.

Oh, lady, I thought. You want to protect the children, and that is good. But you knew there was no danger on that track. You knew the tracks were there for children to safely do what they were doing so they could experience what many children have done.

You missed the joy of watching them, and that is a shame. Many of us get so angry about some things that we cannot see past our anger.

But saddest of all, she missed that idyllic picture when Little Miss Red Stockings' big sister held her hands and helped her up onto the steel rail.

We learned later who the older girl was, and while she walked backward the little one took one step, then another and another.

She was the happiest girl in the world who ever walked a rail.

Had she been around 150 years ago, she would probably have melted the heart of the crusty, greedy head of the CPR. Possibly he would have held up his hand because of that smile of the girl walking on the rail.

"Stop the train right here. I can't disappoint that child."

Port Moody would have skyscraping condos and Vancouver would be the mud flats at the end of a gravel road.

Who knows? History often turns on a smile.

You are who you want to be: someone looking at the tragic side and worrying and blaming and complaining, or someone with a smile, experiencing and loving her big sister and her bigger accomplishment.

The complaining woman said the image made her sick. Sadly, she was right.

ANDREW CARNEGIE

"**D**o you know why there is a Carnegie Library here at this spot in skid row?" I asked a very smart man who was taking a tour with me.

He shook his head. This man is president of a large, successful Vancouver company. He knows many things about the city. But no, he does not know why one of the most beautiful historic buildings in British Columbia is at Main and Hastings, and, "Did you say it's a library?"

Yes, a library. That is why it was built. Later it was changed to the Carnegie Centre when most of the local population stopped reading.

"Do you know why this is here?" I ask a woman who works in the centre at the reception desk in front of the small room that still has books, which is odd to see at Main and Hastings with drug dealers outside and wasted lives in the alley behind the books.

"It's always been here," she said. "It was built for the poor people."

Bingo, half right. Poor people have a lot to do with it. So does the belief that poor people don't have to stay poor.

Let me tell you the story of one of the most amazing people in the history of the world, and how he got what he believed in and how he wanted others to get the same thing.

Andrew Carnegie was born poor, dirt poor, hungry poor. He was the son of a weaver in Scotland, which was a country of weavers. The Carnegies lived in one room with a dirt floor. Mother and father wove yarn into cloth and then tried to sell it, the same as everyone else was trying to do.

The market was poor. No sale.

With no money in their present or their future, they sailed for America in steerage. We cannot imagine how terrible that was. Only the slaves had it worse.

The poor huddled masses in steerage were locked below decks and shared a space tighter than the guest bathroom in some small condo, but there were no toilets. They could not stretch out their arms. They tried to cook over a charcoal stove and sleep and not gag when someone in a bunk above them vomited.

They were allowed on the open air deck for an hour a day, but not all days. Many died on the trip.

At their destination there was more poverty. The Carnegie family got to Pennsylvania. There was no welcome wagon waiting. Andrew worked as a bobbin boy in a spinning mill hopping barefoot over the machinery changing spools of thread twelve hours a day, six days a week. He was paid enough to feed himself for three days. He was thirteen years old.

His next job was a telegraph messenger boy. If you are old enough you know the kid on the bike saying: "Western Union calling."

Andrew did it without a bike. He made enough to feed himself four days a week. He gave all his money to his mother.

But something happened to this poor kid that simply changed not only his life, but much of the world. A kindly old rich man opened his own personal library of four hundred books to the poor working kids in town. They could read on Saturday afternoons for two hours.

If you have an old stack of paperbacks you probably have one or two hundred books. Four hundred is nothing by our standards, but in the early 1800s it was a treasure. There were no libraries to join. Public libraries were rare. For most there was no chance to read outside of school and school was not possible for someone working from bed to bed.

Andrew read and read and sucked in every word. He read Shakespeare and history and math books. Whatever was next on the shelf he read and he reread and he remembered. This was the answer to his wish, his longing, his belief.

This was not casual reading. This was not curl up on the couch and enjoy a sexy novel. This was the chance to learn something that might, just might, make his life and his family's life better. It was all there on the pages.

He read his way through the library and learned so many things. He learned about business and about people and about the past. Then he set out to make his future.

He had saved a few dollars, which was almost impossible, but he did and he invested it in a new enterprise, the Pullman Coach Company. The founders were building passenger cars on trains for first-class travel. Andrew could not afford a ticket to ride in the undercarriage.

The company did well. He put his money into a small oil company before there was much need for oil. Later motor cars came on the scene. Then he worked his way into steel production at a time when America was entering its Civil War. Wars need steel.

In time he became, hold onto your seat, the second richest man in the history of the world. That is according to *Forbes* magazine. The richest man was John D. Rockefeller, who beat him out by a few billion.

If you are thinking of Bill Gates hold that thought. Poor Bill is a street beggar compared to Andrew Carnegie. In today's dollars, Andrew would own Microsoft, Apple, and the state of California with British Columbia thrown in as loose change.

Andrew Carnegie was almost twenty times wealthier than Bill Gates, and that is all in today's money. He had much more than the Queen, more than Russian czars, more than Roman emperors. In today's money, Bill Gates has eighteen billion. In that same money Andrew Carnegie had more than three hundred billion.

Carnegie did well. But that is not amazing. What Andrew Carnegie said and did was mind blowing whether it was 1860 or 2010.

"Money is evil. The amassing of wealth is one of the worse forms of idolatry! No idol is more debasing than the worship of money," he said.

But money gave you freedom from poverty, something that is obvious. How do you get money without worshipping it? Everyone wants money.

He gave the answer. He asked a well-known journalist and writer, Napoleon Hill, to interview him and other rich men and women. Carnegie opened up his methods, his finances, his secrets to Hill. He told everything and he asked his friends to do the same.

When Carnegie asked someone to do something, they did it. There was no holding back.

Napoleon Hill wrote *Think And Grow Rich* based on what he had learned. It came out during the Depression when few could afford a meal, much less a book.

It became a bestseller and it has never gone out of print. You can get it in any bookstore or library. The basic rule that Napoleon Hill learned from the richest people in the world: Believe you will get what you want. Believe it so strongly that there is no doubt.

Yes, of course you have to work for it. You have to have a plan and stick with it, then alter your plan until something works. It is a practical book. It also tells you to be honest, something else the rich people said is a must, and to pay your debts on time.

It is a practical book full of simple, down-to-earth methods. Write the amount of money you want on a piece of paper and look at it every day. Then write down ways of making that money, honest ways. Concentrate on it.

The bottom line, like catching a fish, is that you will get it, if you believe you will.

Many have read the book and put it aside. They are looking for some magical key, some way to shortcut their way to wealth. Critics of the book have been around since it was first published.

They say they are thinking, but they are not getting rich. But they are not working, and they are not believing. Wishing does not make it so.

The book, like Carnegie's life, did not have a trick in it. You first believe you will grow rich, you figure out a way of doing it, or another way when the first way does not work, and then a third way, and eventually you will get what you want.

But Andrew Carnegie did not want the accumulation of money to take over his life. There were so many other important things to do, mostly learning things. He wanted to know things, everything. Building a fortune was like having a collection of bottle caps. At first it is fun, but after a while when the pails are full of caps it just gets to be a burden.

But he could not stop making money because his stocks and companies were earning too much. So he made the only decision he could. He gave away his fortune.

Like Bill Gates is doing now, Andrew Carnegie gave away almost all his money. He kept a bit to live on, and by today's standards he lived well. But if all his money had been put into a warehouse, filled floor to roof, he gave away the equivalent of everything except a shoebox of folding bills. He lived off the shoebox.

He gave to hospitals and other charities and he gave to cultural pursuits: Carnegie Hall. But most of his money went to schools and to build libraries so that others could do what he did: read.

He built more than three thousand libraries around the world, including one at Main and Hastings in Vancouver. The cities he donated to always chose the locations for the libraries. After that the municipality had to do nothing but maintain the building and the books.

"Sign here and the building and books are all yours. No strings attached. Just maintain the building and the books."

Vancouver's city officials picked Main and Hastings when that was the centre of town. Much later, in the 1980s, when it was the armpit of town, the city wanted to tear down the beautiful old library.

The Carnegie Foundation said in brief: No. Sorry. You can't. Here is the contract you signed that said you would maintain it.

"But we want to knock it down. It is out of place in an area that is becoming a slum. We don't want it any longer."

The Carnegie Foundation held up the contract. Sorry, politicians of Vancouver, your ancestors signed this piece of paper. You must maintain it."

Darn. All that money and work has to go into keeping it going. Poor us, said the politicians of Vancouver.

The building was restored. That, in short, is why one of the most beautiful buildings in the city is now on one of the worst corners. The city also had to replace the books, so if you go into the Carnegie Centre the first room you will see is a library. It is not very big. Most of the building is used for social programs.

But there is a library, and it has more than four hundred books. And it is open and available to everyone, especially the poor.

The point: Andrew Carnegie wanted to better his life. He wanted it very much. He believed he could do it and with the help of someone who allowed him to read he went from abject poverty to towering power and wealth.

He did not have any religion. He said he had seen religions cause too much pain to be part of one himself. His only religion was being positive and believing in himself.

He did not move a mountain, he built a new one out of dollars. Then he said that was not a good thing to do, so then he spread the mountain around so that others could build their own.

The answer to escaping the poverty of skid row is written right inside that beautiful old building. There are many books on addiction among the four hundred. There are motivational books. There are books on how to do something with your life.

If Andrew Carnegie were standing outside on the corner as a poor boy, he would have gone inside and started reading, the same as anyone standing outside now can do.

CAROL AND VICTOR

They had their wedding in the little church in the Burnaby Village Museum, which is the recreation of a town in Burnaby a century ago.

If you have never been to the outdoor museum, why not? It is wonderful. Don't make excuses, just go and experience life as it was.

The church in the village square is small because not many people lived in the village back then. The crowd for Carol and Victor's wedding was large. They spilled out past the front door. Outside, they parted as Carol rolled her powered wheelchair up to the front steps.

Front steps? She cannot get up the front steps. The church was from an era that was not wheelchair friendly. You needed to be able to walk up the steps to get closer to God.

She had some help from friends and family who put their hands under her arms to steady her. She leaned on a cane with four posts on the bottom for stability. She struggled to get a foot up on the first step.

The organ played the same notes again.

She got her second foot on the step.

Five years earlier she had been in a horrendous, terrible car crash. Her husband was killed. When they pulled her from the wreckage they thought she was as good as dead. There was no hope for her.

But there is a difference between being actually not of this world and holding on by an unravelling thread while you are kept alive with pumps and generators so that your organs will continue living so they can be removed from your useless body and give life and hope to someone else.

That was Carol, with the pumps keeping her liver and heart and kidneys alive. And then, in the hospital, she had a stroke.

But now, with the church bells ringing and the little organ inside playing "Here Comes the Bride," she was standing with both feet on the first step.

The crowd inside was hushed while the music repeated, and the bells rang all through Burnaby Village Museum. The organ played, again, and again, "Here Comes the Bride."

Scores of visitors who knew nothing of Carol came to watch. They stood in silence as she pulled herself up the second step. They came to see the old blacksmith and the old schoolhouse, staffed by actors dressed for the parts, and now they were watching a bride-to-be in real life, today, not yesterday, overcoming the impossible.

Carol slowly climbed the four steps and slowly, hesitantly, walked through the open front door and down the short aisle while the organ played the same song, over and over. She was walking alone but with many hands ready nearby to help.

With each note she pushed herself. If the music had stopped she might have also stopped moving. And if she had stopped the music would not have gone on. But both continued.

The bride and "Here Comes the Bride" kept forcing themselves to go on until she got to the end of the aisle and paused at the two steps leading up to the altar where her husband-to-be stood, leaning on his cane.

Victor was the bride's groom. Victor who had a stroke a few years before Carol's accident. Victor who was told he would never walk again, or talk, stood waiting for his bride. Victor who walked, and talked, and gave lectures to other stroke sufferers about believing in yourself.

"Believe, and you can do it. Believe and you will do it. Believe," he said. And he did.

Carol heard him talking at GF Strong Rehabilitation Centre. That was after the tubes and wires were removed from her because she refused to die. And it was after her consciousness returned. But before she could walk, or talk.

She listened.

"He told me I could do it," she said, and she said it as clearly as a bride can talk.

"I believed him," she said.

And then it began to work. It is not a pill. It is not immediate. But the belief became what would be, she said.

Carol talked. And walked. And Victor asked her a question, and she said yes. And on this day he was waiting at the top of the two steps while the organ played.

Carol climbed those two steps with one hand of a relative reaching out desperately to grab her, but then pulling back when it was known that she would, she must, do it alone. At the top step the friends and relatives who came for the wedding burst into applause.

They clapped and clapped and you could not hear the organ. The applause filled the church and was heard outside where visitors who did not know Carol or Victor joined in and began applauding.

That was before the ceremony, which was brief.

"I now pronounce you Man and Wife."

More applause. Louder this time.

And then the organ again, but this time the faster, more joyous song that follows weddings and they walked back down the aisle together and outside to be greeted by a crowd of people they had never seen before. The blacksmith and the old school could wait. This was more important.

"I am very happy," said Carol who sat back in her wheelchair and looked beautiful.

"I was so nervous I was worried I'd forget what to say," said Victor, who never forgets what to say.

And they lived happily ever after.

ANVIL BATTERY

Don't Mess With New West.

You see that sign in Texas, except on the bumper stickers they say Texas instead of New Westminster. But in Texas it is an anti-littering slogan.

In New West it is the characters of people you don't mess with.

In 1871 the new capital of British Columbia said "No!" to New West. "No, you cannot shoot off a cannon to celebrate the Queen's birthday. No, you must be silent. No, you cannot honour her because we in Victoria are the new capital and only we can fire a cannon for her birthday."

And to make sure that the old capital, which was New West, would not shoot off a cannon the new capital took away the only cannon that was in New Westminster.

The people of New West were not happy. They loved Queen Victoria. They had had a twenty-one gun salute for her every year for more than a decade since the rough town came into being. Even when they were a tiny hamlet of Royal Engineers and blacksmiths and gold miners and saloon keepers and ladies that lived rugged lives with no complaints they still honoured their Queen.

The biggest holiday of the year in New West was Victoria's birthday. But this year it would be silent because the new capital wanted to be recognized as the only place in the colony to officially salute her.

"I have an idea," said the mayor who was also a blacksmith.

You don't mess with mayors who swing heavy hammers.

He said they could put one of his huge anvils in the middle of the town square. Then they could pour some gunpowder on top of the anvil, and then two very strong men who you would not mess with would place another anvil on top of the gunpowder which was on top of an anvil.

This was looking like much fun and much danger and much excitement. The town's folks were coming out to watch. They might have a holiday after all; a New West Don't-Mess-With-Our-Traditions holiday.

Then one brave man, who you would not mess with under any circumstance, pulled a poker from the forge that was glowing red and stuck the hot end into the edge of the gunpowder. You did not have to count to One before the explosion blew the top anvil, which weighed 125 pounds, three feet into the air. You could hear it all over New West.

When they heard about it in Victoria they said, "You cannot do that. In fact, you are forbidden to salute the Queen with that outrageous noise. Only we can make an outrageous noise." It took a while to get the messages delivered, so the officials in Victoria made the pronouncement official for the following year.

The following year the people of New West put more gunpowder on the anvil and placed the other anvil on top once again and lit it and, in short, they did what they were not allowed to do.

"You can't."

Bang.

"Forbidden."

Bang.

"Stop. This is an official order."

Bang.

"This is your last warning."

Bang.

And there was born the twenty-one anvil salute, the only one in the world.

Some of those firing the anvils were former Royal Engineers, who wore red tunics when they were serving the Queen.

"We should have an Anvil Battery uniform," they said.

Hence, the red uniform of the Anvil Battery.

And because Royal Engineers had ranks, they gave themselves ranks: The Right Hand Hoister for picking up the anvil on the right side, and The Left Hand Hoister for picking up the anvil on the left side.

There was also the official Shooter Offer and after the firing, to cool down the anvil with a wet cloth, there was the official Swabber Offer.

With ranks like this it was hard for the politicians in the new capital to pass orders against them. But just in case there was to be an attempt from a gang of lowly Victoria politicians they would have to confront the new anvil battery with a new name: The Ancient and Honourable Hyack Anvil Battery. That was the "Don't Mess With Us" Battery.

"Go ahead, write an order against that."

Hyack came from a Native word meaning hurry up, and the firemen of New West took it as their name since that is the main thing they had to do on their way to fires. They added the name to the anvil battery because they wanted to. No one argued with them.

Now could you imagine a quill-pushing contingent dressed in formal black frocks from Victoria standing in front of blacksmiths and firemen wearing red coats and lifting anvils and carrying red hot pokers and hammers, and trying to tell them to be quiet?

From 1871 to whatever year you are reading this, the Ancient and Honourable Hyack Anvil Battery has fired a twenty-one anvil salute to Queen Victoria every year, except one—the year she died.

You can watch them in New West on May 24. They fire the anvils in the baseball field at Queens Park. They will fly the British flag and sing to their Queen.

You can also watch all the people in unison in the stands putting their hands over their ears just as the Shooter Offer runs up to the anvils with his red hot poker. And you can listen to the car alarms in the parking lot outside the field yelling their little annoying mechanical hearts out.

The one thing you won't hear is anyone trying to tell them to stop. The point of this? Don't Mess With New West. They believe in anvils and gunpowder. And what they believe, they do. Cover your ears.

PUBLIC DRINKING

It's illegal. Drinking in public is a legal sin. You know that. If you are a teenager you hide your beer. If you are a respectable adult with respectable adult friends having a glass of wine on the beach you hide your bottle.

If the police come by you swear you are having lemonade. Even though you are sixty years old and your hair is white you lie because having a drink in public is a no-no. Silly society.

"Hey, they are drinking in public," said Mike Timbrell, a cameraman who had his first hangover with me in Russia when he was a young cameraman. He was dying, as we all are when we want to die more than anything because we were the life of the party the night before.

In Russia I told him to keep shooting, keep his camera going. His biggest accomplishment that day was not throwing up. You count small blessings as large ones when the chips are stacked against you.

Twenty years later he still has never gone back to vodka, or any hard liquor. A Russia hangover is a lifelong lesson.

"They're drinking in public," he said.

"Maybe it's a birthday," I said.

Two balloons were flying above a bench on Beach Avenue. We pulled over. The two couples standing near the bench turned their backs on us.

"They don't look too friendly. I don't think it's a birthday party," I said to Mike.

We sat for a few minutes in his black SUV with a handful of antennas sticking up from its fenders and roof. Mike lives by police and fire radios.

"They are hiding something, probably liquor," he said.

We did not want to find people hiding beer. We were looking for something sweet and uplifting and kind and memorable, not beer in a bag.

"I don't think they'll talk to us," I said.

"Well, try anyway," he said. Otherwise he would have to drive more and he had learned the secret of my particular kind of journalism. To avoid driving around endlessly tell me to get out and talk to someone.

After that comes into play my fundamental belief in the first rule of journalism: Say hello. If they're breathing that's a start, if not, we work on the non-breathing angle.

Everything and everyone has something interesting inside them. If you turn your back and say there's nothing there, it's your loss.

I walked up to the people at the bench, and I was thinking since they are shifting back and forth they must be conniving and secretive, and I was not expecting a warm reception.

"Hello," I said.

"Yes?" with a tone that was suspicious coming back at me.

That was from a woman with white hair, which is the most beautiful colour in the world because it shows you have suffered and survived the suffering, and you've had some good times, which is what life is for, and you've probably had sex and enjoyed it and had sex and faked it, so you are my kind of woman. White-haired women have lived.

"Excuse me, I don't want to bother you and it is none of my business, but would you tell me what you are doing, because it looks like a nice party."

Being polite is always a good way to start. It's better than leaving a bad first impression, which you can never erase.

"We are celebrating our sister's birthday," said the other woman, whose hair was turning white.

I am trying to do the math. If the party is for their sister and there are only two women here then someone is missing.

"And where is your sister?" I asked in simple honesty.

"She died two years ago."

Oh, sad. Death is always sad.

"But we are very happy today," said the other woman. "Because this is the way she would love us to celebrate, except we can't get caught."

I love these people, sweet and defiant, obviously law-abiding and obviously lawbreakers. And birthdays for the dead are as good as birthdays for the living. You give gifts and cake and song to the living, you give memory to the dead, which gives meaning to the gifts and cake and songs that went before this time.

"You looked like you were hiding something," I said.

That is the honesty button. Push it, it always works.

"We thought you were the police in that fancy unmarked car," said sweetheart white-haired woman. "We have our beer and vodka for our sister. She liked a drink in the afternoon."

From out of their coat pockets the two women took two tiny bottles, the kind that are sometimes attached to full sized bottles, and the men took two beer cans from paper bags. They wished a happy birthday to a woman who was there but we could not see her.

The liquids in the small bottles were now being mixed with tears that came very quickly.

"She really preferred Scotch," said the other woman, "but we couldn't get any small bottles of that."

She was, or still is, Maureen Nicol, born in April 1942, and passed away in February 2007.

They honoured her with a plaque on a bench that is in front of her apartment on Beach Avenue.

"We would go up there on the roof in the summer afternoons and have happy hour and look at the shining water," said a neighbour of Maureen's who came by when he saw the party down below.

The plaque on the bench says: "Look for me in the beauty of the shining water."

"So what do you have if you couldn't get Scotch?" I asked.

White-haired lady smiled.

"She went to Mexico once so we got tequila. She'll forgive us."

Then they all toasted Maureen, holding their illegal drinks up high, defying all the rules and regulations that are meant to keep us civilized.

"Happy birthday, dear Maureen, dear sister, we miss you."

They each took a sip of their own drinks and poured the full small bottle of tequila on the ground in front of the bench.

"She's dancing," said another neighbour, a woman, who also came down for the gathering. It was turning into a regular party.

"I feel so good I want to cry," said the white-haired sister.

They let the balloons go free, connecting the ground with the sky, and then they left, slipping their cans and bottles into their pockets so as to leave no mess after the party.

If the police had come by we suspect they would have taken off their hats to these fine lawbreakers. The one law that they did obey, right to the letter, was remembering.

Happy birthday, Maureen. You have a good family.

This is not positive thinking or believing in something, but it is believing that you will remember someone, and there is nothing more positive than that.

SLEIGHT OF HAND

W hen I met these two people, who never met each other, I had no idea how the small things they were doing gave them everything they wanted. They became a tale of four hands that were weaving their own lives.

Again, it starts with the question, what do you want to be?

You want to be happy, you want some money coming in, you want to be productive, not bored, and healthy. Healthy, of course, because we all say without that you have nothing.

But you also want to have friends and you would like to be busy, too busy to have problems. It would not hurt to be useful and have a roof over your head and have people admire your accomplishments, and that means you have to have something you've accomplished.

Those are big ticket orders, especially if you have cancer and haven't done anything really noticeable in your life except raise a good family. But now you are a widow and alone and have that ugly big C.

That's one pair of hands.

The other pair of hands is backed by a voice that has gravel in it and is worn: "I was living on the street. I was lost. I had no idea what to do or who to go to. It's not easy being lost and homeless."

The first pair of hands, still soft despite the years: "I knew the end was coming soon, and I didn't think I had really done anything in life. I had raised a family, but that was the top line on my resumé."

But each had been taught something when they were young. She: crocheting. He: knitting.

She, Lucille Charters, had an idea. Where do ideas come from? In each of us they come from places you can hardly remember, something you see or hear about, and then they take root in your mind and suddenly spring up as your own.

"How did you think of that?"

"Don't know. It just came to me."

It was only a half-dozen years ago that saving the earth was getting to be big, daily news. Plastic bags, which were once the greatest inventions after Styrofoam, were being called evil. Permanent, cloth, reusable shopping bags were being promoted by save-the-earth groups in an effort to get rid of plastic bags.

Lucille was carrying her groceries home to her tiny apartment in a couple of plastic bags. She had a drawer full of the bags in her kitchen.

"I wonder," she thought.

That was all. She had been diagnosed with cancer. She was living alone. Her bed doubled as a sofa in the day leaving only enough room to take four steps one way in her apartment and four steps back.

"I wonder," she thought. "If only . . . could you imagine if there was some way I could do that?" Then alone in her apartment she said out loud, "Of course! I can."

There was a way to save the earth and do something with her time and her life. It came in a flash of insight and brilliance that only a woman who had spent a lifetime crocheting could think of. First it was baby clothes, then decades later it was a way of passing time, slowly moving through minutes by hooking yarn and wrapping it around more yarn when she became a widow. Crocheting was better than sitting, staring out of a window.

Her idea: Stretch plastic bags out straight, cut each one across the bag in slices so that you have a circle of plastic, then loop each circle through the other, making basically a chain of plastic, which then became yarn. Join white bags with the red lettering from other bags. Use green bags as a start, then blue, then every other colour you could find.

"Plastic bags, wonderful! Bring them to me."

She slid her crochet hook under one strand of plastic and started doing what her fingers knew so well. In four days she had produced not another sweater or scarf, but her very first plastic, reusable shopping bag, made up of more than 125 plastic shopping bags.

"Look," she said to me after several years of making beautiful plastic bags, "Start filling it with those cans of pears and peas."

I did until the bag was full. I could barely lift it. The bag did not break. It did not stretch. It simply put a strain on my shoulder.

"It doesn't wear out. I've been using that one," the one I was trying to lift, "for three years. It looks the same as when it was new. And you can wash them and," she was on a roll, "that's 125 bags that did not go into the landfill."

And she was smiling.

And her cancer was in remission.

How is that possible?

When you do something that takes over your life, something that you want to do, something that you believe in, things change. Is it the miracle of the plastic bag, or the miracle of living for something that fixes things?

You can't tell Lucille it's anything but the joy she has of making them, giving them away to friends, selling them at craft fairs, making a little extra money and always being asked: "You really made these? That's amazing."

It's enough to keep you alive.

And then there was Mr. Knit, sitting on a windy corner of a rainy street in New Westminster.

"Got any scarves today, Mr. Knit?"

That was a sweet little old lady walking by on the sidewalk holding an umbrella over her head because the rain had changed to snow.

"Why are you asking for his scarves?" I asked. "Don't you knit?"

"Did you notice the weather, young man?" she said to me.

I love this woman.

"I need a scarf, now."

Mr. Knit held up three, all different colours. She picked the red one.

"Four dollars," said Mr. Knit.

I knew downtown in a department store that scarf would have been thirty dollars.

The woman paid and wrapped it around her neck.

"Very warm," she said.

"How's his knitting?" I asked.

"As good as mine, young man." Then she added, "Do you knit?"

No, of course not. Knitting is for women. Men look at motors and pretend they can make them work.

"You should, then you wouldn't be so cold."

You don't have to go to a theatre to find a one-act play.

She left and I asked Mr. Knit why he was sitting on a corner on a tiny folding stool, knitting. But before he could answer I asked what I really wanted to ask:

"Isn't it odd that a man is knitting?"

He ignored my second question.

"I was homeless," said Mr. Knit. "No money, no job, nothing, and that's a rotten feeling."

How he got that way I don't know. It doesn't matter. He got that way. That was all that did matter.

"What did you do?"

"I needed a hat to keep warm. My grandmother taught me to knit when I was a kid, so I got some wool and needles and made one. Someone asked if they could buy it. Suddenly I had a job."

He has no factory or office, so he works on the street, usually near Belmont and Seventh, which has an overhang so he can keep dry in the rain and snow. And there he sits and knits.

"This took me off the street and gave me a home," he said holding up his needles and wool.

Of course he gets government money. We are not here to say he should or should not. He gets welfare and that is that. But what else he does is click his needles together and make toques and bookmarks and baby socks and scarves.

A group of teens were coming down the street. This is the acid test, especially the boys wearing hoodies. They don't knit.

"Stop. Come here for a second," I said.

That was a challenge. They are ready for anything, especially if they can prove their toughness.

"What do you think of a guy who knits?"

They looked at me as though I were a teacher, and they did not like teachers who asked them questions they might have to answer because that might require thought. And they were not in a thinking mood.

Then they looked at Mr. Knit as though he was something that did not fit into their view of the world where everyone is against them.

A full thirty seconds of studying the flying fingers, the fingers that were stained and wrinkled with raised knuckles and dangerous looking. They were fingers that had survived numerous battles.

But these same fingers were weaving soft yarn into an object that they could recognize. Something was happening before their eyes, but it was not supposed to happen this way. If they had ever seen knitting it was a woman doing it. This was a man of the street with a straggly, uncombed beard, and eyes that had seen many things that the teenagers had not. The eyes jumped around, not letting anyone sneak up on them.

"Holy blank," said a voice from the darkness of a hoodie. "That is one tough dude to be doing that."

"I wouldn't have the guts to do that," said another voice from deep inside another hood, which is one way to face the world.

"Why?" I asked the faceless duo.

Their friends were examining the flying fingers.

"Cause that's what women do, and he's no woman," said one.

"You are truly an M.O.," I said.

"What's that?"

"A master of the obvious."

I saw a head jerk. He was not sure if that was a compliment.

"I was like you guys once," said Mr. Knit. "You should really learn to do this in case your life doesn't turn out like you think it will."

That is when they left. They were sure their lives would turn out like they thought they would.

"I wish them luck," said Mr. Knit.

"So you just knitted yourself out of homelessness?" I asked.

He nodded. "Once I started doing this I knew I could have a good life, and that's what I have now."

Mr. Knit's real name is Wayne Rideout. You can find him on a corner most days earning a living, not begging.

"How do you feel while you are doing this?"

"Like I am in charge of my life, and I feel that way because I am."

Then his fingers went back to work.

There are alternatives to the lives of Mr. Knit and Lucille. You know some of those who suffer though them:

"No, don't be stupid, I'm not going to sit on a corner and knit stupid scarves. My grandmother showed me how, but I forgot. And besides, people would laugh at me."

And:

"What do I care about saving the earth? I don't have much time left on it anyway, and besides, who would want to use a plastic bag made out of plastic bags?"

Luckily Lucille and Mr. Knit both wanted something different and, as a result, got the lives they wanted.

THE POWER TO COME BACK

They were painting and cleaning. They were volunteers, a North Shore running group of women who decided to do something to help. Someone in the group knew someone who knew someone else who told them about a street mission on East Cordova.

The women, all well dressed, well combed and brushed, put on latex gloves and painted the walls and had a good time. The street people working with them had a good time. It was the first time many of them had seen people like each other.

While they were doing it I saw one woman, a worker in the mission. I could not help noticing her because she was in a wheelchair. She had been badly burned. Her face was disfigured. Her hands were misshapen. And she was missing one leg.

I saw her and she appeared in the story, but briefly. She was just too hard to look at. We all do that. We avert out eyes.

The story of the volunteers helping out was fine; women with bracelets and neatly applied makeup were painting over the cracked walls while standing next to men and women whose only bracelets had been when the police put handcuffs on them for public drunkenness.

Each inspired the other, whose eyes were opened by the other. It was good.

Just as we were leaving, one of the runners from West Vancouver opened the rear of her expensive car and took out several flats of spring primulas.

"They were donated by a nursery in Southlands," she said to me.

Southlands. Shaughnessy with horses. Southlands, where the homes have more floor space than some entire single room occupancy hotels on the Downtown Eastside, and where the homeowners go next door to visit their horses in their private stables.

Some nice people live there. They do not have much in common with Main and Hastings, but that does not stop them from being nice. If you get the chance you should wander down there, south of Southwest Marine Drive. It may inspire you to work harder.

And some nice people there donated some primulas to the women who were volunteering in the Downtown Eastside.

"I've been told they won't last the night," said one very lovely woman who was wearing a jogging outfit that was not used for jogging. This was sort of an après-jog tog that could be worn in Park Royal.

She and another volunteer planted the flowers in two concrete pots in front of the mission, and then they all left.

A month later the flowers were still there. The woman who had been burned was tending them, pulling weeds out of the pots while she sat in her wheelchair.

"The people at this mission protect them," she said. "We say they are so beautiful, leave them."

And because they said so, they were left, in peace and beauty. Sometimes it does work that way.

"Tell me about yourself," I asked.

Five years ago she had been walking across Oppenheimer Park when someone poured gasoline over her and lit her on fire.

"Oh, God. Why?"

"I don't know," she said.

"What happened?"

"I don't remember."

She spent two years in hospitals and rehab wards. She had operations, her leg amputated, and counselling and skin grafts and more surgery.

"How are you now?" I asked a woman with one leg and a changed face.

"Fine," she said. "I have friends here," she gestured to the mission, "and up there." She gestured to the sky.

"And now I am taking care of these flowers."

And then she smiled.

"How do you do this?" I asked, meaning how do you keep your spirits up when you are in this position, and she knew what I meant. And then she gave the most profound answer to a question about overcoming hardships that I have ever heard:

"If kids with cancer, kids who are dying, can smile and laugh, this is nothing. I've already had my childhood and I am still here."

A staggering, swearing, smelly passerby passed by and objected to us being there and said a profane word to us. We with a television camera did not belong in this neighbourhood, he said.

All Linda said to him was, "Hello, sweetheart."

You know how that greeting made one old, foul man with bad breath and bad skin and a bad attitude feel? No one hears themselves being called "sweetheart" without involuntarily feeling something good.

"Don't look at their drugs and drink," she said. "There is a human being under there. And that person needs love."

As we left, Linda said, "See, there is good news down here."

She pushed her wheelchair back into the mission. She is working as a secretary, custodian, caregiver and primula guardian. We need more Lindas.

TWO OTHER GUYS

At the risk of saying too much about East Hastings, I want to tell you about these two guys.

I got a call from Jason's wife.

"You are spending time in the back alleys?"

"Yes."

"You want to meet someone who was there?"

"I know many who were here, and are still here."

"You want to meet someone who was and isn't?"

"Okay."

Promises by phone are sometimes overstated.

"We'll be there in half an hour."

That is a good start.

A high-end SUV pickup pulled up to the curb.

"Whoever they are, they have way too much money," I thought in my bigoted way.

Two kids and a woman got out, then a tall man, good looking, strong—a family that is hard to peg.

They came to me. Obviously this is the promise, and it seems to be coming true.

"I want to show you where I started out," said Jason Diffner.

We walked past the drug dealers who were crowding the alley just behind

tHE EXPANDED REILLY METHOD

the Carnegie Centre. The dealers are big and tough-looking, but Jason was bigger, and he looked tougher, and he obviously had no fear.

He walked past them with a young girl and boy and a pretty woman at his side. This is not the family of the back alley.

"I used to shoot up behind that dumpster," he said, looking at a dumpster behind which a young woman was sticking a needle into her arm.

"I spent half my life here," he said. "I quit, and then in 1998 I went back, hard."

He had what almost no one has, he had a motion picture history of himself back here, where rats are higher on the existence scale than humans with needles in their arms.

The police videotaped Jason when they arrested him. He was shirtless and screaming and flailing his arms and fists at the air while he lay on the ground, which had broken bottles spread around his shirtless body.

"That was me," he said. "Not much to write home about."

His son and daughter stood next to him.

"I'm glad he's back," said his daughter. "This is so scary."

His son looked around and his face said more than a university course in the social dynamics of alternate lifestyles. In short, Jason's son will not end up here.

Then they left. They walked by the dealers, who opened up and let this family pass. The drug dealers, who come and go and change languages frequently and have wads of cash in their pockets, had no idea who he was.

The drug dealers have almost as short a life expectancy as the drug addicts. It is not overdoses that dispose of them, but other drug dealers.

But when Jason walked past them they saw someone they knew they would not even try to sell their poison to. He was proud and brave and the dealers do not sell to people who are that.

Jason has his own construction company and runs a program helping others escape.

"Why? How?"

"I had no choice. Leave or die. And I believed I could get past it. So I did."

When you believe, really believe, even death can be cheated.

The day before I talked to Jason I met Randy Tait, a native counsellor. He was like Jason. Both had more than a half dozen years of clean freedom behind them and a strong will keeping them going.

Natives have it worse than whites or blacks or yellows when it comes to drugs. For reasons that are deeper than I understand, they have less hope. Maybe it is because everything was taken away from them by the government and the church and they were told to be like us, or they would have nothing.

From nothing to nothing. What a deal. When they rebelled they were hung or beaten or raped. Their choices were limited. When they consented to having their children taken away for a better life the children were put into miserable schools and brainwashed and had a worse life.

That was a few generations ago, but the emptiness remains and the drugs fill that emptiness, at least it seems they do. Or it is a good excuse.

Randy's escape route from reality was the same as Jason's. Breathe it, swallow it, inject it. Then the bottom.

"You've got to believe you can do it, and then you do," he said. "There is the only magic formula."

He believed and he did.

When I last saw Randy he had his arm around a lost soul who had come to the corner of Main and Hastings looking for drugs, and now they were walking to a coffee shop. The only thing Randy lives for is to help others escape. There is nothing finer in life.

You believe you can catch a fish, or get off drugs, or change the world or change your life, and you will. But you have to believe you will. The proof is there. The shirtless man screaming on the ground looked like he had no future other than to be locked away and let the cockroaches eat him alive. An ugly thought, and not uncommon down there.

Instead, he held open the truck doors for his wife and kids and drove away in an expensive piece of steel. He drove away from Main and Hastings. He drove away from a past that some say is impossible to leave.

If he looked back in his mirror he saw the buyers and sellers of chemical dreams who end up on the ground without a shirt. I don't know if he looked back. I do know he kept going forward—that was all that mattered.

HOW TO FIND ANYTHING, AND HOW EVERYTHING WORKS OUT, NO MATTER HOW UNBELIEVABLE IT SEEMS

Those self-help books have a long process on how to improve your outlook by following a set of exercises that you can learn if you buy their DVDs and study them. Then you go on to the next lesson, which you must buy.

They say if you want to remember where you left something that you cannot find and that you desperately need, simply associate what you are looking for with your actions over the time that you misplaced it.

What the heck does that mean?

Then if you still can't find it go to the next lesson where you picture what you are looking for, getting everything else out of your head, concentrate on it, concentrate more, no, you are not concentrating hard enough.

Forget eating, forget sleeping, concentrate. Forget work and play. Forget where you are. Forget where you are going. Forget where you have been. Forget everything.

This works every time because by then you've forgotten what you were looking for and probably didn't need it anyway.

How would you like a simpler success? Like when you are looking for your keys, or can't find a street on a map that you are staring at, or you lose your wallet—anything. Those are all disasters and things we all face repeatedly.

Reilly said you get what you believe you will get. So try it with lost items.

Wait a minute. That's impossible. You only get what you want because you change your own outlook. You do not change the world. You do not change reality, you only alter your own outlook on reality. You do not move the lost keys out of the sofa and put them where you can see them.

Oh, yeah. In the most strange way, you will find what you are looking for if you simply believe you will find it.

I want to buy a bottle of Kim Crawford wine for a long-time friend. It is her birthday. She loves Kim Crawford wine.

I have very little time because we are going to see her tonight and I am now in City Hall doing a story about the new poet laureate of Vancouver and it is almost 5 p.m.

It is late because poet laureates are the last thing on any official docket. You can't very well put poetry ahead of the issues of garbage collection or taxes. On the other hand, if they did have poetry earlier in the meetings the officials might be more relaxed when they got around to garbage issues.

No matter. The new poet of Vancouver is a tall, balding, serious-looking man. What am I going to report about him?

"What is your favourite poem?" seems to be a good place to start.

Brad Cran starts reciting a lengthy monologue of existential existence. My eyes are growing wider. I don't understand it and, worse, a minute has gone by without him taking a breath. The story is only two minutes long. One more breath and we will be done and I will not have a clue what has just gone on.

This story will work. I believe it will work. I don't know how, but it will. There is Reilly sticking his poetic nose in again.

Some grade two children arrive who will be part of the poetry ceremony.

"What is your favourite poem?" I ask them.

"Alligator pie, alligator pie. If I don't get some I think I'm gonna die," they shout.

That's poetry.

I ask Brad if he knows "Alligator Pie."

Without batting an eyelash he smiles and says: "Alligator pie, alligator pie. If I don't get some I think I'm gonna die."

And then he knows the second verse, and the third verse. I am in heaven. He speaks the poetic language of children. I am thinking that my daughter is about to have a second child any day now and I will make sure she knows "Alligator Pie."

One of the children is watching and listening. I say to her, "He knows it. Are you surprised?"

She shakes her head and says, "Of course he knows it, he's my father. He taught me."

I am higher than heaven. The new official poet of the city knows "Alligator Pie" and has taught it to the next generation. What more could you ask for, except a bottle of Kim Crawford?

But I know I will be okay because one of the best liquor stores in the city is just one block down the street from City Hall, and because it is so late in the day one of the mobile editing trucks is being sent to the City Hall parking lot for me to work out of.

I have only been in this liquor store once before. It is way out of my usual patrol area, which does not normally include City Hall.

The editor, Darren Twiss, is skilfully putting the pictures together and he tells me that I probably did not know, but while I was away the previous few weeks the son of the cook at the cafeteria at the TV station died.

Sad. It is always sad when a child dies. For a moment I do not think about Kim Crawford or poetry, just the pain that every parent fears and many have to learn to endure.

We finish the story and Darren sends it to the station by microwave. Amazing thing. He raises a mast two storeys high and beams the images and words through the air.

"But the station is the other way," I say.

"City Hall is in the way," he says, and the microwave must go in a straight line.

So to get around City Hall Darren shoots the electron beam to the Wall Centre downtown where there is a relay antenna on the roof, which ricochets the wave to Mount Seymour where there is another antenna, which shoots it to an antenna on the roof of the station in Burnaby where it is rebroadcast around the province.

No wonder the post office is having trouble keeping up.

And now Kim Crawford.

I wander the aisles. I think it is from Australia. I look at all the bottles from Australia. It is not there and the clerks are too busy to ask. It is also just an hour before one of the Canucks' playoff games and so stores that sell beer are the busiest places in town, outside of stores that sell chips, the diet of a hockey fan.

I still cannot find Kim Crawford. In the world of gift giving this is a disaster. If only I had thought about it earlier, like yesterday, everything would have been all right. But now, catastrophe.

Then someone says hello to me. It is the cook from the TV station. His name is Coster and he was buying some beer to watch the game.

"I'm so sorry, I heard about your tragedy," I said. "I just learned about it. I was away at the time."

He thanked me and told me how he misses his son. Lou Gehrig's disease, he said, which his son got in his thirties. When a child dies the age does not matter. It is your child.

"It was a terrible way to go," he said.

I felt so sad for him, but I knew that, for whatever infinitesimal small moment of relief it brought him, he was glad that his son's death was known about and acknowledged.

How did I learn about his son just a half-hour earlier? How was it that I went to that liquor store, which is near where Coster lives, even though I did not know that he lives there?

He left. His head was down. Perhaps for a few moments the hockey game would numb the pain. Then I went on looking for Kim Crawford.

Reilly says just believe. Okay, kid, let's see if that works.

This will sound stupid so I will only think it. "I will find Kim Crawford. I believe I will find Kim Crawford. I know I will find it, truly, absolutely and totally. I base this on the fact that it is a popular wine because my friend is a trendsetter and she knows good wines and if she is drinking it others will drink it and so a good liquor store will have it."

Fortunately no one can hear me thinking, because if they did they would say I should be served nothing more. I walk down one more aisle.

There! Right there. Second shelf down, right about my knees, it's true, believing works. The sign: Kim Crawford. How did I miss it?

Of course I knew how I missed it. The shelf was empty, there was only a sign.

Reilly said I would get what I believed I would get and I did, sort of.

It is just that neither Reilly nor I can control the popularity of something.

I left thinking that flowers without wine will have to do for a gift. Darn. She would have preferred wine without the flowers, but it was really too late to stop in another liquor store after picking up my wife. Then my wife called.

Our daughter just had her baby. Wonderful. We have to rush over and pick up our daughter's other daughter and babysit her tonight.

"Sorry we can't drop off the wine that you said you were getting," my wife added.

I got what I wanted. The Kim Crawford was delivered a few days later along with pictures of our new granddaughter. And a few days later in the cafeteria Coster said he appreciated me mentioning his son. Nothing relieves the pain, but sharing helps. If I had not known about his son the moment of meeting would have been painful for him. Should he mention it or not? Tragedy has many layers. I am so thankful I knew.

And in addition to that, "Alligator Pie" was recited in the chambers of City Hall for the first time in history, all because of a group of kids. You can't beat that for finding the perfect thing at the perfect place at the perfect time.

Reilly was right.

NEW YORK WANTED SAFER STREETS, SO IT MADE ITS STREETS SAFER

I got a ticket. A parking ticket that I did not deserve and I am ticked off. Okay, I did park too close to the fire hydrant, but here is the reason for that.

I was on my first day of vacation in New York visiting a sweet little old lady whom my wife and I see every year. We took her on a long drive to a cemetery to visit her dear, departed husband's grave. After that we showed her some pretty scenery and then went to dinner and by the time we got back to her apartment in the city it was almost midnight. There were no parking spaces.

Of course not. It's a crowded city.

I stopped by the fire hydrant just so she could get out and we helped her up her stairs to the second floor where she lives and I took out her garbage and hurried back to my rented car to go hunt for a space and there was a ticket under the wiper blade.

What? I was helping a little old lady. I'm not a lawbreaker.

And secondly, who the heck gives out tickets in this neighbourhood at midnight? This is not a good neighbourhood with police protection. This is not a neighbourhood where they care how you park, at least it wasn't when I lived here, or even if the car you left was abandoned or stolen. In fact, when we left New York this was a neighbourhood under siege by criminals. There

115

was gunfire at night. Sometimes in the day. No one gave out tickets. There were just people ducking.

Now, this neighbourhood is safe, like all of New York.

The sweet little old lady used to tell me, "Don't go outside. They shoot people here."

Now every day she walks slowly down the street to get her newspaper. No one bothers her. Neighbours sit on their front steps and say hello to her.

So who gave me the ticket?

My wife and I saw a lonely figure a block away with a police hat. I walked quickly and caught up to him. He was way too young to be a cop, but he had the uniform and a gun and badge. When the cops get young you know you are getting old.

I suspect he was thinking this guy is too old to be out on the street so late.

"Did you give me this ticket, and who are you and what are you doing here?"

I had a lot of questions for someone whose car was parked close to a fire hydrant. But I had never seen a cop on this street before and I have known this street for forty years.

"You were parked illegally."

"But I was helping a sweet little old lady up the stairs."

He looked at me with his youthful, lawman eyes and said he was sorry. If he had known he would not have given it to me.

Then I stopped asking about the ticket. There was a bigger question here: "What are you doing here?"

Before he could answer I saw more cops.

"What are you all doing here? Has there been a murder?"

"No, sir," said one with stripes on his sleeve. "Just trying to keep that from happening."

Now here's the story and, as it turns out, I've been fibbing to you. Yes, there is crime in New York.

True, there is no Main and Hastings any more. There used to be Main and Hastings everywhere. The famous Broadway was one long Main and Hastings. Grand Central Station used to be Main and Hastings. The South Bronx and all of Brooklyn used to be Main and Hastings.

When we left New York in the early 1970s Times Square was worse than the back alley behind Main and Hastings. There was open drugs dealing and drug taking, and open prostitution, and open wounds of the freshly stabbed and shot. The famous lights around the theatre streets had gone dim. The big, glowing billboards that you ooh and ahh at now were dark.

Now, Times Square is a twenty-four-hour Disney-inspired vacation land. The lights and laughter and amazement and excitement are non-stop. Families are on the street at 2 a.m. taking pictures of the squads of police who smile and pose.

You almost get the idea that the only duty of the police is to have their photos taken by visitors from Kansas and British Columbia.

There is no crime in Times Square. Well, of course not. The police are standing right there, and there and over there across the street. That is a very reassuring sight, unless you are a criminal and then you go elsewhere.

But where is elsewhere? There are police strolling around Grand Central Station. Can't go there, if you are a crook. If you are a tourist or a taxpaying citizen you say, "My gosh, this is comfortable. There's no crime here."

Go to the world famous Macy's Department store on 34th Street, the biggest single store in the world, and there are no criminals who will take your packages or your money.

In fact, you can't go anywhere in Manhattan and stumble into a bad neighbourhood, even the infamous old Hell's Kitchen or Lower East Side. It doesn't matter if you don't know where those places are, there was a time only ten or twenty years ago when the only reason you would want to know where they were was to not go there. Now they are so safe you tour them at night and go home talking about how safe you felt.

That is one topic that does not get boring with repetition. Why? Because in the centre of the city there is a cop on the beat, no, there are two, wait, another block away there are more, and you know that the worst thing that is going to happen to you is a heat wave or a snowstorm or a parking ticket.

So if you are a criminal where do you go? That is a problem.

Well, you go to my old neighbourhood in Brooklyn on the outskirts of New York. It is far from the skyscrapers, it has no tourists that the city wants to protect, and who would care if a crime is committed here?

And for a while, the criminals had that figured out. In this neighbourhood of apartment houses and row houses and tire shops and auto body repair shops and a couple of corner food stores, crime started rising.

It was a trickle at first, then as criminals got away with it, more and more crime. The newspapers and TV news had stories of shootings and holdups and sex assaults in pockets of neighbourhoods around the city. If you were visiting the city you had no idea this was going on, except by reading about it. You would never go to these streets. You would not even know how to get to them. And if you asked your tour guide how to get there he would look at you with crossed eyes and say, "That's not the real New York. There are no museums, no shows, no art galleries, no department stores, no restaurants, and you can't even buy a T-shirt there. Don't bother going."

But this is my neighbourhood. It is where I stay when I go to New York and on my first night here this year there is this most incredible sight: Cops walking around the streets. My street as I knew it had never felt the bottom of a beat cop's shoes. Before we left for Canada my street had gotten worse and worse with crime. The only police that were here then came in cars, picked up the casualties, then drove away.

Now, at midnight on a cool April night three cops were walking around the neighbourhood.

"Why? How? When?" I asked not actually believing that I was seeing cops on the beat, on foot, not in cars, out in the open, right there, right in front of me—you get the picture—and there were no tourists around to take photos of them.

"This is a high crime area," said one of them, "And this is our high impact response team."

That sounded like official speak, but I did not care how he was saying it, just so long as he was there to say it.

He said there were forty-five cops assigned to a six square block area. They had been there for the past nine months, twenty-four hours a day, every day. There are thirty-six streets with roughly thirty-five thousand people living in them, many in apartment buildings.

In the first three months of walking and talking and watching and arresting, crime fell fifty percent. In the next three months it was cut in half again. After that it really went downhill and the neighbourhood went the other way.

When someone calls 911 there is a cop at the door in two minutes, sometimes less, with no sirens and no screeching tires. If someone is screaming there will be a cop running to help before the second scream comes out.

The cop on the beat, old-fashioned policing, just being there, is all it took. There are books and college courses and lecture circuits on how New York was cleaned up and saved. But basically, someone in a uniform walking down the street means there will be no crime on that street, whether it is Times Square, or East 93rd Street in Brooklyn, or Main and Hastings.

When the criminals move on, so will the cops. They may be one step behind, but when that step carries a badge and a gun eventually the criminals will run out of places and maybe get a job. Okay, that is wishing too much. But the point is when crime starts to increase somewhere the police move in and walk around the neighbourhood. Then, before it gets out of hand, the crime goes down.

It is like getting rid of graffiti by painting over it. It works. After a while the graffiti appliers get tired of seeing their work disappear and they quit or move on. The end result, no graffiti.

With cops on the beat my old street is safe. Even from those who park illegally.

It is the first time I ever got a parking ticket on that street and I said thanks.

And if that forgotten street in Brooklyn, New York, can be made safe, cleaning up our Main and Hastings is a cinch. Someone just has to believe it can be done and tell the cops to walk around the block and then walk again.

Believe me, you can believe that.

SHINE A LITTLE LIGHT

The streets were hot. Sometimes in late July and always all through August the tar on the street would get soft enough to bend if you squished your shoe into it. But you didn't want to do that because the heat would go up through your sole and made you hotter.

And then when the sweat was coming down and you did not have the energy to play or even read a comic book someone would sometimes ask their father or mother to take us to the beach, the real one with sand that was next to the ocean, not the pile of cardboard boxes that we dove into next to the factory and pretended we were swimming.

We needed a parent because we were only seven or eight years old and the beach was two hours away on a combination of subways and buses and if just kids went, more than likely somebody's little brother or sister would wander off and get lost and the older kids would not stop and think if anyone was missing.

"We're not going to Coney Island," the parent would say. "I don't want all that noise."

Coney Island was the famous beach of rides and hot dogs. We booed because we wanted the noise and the rides and the hot dogs. The reason the parent did not want that was because there everything cost nickels, dimes and even quarters, and this was a neighbourhood where there were few coins.

But subway tokens to the other beach were affordable and you could always squeeze two or three kids together through the turnstile. A token saved is a token to get home on.

"We're going to Riis Park."

"Boo."

Riis Park was at the bottom of the city, below the teeming streets of Brooklyn, on a spit of land that was really just sand. It had the ocean on one side and a bay on the other and there was nothing to stop a breeze coming off the Atlantic that would cool a sweaty face.

"But there's nothing to do here but swim," we would say.

"That's the point of going to the beach," the parent would say.

So we swam and had a wonderful day and had peanut butter and baloney sandwiches brought from home and water from the water fountain to drink.

More than a half century later my wife and I were back at Riis Park. She and I had gone, both as kids, but we never met there.

"It looks the same," she said. "There's nothing here. And now, I love that."

During that trip we had left the city to get away from the city and get some fresh air, and fresh air is what you get at Riis Park, which is still in the city.

But now they had added a visitors' centre. I could use the bathroom. Inside was a display of photos of slums and hollow-eyed, dirty-faced frightened people, staring into the camera.

More pictures of back alleys that were like those behind Main and Hastings, only they were packed with people and they all looked like death was close, but not close enough.

What? Who? Why?

The nice lady at the centre said this is why we have Riis Park. It was opened long after Jacob Riis died, but it was dedicated to him because he did the impossible. He cleaned up the slums.

Who? And don't forget how? And how come I don't know about him?

Jacob Riis was from Denmark, one of fifteen children in a poor family. Like many others in this predicament, he went to America for a better life. Like many others, he did not get it.

To say the streets were crowded does not come close to an accurate picture. You squeezed your way through, always bumping into someone like yourself, poor, truly penniless, hungry, alone, no jobs because too many people were arriving who were just like you looking for work and there was none.

You tried to get into a tenement to get out of the cold and the rain, but they would not let you in because you could not pay the ten cent a day rent to squeeze into a single room with a single bed. The single room occupancy hotels in Vancouver's skid row are terrible and have roaches and mice and no toilet and they overcharge. But in New York in the 1870s the same sized rooms had six occupants, half of them sleeping on the floor.

So Jacob Riis went to one of the poorhouses looking for shelter. They were much much more terrible than the tenements. The poorhouses were run by the police and they were so filthy and vile and there was so much violence that this immigrant young man said sleeping on the sidewalk in the snow was better. Except if you did that the police would beat you with their night sticks.

But Jacob Riis was lucky. He could read. His father had taught him, and because of that, Jacob Riis was unlike many of the poor. He walked into a newspaper office and got a job. He would be a police reporter, because crime news always sells, and he said he was not afraid to go into the slums where the worst of the crimes happened.

His stories were a sensation. He went where few other reporters dared to go. He wrote about the grit and sleaze and endless violence first hand. He did not get a press release from the police, he got the news with his eyes and ears and wrote the inside stories from the inside.

But he said to himself that this was not doing any good. It is not the news of crime that should be reported, but rather why is there crime? Why is there pain? And why is there a hopelessness that leads people into deliberately wasting their lives?

He knew the answer. It was right in front of him. It was in his personal history. You cannot live in nasty filth surrounded by people hurting others and come out of that with your hair combed and a shine on your shoes.

He swore to himself he would help them.

So Jacob Riis started doing stories on the people in the slums and the rat holes they were living in and the streets that were too scary for those living uptown who had money and jobs and carriages and food to ever think of thinking about, much less ever think of visiting.

Like Main and Hastings, the slums were shunned by those not forced to live there. They were spurned with head shaking, and then ignored.

That is until Riis started writing about them. And he wrote and wrote, ceaselessly. He spent his nights learning about the lost hungry souls on an individual basis, and then spent his days writing about them. No one had done that before.

Then came the camera. Photography was a baby invention, but Riis knew that one picture of a mother in rags holding her baby in an alley surrounded by dangerous looking men is stronger than describing the same scene in print. So he took the infant of a camera and learned to coax pictures from it and went into the streets.

Most New Yorkers who did not live in the slums had never seen them before. His pictures caused a shock wave in the city.

"Something should be done. Something must be done! Look at this, and this. That poor woman. Those hungry, ragged children. We must do something."

He wrote hundreds of stories with pictures attached. He was like a boxer with a one-two punch. He kept writing and photographing, a left jab of a picture, a right cross of a story, left, right.

Then came the knockout punch.

He went inside the police run poorhouses where he had found life unbearable.

But how do you show what is going on inside when behind the walls it is always night?

There were no gaslights and no windows in those hellholes. The only lighting came from candles. And if you are thinking about how often there were fires with people trapped inside, you are right.

And of course the other problem: the cameras of those days would not work with candle power.

Riis learned about experiments with flash powder, sort of a gunpowder concoction that was difficult to use and dangerous. He tried it, and tried again and again.

And then suddenly on page one of his newspaper was the first look anyone had ever had of conditions inside a police-run poorhouse. It was sickening. It was inhuman. It was not sensationalizing. It was true, and it was skin crawling.

He shined a light into the darkness. Then more photos, many more.

Teddy Roosevelt, who had led the Rough Riders during the Spanish-American War and would later become president of the US, was at that time police commissioner of New York.

"I did not know about this," he said.

In a short time the poorhouses were closed and replaced by livable housing. Then a movement began to plough down all the slums. Of course taxes had to be raised. Of course the rich protested. Of course the transition was difficult and confusing and had setbacks. But within ten years the slums were gone. Crime nosedived.

Teddy Roosevelt said Jacob Riis was the finest, bravest man he had ever known.

Much later Riis Park was opened and dedicated to the crusading reporter. It was intentionally made without rides or amusements so that you could go there and breathe clean air and have peace.

I didn't know that when I was a kid. But we all knew it was good to get away from the city.

Again, the question, what does this have to do with the belief that you get what you want?

Again the answer is it has everything to do with that: Jacob Riis wanted to move the mountain of pain and poverty, and he did.

PS: The more we know about Main and Hastings, and the more we shine a light on it and talk and write and open it up, the less it will be known as Pain and Wastings, and the more some fresh air will blow across it.

THE TOUR GUIDE

One more brief story from New York, basically proving all things are possible, especially those things that seem impossible.

In the 1970s and '80s the South Bronx was known as the most dangerous place on earth. It was right around Yankee Stadium. Not many went to the games.

The nickname for the police station there was Fort Apache. That became a movie called Fort Apache, the Bronx, with Paul Newman.

Like Paul Newman without the looks, I worked in that police station as a young crime reporter. I had just gotten out of the air force. When I turned in my M-16 I told myself I would never again carry a gun. Because of that, I was the only reporter assigned there without a pistol next to my note pad.

The area was much too violent to support human life in any condition that would be called normal.

Firemen in the South Bronx could not fight the fires that raged in abandoned tenements because after the local street rats started the fires they would go on adjacent rooftops and throw bricks down at the firemen six storeys below. The fire department put thick plastic roofs over their trucks and the firemen could not take one step out past them without risking death, while they still had to fight the fire.

Chaos ruled.

Curtis Sliwa, a very tough guy with a feeling that he wanted to make things better, organized a group called the Guardian Angels. The members were all advanced in martial arts. The idea was, they would wear a red beret so you would know who they were and they would patrol the streets of the South Bronx, unarmed except for their fists, which in many cases were faster than a trigger finger.

At first the police were suspicious, but they quickly found the Angels were helping them. Eventually the Guardian Angels patrolled with the police. Residents liked them from the first day.

Their numbers grew, they did heroic acts protecting everyone they could and the term Guardian Angel was accepted into the language meaning citizens fighting back. During the 1970s and '80s four Guardian Angels were killed while trying to stop violence in and around New York.

Move ahead to now, a long distance of time if you've lived through it. Curtis Sliwa, who has been shot twice and beaten uncountable times and escaped from a kidnapping, is still in the South Bronx.

But now he is giving tours to a new generation who only heard about the bad times—tours of how it used to be.

"Over there were the burned-out buildings. And there, where you see those community gardens, were the shooting galleries for addicts. And there, where you see those neat row houses with pretty flowers in front of them, was the scene of gun battles almost every week."

He speaks with a Brooklyn accent from where he was born. He still wears his red beret. He hears some say it could not really have been that bad, because it is so peaceful now.

It does not matter if they cannot imagine it. It is true and it is over.

How? Simply, people wanted it to change. In not simple terms, it took massive government action to bulldoze the tenements and slums and rebuild the area with neat homes that were affordable for ordinary people. The ordinary people wanted ordinary things, like peace and safety, along with their tiny gardens in front of their homes.

It also took massive police work to arrest the evil doers, and hikes in taxes to build more jails to keep the bad people away from the good people. Then it took programs for the bad people to go to when they got out. It also took the reality of sending them back to jail if they were bad again.

In short, it took common sense and it took a long time.

"And over here, where you see those kids playing on a swing under that tree, a child was shot to death when he was caught in the middle of a gunfight."

Curtis Sliwa is pointing to a quiet corner in the South Bronx.

"There was no tree growing there then."

The change is amazing. And like a person can change the life he or she lives simply by wanting it and making it change, so can a city.

It is not easy. It is not easy to move a mountain. It is not easy to catch a fish.

But some day: "Welcome to fabulous Main and Hastings, the trendiest place in town." That is just like "Welcome to the South Bronx, a good neighbourhood to raise children."

Believe it. If you don't, who will?

HOLE IN THE CLOUDS

I'll tell you where I get my help. It is through the holes in the clouds.

At least that is what I believe, and when you believe something, it is true. I used to believe in lucky sticks, and they worked, but sticks were too hard to hold onto.

So I switched my faith to lucky rocks. Now rocks are something that you can keep. Mike Timbrell, the chief cameraman, carries lucky rocks for me in his ashtray. What am I saying? We don't have ashtrays any longer. The lucky rocks he keeps for me are in his coin tray. That is already lucky. They are rubbing up against the Queen, which makes them luckier.

When we can't find a story he says, "The rocks are waiting. They have slept long enough."

I pull out the tiny sliding drawer and try to get my fingers around one of them. They don't like to be disturbed. They are in almost constant hibernation.

"Did you get one of them out yet?"

"I'm trying, but they are fighting me."

"Try harder, they are not smart enough to fight back."

"That's what you think."

This is an actual conversation between a cameraman with twenty-five years' experience and a reporter who started in the business before he was born.

How do you find your stories?

Rocks. Lucky rocks.

But no longer true.

Now it is the hole in the clouds. That is the way God looks down, and when God looks down everything turns out good.

Don't freak out. We are not going to get into religion, we are into holes in the clouds.

No religion, because my father's family was from Ireland and they were Catholic and hated the Protestants. When I was born my mother looked around for a church in which to baptize me.

There was one down the street, it was covered with vines. It looked pretty. It was Protestant.

My son's godfather is Jewish.

"You can't have a Jewish godfather for your son," said the Anglican priest who was going to baptize our son. "If you die he will be raised Jewish."

"That's nice," I said. "Some of my best friends are Jewish, including my son's godfather once you perform the ceremony."

You get the picture. A Jewish guy with a skullcap standing under a cross promising to provide religious instruction to a tiny baby in a church while the priest is hoping no bishops walk in.

Religion can kill you or make you. You can forget it or worship it. I simply prefer the holes in the clouds. That is direct access.

It started when the rocks were not working well enough. I looked up. There was a hole in the clouds. I used to joke about the Story God. But it was late in the day so I went directly to the big guy.

"God, help me find something of interest that will work and save my day and probably my life and certainly my job."

That is not in the Book of Common Prayer.

Bingo. Around the corner was the man on the scooter with his little dog who saved his life when he passed out. The dog barked until someone came to help. I am not kidding. And I do not mess with success.

Another hole in the clouds. We have to get done quickly because there is a shortage of cameramen. "God, etc. Please, please, please. I cannot keep others waiting because I cannot find something."

That is not like a big-time prayer. It's more a prayer of desperation. "But first, I have to go to the bathroom," I say.

The earlier stuff about keeping your mind off your bladder works fine unless there is no need of it. When you are in the dentist's chair and basically upside down while a drill is going into your nerve you say, "I do not have to go. I do not."

It works. The pain in your tooth also helps keep away the pain in your bladder.

But now there is no need to hold it in. I have already asked for a story and I know, after hundreds of times of asking, that I will find something, so I turn my attention to other things.

We see a couple kissing. That is nice. "Stop."

It is awkward to interrupt lips wrapped around other lips and tongues that you cannot see, which are touching behind the lips that are wrapped around each other.

"Uhhh, excuse me."

They do not budge. I try again.

"Excuse me, I hate to bother you."

They separate, with both of them looking as if they do not want to.

"Did you just get engaged or something?" I ask.

"No," says the man and they resume locking lips.

This is not going to work. If you cannot separate lips you move on. We drive to the Hollow Tree which is being saved by people who do things like that.

"We will be doing big things in a couple of weeks," says one of them.

"A couple of weeks" is not today. "Please go down to Third Beach," I say to the cameraman. "There is a bathroom at Third Beach that is open all year round."

I go into the bathroom. The cameraman, Roger Hope, says he will wait outside.

When I come out, smiling, he is smiling.

"Look," he says, pointing down at the beach.

I look. There is a woman dancing on the beach. If you started this book from the beginning you know the questions that followed.

How is something wonderful like that found? I had to go to the bathroom, yes. We stopped to look at a couple kissing and wondered if they had just gotten engaged. No. We looked at people trying to save the Hollow Tree, which took up a few minutes.

The timing of each of those slowed us down until we got to Third Beach and we only got there because I had to use the facilities. And because of all that, we found the woman who was dancing on the beach.

What a beautiful sight. She was like Zorba the Greek, alone, listening to the music of the heart and dancing with his arms up and his life even higher.

If you have never seen the old Anthony Quinn movie, *Zorba the Greek*, you could do yourself a favour and spend a black and white evening getting connected with the power of life.

This woman at Third Beach looked like she was connecting with something.

We hurried down the long stairs and walked carefully across the sand. When someone is dancing alone you don't want to surprise them. You don't want them suddenly to see you and be embarrassed, because you will see no more dancing and, more importantly, you will ruin whatever it is they are dancing for.

We stayed well back. Then she stopped and took out a camera and started taking pictures of her footprints in the sand.

"Excuse me, I hate to bother you, but you looked wonderful dancing."

She smiled. That is always the best moment in a dance.

Her name was Irene and she said she was on vacation in Vancouver and her daughter told her to have fun, and make sure she danced on the beach.

That was so sweet.

She was here alone. She had no one to take a picture of her dancing so she would just take pictures of her footprints.

I offered to take a picture for her and she was excited about that. She then said she was from a Native reserve in Saskatchewan and had never seen the ocean before.

Irene said she worked in a drug and alcohol rehabilitation centre and she had been clean for five years.

She had reason to dance.

She told us she had cancer and not long to live.

"I'm so sorry," I said.

"I'm not," she replied.

There are always moments in life that you cannot be ready for. That was one of them.

"What I mean is, better me than my daughter."

I have no idea how she would think having cancer would save her daughter. We know cancer does not happen that way. But she thought so and that was all that mattered.

We said if we took pictures of her for television her daughter could watch it on the Internet. We were lucky. We could offer that.

At that moment, the meeting of technology and timing turned into a gift that a dying woman could give to her daughter.

What the TV audience watched that night her daughter watched on her computer the following night.

The sweet woman was crying when she was dancing. Perhaps her daughter was, too, when she was watching.

If we had not stopped for the kissing couple or the Hollow Tree or if my bladder was properly working, we would have missed her.

Was it the hole in the clouds?

No, of course not.

It's doubtful whether God, if you believe in a god, would wait for a hole in a stratocumulus to intervene in someone's life. Most of the world's religions started in the Middle East where there are no clouds. And none of the world's religions recommend waiting for a hole to communicate through.

But there is no chance in the world we would have found her if I hadn't looked up through that hole. It could have been the rocks, but Roger doesn't carry rocks.

It was the faith that as soon as I asked for help through the hole I knew the day would be saved. I knew it. I believed it. You could have put me in front of the CIA and their now-infamous interrogation methods and I would not have altered my words.

I am not saying you should put your faith in any religion. All I am saying is you get what you believe in. It is simple, and it is profound. I am not urging you to look for holes, or rocks, or sticks. I am not suggesting you get a Jewish godfather.

But once again, as I have said before earlier in this book, for more than a thousand consecutive days I have relied on a hole in the clouds. Never fails.

Before that, rocks. Never failed. And sticks. That was different. A stick I was carrying once poked a cameraman in the crotch when I turned and he turned and the stick didn't. That was a bad day.

But you have to believe. You get what you believe in. I believe. I totally, without reservation, without doubt, without hesitation, believe something good will appear before us.

Anthony Quinn believed in *Zorba the Greek*. It was a story about the joy of living. It was a low budget film shot in six weeks in 1963, the same year *My Fair Lady* was produced, which took half a year to film and cost $20 million and was done in Technicolor on a super-wide screen.

Zorba cost $600,000. Instead of a star's salary, Anthony Quinn asked for a cut in the profits of the film. Many believed it would make nothing.

Two days before the scene of him dancing on the beach was shot he broke his foot. They could not hold up production.

Anthony Quinn's foot was taped tightly, then the bandages were taken off just before the cameras rolled. He said the pain was close to unbearable. He could not jump in the traditional Greek way, so he dragged his one foot through the sand.

The scene is considered to be a classic in its own right. It was, according to many, the most dramatic moment in Anthony Quinn's life in film. And because it was seen so many times by millions of people, the way many people dance on a beach now, pretending they are doing a Greek dance, is the way he danced—no jumping, just shuffling with arms, head and spirits all held high.

Almost no one who saw it knew about his foot or knew that it was a dance that was hiding the pain, which is the same way Irene danced on the sand at Third Beach.

They both believed they had to dance, and they both did. At least once in your life, dance on the beach. All the pain goes away.

And while we are talking about the power of the hole in the clouds leading us to the power of dancing on the beach, there was the dog sliding down the hill on his back.

"Are you kidding?"

"No, look, there is a dog sliding down a hill on its back."

I have seen many dogs loving the grass and rolling over in it.

"But he's not rolling," said I to myself. "He's sliding straight down the grassy hill off Beach Avenue to the beach, pushing with his hind legs."

And when he got to the bottom he limped up to the top and started again. This is the stuff that television was made for. This is real life. This is better than politics.

That story coming up next. That is like a promo on the news.

But first, thank you, hole in the clouds. Did I ask the hole in the clouds for something, not knowing about a dog on its back? You bet. Did I pretend I was only checking the weather so the cameraman would not think I was asking a hole for help? You bet.

Did the dog appear five minutes later?

You bet. It was on television an hour later, and half a million people got a chance to say, "That is an amazing dog."

How did it happen? The hole? The belief? Luck?

I know you are still saying that is idiotic. You are not going to believe that a conversation through a cloud is going to lead you to anything.

Perhaps luck will, but luck is only good when it turns out that way and before it hits you have no idea that it is going to be there. In short, luck is what you give credit to when something turns out good and you did not expect it and were just hoping for it.

"Wow, I got lucky, I won two dollars on this scratch and win ticket. I only had to spend twenty dollars. My luck is getting better."

Well, yes, that is luck.

But do you think I am going to question the hole in the clouds, or the rocks, or simply the faith that something good is going to happen when I have the dancer on the beach, the dog on the grass, and the kitten in the office?

That was earlier in the week, but the same faith in the same process. It happened this way:

There was a shortage of camera time again.

"I hate to ask this, but can you be quick?" says the camera coordinator.

How can I be quick? I have no idea how reality will turn out. But try the hole in the clouds, I think.

Whoops. It is raining.

Try penetrating the clouds. Imagine a hole.

"We have to hurry," said the cameraman.

I go into the maintenance office of the PNE because that is where I learned about CJ's cup and I heard a month earlier that a fellow who works behind the roller coaster collects clocks. He has a small office and has fifty timepieces in it.

Great.

I go into the main maintenance office and ask. But before I finish asking there is a squeak.

"Is that a bird?" asks the cameraman.

The woman behind the desk shakes her head. A kitten jumps on her lap.

Oh, thank you overcast rainy sky.

She had asked someone who was giving away kittens for a picture of one of them. Instead, he brought in a living, breathing ball of fur. She fell in love and kept it, of course.

Nice. But unbelievably, we were there just after he dropped it off.

And the story was much better than just a new kitten because the other woman who works in that office told the man giving away the kittens to bring the real thing instead of a picture.

"She fell for it once before, when I wanted to give away a black kitten and she said she wanted anything except a black kitten," said the woman's co-worker. "When I brought in the black kitten it was game over. The black kitten had a new home."

But the story was better than just a co-worker who tricks her friend into taking home a new kitten.

The woman with the new kitten was going away for a vacation the next morning. Her sneaky friend forgot about that.

"Could you babysit the kitten, starting tonight?" asked the woman who had a new kitten thanks to her co-worker.

The tale from an ordinary office.

How?

Simply, the belief that a thought can penetrate a cloud.

This all sounds silly, I know. What is the big deal about stumbling onto a kitten or a dancing woman on a beach or a dog sliding on grass? Nothing, and everything.

They are what I wanted. And after I asked, I believed. And after I believed, they were there, almost waiting for me. Try it. Take one belief and call me in the morning.

THE NATURAL WAY

"He's sliding on his back."

"Who?"

"The dog, right there in front of you, you idiot."

The kindly remark is from the cameraman Mike Timbrell, whose brother has just given up being a cameraman and joined the Mounties.

"The very first time with a gun and he got twelve bull's eyes in a row," said Mike who is proud of his brother and was telling me that just before he saw the kids on the beach doing cartwheels.

A well-known rule is don't argue with someone whose brother gets twelve bulls' eyes in a row.

The second is if someone says something to you that you have not thought of or seen on your own or previously considered, don't take offence. That's the way life is. Don't say "I wasn't looking that way because I was checking to make sure it was safe to cross the parking lot." Don't make excuses.

Just for heaven's sake look at or think about what the other person has said and presto, it may improve your day. No argument, no hard feelings. In short, grow up.

There was a dog sliding down a hill of grass just off Beach Avenue where we saw some kids doing cartwheels. Cartwheels are fun. Maybe that will make a TV story. I knew the cartwheels would work because I had already spoken secretly through a hole in the clouds. Cartwheels popped up right after that. Amazing.

But first a moment with the dog sliding down the hill. If you know Beach Avenue you know there is a grassy slope that starts at the sidewalk and goes down to the pedestrian path. It is quite steep. If your bones are past fifty they would not like to take the challenge of climbing it.

But if you are an Irish Setter you can make it. And that is when the comment, "Look, he's sliding on his back" came.

Which was where the "What dog and where and when?" came in, which was followed by the "Right in front of you, you idiot."

In five seconds we have a battle between two friends.

I only add gasoline to the fire by saying, "You think you can get a picture of that? It will contrast well with the kids."

I like to take charge. But, of course, would a cameraman with a camera who has just seen a good picture not take it?

And what would such a cameraman, who is already taking a picture of said dog, think when he is asked to take a picture of it? The same thing as your wife or husband or child who has just sat down for dinner and put a napkin across a lap and is then told, "Be careful not to spill anything."

The simple solution to most problems of communication is to shut up and say nothing.

But now we are both wondering how long the dog will stay upside down as he slides down the hill. Your dog has done this, many dogs have done this, in fact, every dog has done this. It will be funny for five seconds before the dog gets up and we go on to the kids turning cartwheels.

But the dog does not stop. He pushes himself down the hill with his hind legs. He has a ball in his mouth, the same as any dog returning a ball except he is upside down. He pushes and pushes and rolls on his side, then throws his feet straight up, adjusts his body, and with his fore feet pointing at the clouds with the hole in it, pushes with his back feet and slides down the hill.

This is wonderful.

It will work beautifully with pictures of the cartwheels. We are lucky we captured this moment, which is surely going to end in less than a moment.

"He's been doing this all his life," said Steve, the man with the leash that he did not need who was standing on the path at the bottom of the hill.

The story, in short: Cleo, who is not a he but a wonderful she, was born with a deformed leg. Arthritis set in early. She could not walk.

"We couldn't go around Stanley Park or go for outings like other dogs," said Steve.

But she could slide. She rolled over, pushed herself, and slid.

When Steve found this spot, which was made for sliding, Cleo found heaven. She would limp up the hill, then roll on her back and slide down. For eight years she did this.

Residents of the area affectionately gave her the title: "The Stupid Dog Who Slides Down the Hill," Steve said.

You can't take offence at an insult that praises your best talent.

Then Steve heard about an operation that would give Cleo an artificial joint in her elbow, the first in Canada. It had been done in the States a dozen times, but now he could get it for his tongue-licking back-sliding friend.

One problem: $10,000. But Steve paid. After all, Cleo was not just a dog, as all dogs are more than that.

The operation was a success. And Steve went out with Cleo, and Cleo kept sliding. Just because she had had an operation and it was successful and she could now use her leg, all that expense and bother was obviously not her idea. Sliding was good enough, and besides, you don't get your back scratched when you are walking.

Steve still tries to get her to walk on all fours, but Cleo is happy hopping up the hill on all threes and sliding down.

"Eventually she'll walk," he said.

And probably she will. When she gets tired of looking at holes in the clouds she will act like a dog and stare at the ground while she is walking. Or maybe the sky and the hill are too beautiful to give up just for the sake of being like everyone else.

The story was good. Dog lovers loved it. But I realized something when I thought about Cleo later that night.

She never whined about having only three working legs. She adapted. She wagged her tail, upside down. She licked Steve's hand, both before and after the operation, upside down.

You may have had a dog or a cat or a turtle with three legs. You probably called her or him Tripod, as another cameraman called his three-legged cat, which he rescued from a miserable life from under a rotting pier.

When I was young, the kids on my street in New York befriended a one-legged pigeon whom we called Stumpy. Everyone has seen one-legged pigeons.

I learned later in life that pigeons are originally from the barren, rocky cliffs of North Africa where the weather is always warm. They were imported into northern Europe long ago to be used as food, before chickens. They adapted to city life because roosting on buildings is like being on rocky cliffs.

What they did not adapt to is winter, and pigeons are one of the few birds with fleshy feet. In winter their toes sometimes freeze, then gangrene sets in and their feet rot off.

It's not a nice way to spend a night without Tylenol.

But the pigeons do not give up. One-legged pigeons still try to push two-legged cousins out of the way to get breadcrumbs.

Three-legged dogs do not mope. They run, except for Cleo who slides, and play and wag their tails. Even when they do not run as fast as other dogs and never win a race, they do not quit. They do not sit on the sidelines and wave their stumps in the air and say, pity me.

There is obviously something in dogs and cats and pigeons and turtles that we can learn from.

Rick Hanson inspired millions by going around the world in a wheelchair after he lost his legs. Terry Fox, as I have said in an earlier book, is my life's personal hero.

You just read about Jim Byrnes. And in the Telethon story the teacher, Tammy Corness, teaches from a wheelchair.

They have found what is inherent in every living creature. You don't quit. Quitting is not an option. It was not for Cleo and not for anyone you see who is waiting for a bus while sitting in a wheelchair in the rain and is going to work.

It was not an option for Reilly. He knows he is different. He does not know how he is different, just that the world sometimes seems all screwy and sometimes he just wants to scream. But he is going to catch a fish and to do that he has to stay calm and quiet and keep his line in the water. And that is what he does because he believes he will catch a fish, just like Tammy the teacher knows she has to get to school every day in her wheelchair, otherwise how is she going to teach the kids? And Rick and Jim both know the same thing.

Somewhere deep inside Cleo, pushing through the grass on her back, is that belief that the mountain can be moved, even if Cleo has no idea that she believes it. It is in her soul or DNA or spirit or something. And if it is in her, it is in all of us.

THE LAST LAUGH

I t is good to get the comedy right on the street. Comedy is when someone laughs. It is even funnier when someone laughs at someone else's expense, so long as the someone else is not hurt, except in their pride.

Dave was trying to get the coat hanger in through the crack in the top of the driver's side window of his pickup truck. He was trying to do this because the keys were still in the ignition.

Barb was watching him.

"I'm glad I didn't lock them in there," she said. "It's always the woman who gets blamed for things like that."

Barb and Dave work together in landscaping. Dave had been struggling with the lock for about ten minutes and those darn keys were starting to cost them money. It was time they were not getting to the place they had to work.

"I almost got it," said Dave who was twisting his face in as many contortions as the wire that was almost hooking under the latch, but not quite.

"Can I help?" asked Barb.

"No, I almost got it," said Dave who almost got it, but not quite.

It would be tough to be upstaged, and besides, he almost had it.

"You got a piece of wood?" asked a guy who was passing by.

"Yeah, I have some wood," said Dave, who was willing to take help from a stranger with an actual, workable suggestion.

Dave got a piece of wood from the back of the truck and the two men tried to wedge it between the door and the frame of the truck.

"Can I help?" asked Barb.

"No, we almost have it," said Dave.

And they almost did have it, except the door was made very well and would not be wedged away from the truck.

The man left, with apologies, and said he had to get going.

"So you have to get the wire around that latch?" asked another man, who had crossed the street and was staring through the window at the wire trying to hook around the latch.

"Yeah," said Dave, "I almost got it, but it won't get over enough."

"Let me try," said the man who figured he could get the wire over the latch and save the day and Dave let him hold the wire and try.

"I almost got it," said the man who was excited.

And then he didn't have it.

"That's the problem," said Dave.

"Can I help?" asked Barb.

"No, we almost got it," said Dave.

The man who almost got it with Dave left, with apologies that he had to get somewhere.

A half-hour had now passed. Time flies when you almost have something figured out.

"Maybe I could do it," said Barb.

"No, I want to give it one more try," said Dave.

"Did you try a second wire to hold the first wire in place?" said another man who had been watching Dave for a few minutes.

"That's a good idea," said Dave who asked Barb if she could find another coat hanger in the back of the truck.

She looked and said there were no more hangers and the one he had was only there because she used it once to hang up her jacket while they worked.

Dave frowned. No more coat hangers.

"Well, break this one in half and then use one piece to hold the other piece against the thing and you'll have it," said the man who suggested two wires would be better than one wire.

"Could I try just once before you break the wire?" asked Barb.

"No, I think this guy's got a good idea," said Dave.

He pulled out the long coat hanger and began bending it back and forth to break it in half.

Then he squeezed the one wire which still had a hook at the end through the crack in the window and the other man squeezed his wire through the crack and both wires made it down to the latch and the new wire hooked onto the old wire.

"No, you got to get your wire behind my wire," said Dave.

"I know, but I can't get over there, your hand is in the way," said the other man.

They tried again with the two men's knuckles pushing into each other and the wires in a duelling dance around the latch.

"It should work. We almost got it," said the man, "but I just can't get it around yours."

They tried several more times and now an hour had gone by.

The man said he was sorry, but he had to go.

Barb started to say something, but stopped.

A fourth man seemed to have been waiting for his turn and he bent down and looked through the window and stared at the latch and said, "Hummm," several times.

"It looks like it's slipping off the latch. If you had something sticky that would grab onto the latch it would probably work."

Dave thought that was a good idea and pulled the wire out and went to the back of the truck and got some tape to wrap around the hanger and then he could hook onto the latch.

Barb did not say anything. She was using a different tool, found between her ears.

"Agh, the tape came off," said Dave who had spent five minutes wrapping the tape around the wire and then another several minutes pushing the tape and the hanger through the crack.

"Well, it was worth a try," said the fourth man who wished Dave good luck as he left.

Then the tow truck that Barb called pulled up and a guy with a large belly and a cigarette in his mouth got out.

"You called?" he said to Dave and Barb, not caring who answered, just so long as he got a nod.

Barb nodded.

The driver took his metal bar, the tool that he uses ten times a day to break into cars that are in no parking zones and slipped it between the window and the door frame and in four seconds opened the door.

The cost, much less than the time they had spent missing work.

"I almost had it," said Dave.

"You want me to lock it up again?" asked the tow truck driver.

Barb tried very hard not to laugh, but failed.

Again, what does this have to do with Reilly and his rules?

Well, one: Don't be stupid. Two: Don't be Dave. Three: Don't be pig-headed. Four: Don't say no to someone you want to be better than. Five: Don't be Dave.

In short, if someone said to Reilly, "Let me show you how to hold your pole," Reilly would have handed over his fishing rod.

He believed he would catch a fish. He did not say he would show up anyone else while doing it.

THE FUR COAT CAR

It had a garbage can in the front, sticking out from the grill and bumper. It was a regular, full-sized twenty-gallon steel can.

But you didn't notice that at first.

It had tiki lights sticking up from the roof, the pretend torches that used to be in tiki bars with pretend thatched roofs where you had mai tais with paper umbrellas sticking up from the top of the glass. We have an extremely inventive culture.

But like the garbage can, you didn't notice the tiki lights, at least not at first.

What you did see was the blue fur that covered every bit of the car, the roof, fenders, hood, the whole automotive works.

Of course it was not real fur; all blue animals are extinct.

"May we ask you about your car?" I asked.

"It's just fun," said the driver as he got out. "You should try not to take life too seriously, it's too short for that."

"Why fur?"

"I like it."

"Why blue?"

"I like that too."

Then we noticed the garbage can, which had some garbage in it—a few paper cups and a banana peel.

"When it's parked people put things in there. It's better than on the street."

So, okay, he's doing a public service and for that I like him.

Then we saw the tiki lights.

"How could I resist? I saw them in a yard sale," he said.

And the fuzzy dice hanging from the rear view mirror? No point in asking; I knew what the answer would be.

He did not have long hair or a tie-dyed T-shirt. He was clean-shaven and wore a shirt with a collar. It was almost as though he was coming from school.

"Would you tell me why?" I asked, looking at the car.

"It's the child in me that wants to get out and have fun," he said.

I have heard this before, releasing the "inner child," but usually it is from some serious academic trying to explain a thesis on behavioural misconduct.

"My childhood was rotten, wasted, I was dumb. Now I'm doing it the way it should have been."

"Would you tell me about it?"

He said by twelve he was smoking marijuana. That meant at eleven, or ten, he probably did not have much guidance. By his early teens he was into heroin and cocaine.

That is not a good way to live. There are many kids in their late teens at Main and Hastings who use the same drugs and are not living at all. Existence just for the purpose of putting drugs into your blood has nothing to do with living.

Then he reached rock bottom. All things were bad. You hear this from alcoholics and drug addicts when some last straw in their lives is screaming "Stop, or I will break." Sometimes the lost, mind-numbed souls hear the screaming and get up enough courage to put down the bottle or the needle.

And then comes one day of sobriety, or one day of being clean, and the shock in the morning of waking up without a splitting head or missing teeth is almost the religion of being reborn. Is it possible not to have the pain that I cause myself?

And then comes the day full of temptation and struggle and sometimes you make it to day two.

I can't believe I feel so good.

Then comes the stronger temptations because you feel so good that just one drink or one jab of the needle or one lungful of smoky crack will make you feel even better, like you are in heaven.

And sometimes you don't make it through that day, and the gates of hell open again for you.

But sometimes you hold on, and the days become a week, and the weeks pass by with laughter and thought that is clear and you say what everyone who gets to this point says: "I feel free."

You have to hold on for the rest of your life, but at least you have a life and you have today.

"I believed I could do it," said André. "I wanted to and I believed I could."

That was André Gainsford, with his blue, fake-fur-covered old station wagon.

"Most of us spend our lives trying to get things; cars, houses, things. The only thing we really need is to get ourselves. When you die, it doesn't matter what you have, only if you are happy with yourself."

"What do you do for a living?" I asked.

"High school counsellor."

"You are kidding?" I said. "You are too weird for that."

"It's my life," he said. "I just want those kids to love being alive and not try to kill themselves."

When that car is parked outside his school, the kids inside are some of the luckiest on earth. Each one's "inner child" has got someone to play ball with, and maybe ride in a car covered with blue fur.

You get what you want.

But sometimes you have to be shown what you would want by someone who has found it, and a teacher with fuzzy dice and a garbage can on the front of his car will show you things you can't imagine.

You let the inner child go out to play, and finding a car with a garbage can on the front will give you more joy than a needle in a back lane.

YOU WILL NOT HAVE
AN ACCIDENT

That's impossible. You cannot will yourself not to have an accident.

On the other hand, yes you can. It sounds impossible, but really, you say to yourself I will not have an accident. I simply will not. I will get back home tonight as healthy as I am at the starting line and presto, you back into a parking spot at the end of your day's travels and you are still alive

If you say to yourself "I will not have an accident," you will use the number one safety device to its fullest extent: your attitude.

"I will be safe. I will not get angry. I will not speed up when someone passes me too closely. I will not have an accident."

You will look through your windshield, which is a good driving tip for keeping you alive, and see the idiot who is going through the stop sign and you will stop in time.

That wasn't so hard, and it saved your life.

You will see the car that is going way too slow, then suddenly speeds up and is going way too fast, half in one lane and half in another.

You will know he is on his cellphone on the way home from the pub and is dialling his girlfriend to tell her he's in love, but not with her.

You will slow down as he goes off the road.

You will see the super idiot who cuts ahead of you, missing your car by one fingernail, because he wants to get off at the exit that he has no time to make and he jams on his brakes and then shoots off over the traffic island.

That situation will take advanced positive thinking to overcome. First use your brakes; second, pray; third, while he is losing his undercarriage as he goes over the concrete bumpers you can secretly feel good.

If you want to have a good life you should never wish someone else ill. But if it happens after they almost kill you, well, you are only human.

But if you start every trip by saying you will not have an accident and that everything will be fine, it will be like starting every day the same way with your life. Once you make up your mind that is the way it is going to be, your chances are pretty good.

Except for the accident I had.

"Drive carefully," said our friends Freda and George as we left their home in the Cariboo in the dead of last year's frigid winter. "The roads can be slippery."

Me drive carefully? No one watches more for every ant crossing the street. I once hit a turtle with a large military truck at an air base in the southern US and I am still in mourning over it.

I had never driven before and after they gave me a gun, which I had never shot before, a sergeant told me to move that truck down the road.

"I can't drive a truck," I said.

"Boy, when I say move that truck I mean move that truck," he said, loudly.

It was impossible for him to conceive of a semi-adult male not being able to drive or shoot a gun. He had that southern drawl that is learned while shooting and driving.

Another understanding recruit showed me how to push the clutch, put it in first gear and slowly lift off the clutch. We lurched and bounced and stalled and started again and then I saw the turtle coming out of a swamp.

"I'm going to hit him," I yelled.

"Steer around him," said the recruit.

"How?"

"With the steering wheel."

"But I have my foot on the clutch."

He did not understand that multi-tasking in the driver's seat was not something you learned on the streets of New York, where no one I grew up with ever sat in a car.

"Run, turtle," I yelled.

But it was too late. I killed a turtle in defence of the United States. That would be called death by friendly tire. That was before I learned about Reilly's rule and I have never since then hurt anything on the road. I believe I will not hit turtles.

"We'll be careful," I said to the Cariboo and drove south.

There were shadows on the road; I slowed down because I know ice forms in them. At every curve I slowed.

But then there was this straightaway north of Spences Bridge. Still going only at the speed limit, I hit unseen ice and my front wheels started sliding while my back wheels decided they would go in front of my front wheels.

"Darn," I said, using a different word, a very bad word, very loudly and repeatedly as the world on the highway passed in front of my eyes from left to right all the way around.

"Darn," I said again, even louder, repeating that word that my wife never allows me to say.

Take your foot off the brake, no put it on because we are heading right for the side of the road that goes over the side and ends far, far down. "Darn."

I spun the wheel this way and that way and the other way and it spun back. And then we went across the highway backward and ended up in a ditch against a rock wall.

"You saved us," my wife said.

"I didn't do anything but say 'darn,'" I said.

"We would have died if we'd gone over that side," she said.

"Yes, but we didn't," I tried to say, but I was shaking too badly to say anything except to repeat a slightly less offensive word.

"I don't care what you say, you saved us," said my wife.

Who am I to disagree when my hands are trembling and I am watching someone slowing down on the highway and leaning out and taking a picture of our car, which is in the ditch.

So this is what it feels like to be in an accident and see the news cameras. I have more understanding now.

We got towed. The car got fixed. I eventually stopped trembling. But what happened to Reilly's method? "I will not have an accident."

Nothing. Just believing you will not have an accident does not mean you will never have an accident. You don't change reality. You don't get rid of the ice.

But since I have been saying "I will not have an accident," all turtles have been safe, as well as other cars and walls and fire hydrants.

Reilly at least deserves credit for that.

YEAH? AND THIS TO YOU, BUDDY

There is no room left for more stickers on Alan Tin's minivan. But a couple of things were really strange.

Minivans usually have kids on the inside, not oddball stickers on the outside. This is a family vehicle we are talking about and Alan has a bunch of kids of his own to carry.

The other thing strange was Alan, like André with the blue fur car, who did not look like the young, self-expressive eternal hippie type. He looked like a family man.

But his stickers were funny, some of them religious:

GOD ALLOWS U-TURNS

And,

JESUS IS COMING, LOOK BUSY

But not all of them:

ARE YOU DRUNK OR ON YOUR Cellphone?

THERAPY HAS TAUGHT ME THAT IT'S ALL YOUR FAULT

"I like this one best," said Alan.

I USED UP ALL MY SICK DAYS, SO I CALLED IN DEAD

"The boss laughed."

I couldn't tell if he was really religious or not because he had the little metal plaque with the sign of the fish with the Greek letters in the centre that spell the name Jesus, but nose to nose with it was another little metal plaque with the letters 'N' CHIPS inside the fish.

"Are you religious?" I asked.

"I believe in God, but that's it," he said. "I've had good experiences in church and I've bad experiences in church. I've met some very good Christians and some who are, well, not doing their faith any favours."

He was standing next to a large sticker that said:

DON'T MAKE ME COME DOWN THERE—GOD

There were more than a hundred stickers:

THINK. IT'S NOT ILLEGAL YET

"My kids love them and hunt for them," he said.

GOD ANSWERS KNEE-MAIL

And,

GOD PROTECT ME FROM YOUR FOLLOWERS

"Most pastors laugh at that, but some people in church don't," he said.

And then of course, "But why do you do this?"

"It started ugly. Another driver cut me off and gave me the finger. My reflex was I'll give him the finger. This went on for about five blocks and suddenly I thought, 'This is stupid.'"

Then Alan had an idea. "Maybe I can make them laugh."

Earlier in the day he had seen a funny sticker in a store, but he didn't buy it. He was a middle-aged man with a minivan full of kids. Bumper stickers were for younger, more exciting guys.

But after the finger incident he turned his minivan around and went back to the store, and stuck it on his bumper:

IF YOU CAN'T LAUGH AT YOURSELF,
LET ME DO IT

Then he added another:

CHANGE IS INEVITABLE,
GROWTH IS OPTIONAL

So long as it was not nasty or ugly he stuck it on. In time he noticed something. Drivers looked, but fingers did not rise. He became a breeding ground for smiles rather than anger.

Of course you could say he might cause an accident when others try to read his van. There is always a negative way of looking at anything. But so far, no accidents. Just smiles.

And also since he started this, several years ago, no anger.

"One guy cut me off trying to get ahead of me, then he slowed down until we got alongside him. I thought he was going to give me the finger, but he was trying to read the signs."

Alan pointed at:

LORD, HELP ME TO BE THE PERSON
MY DOG THINKS I AM.

They are large signs, large enough to read on the road.

"Or maybe it was that one:"

YOUR MIRROR IS NOT LYING,
YOU ARE MISERABLE

"He stayed alongside me and then looked out his side window and then he gave me the finger," said Alan.

I felt so sad.

"It was the thumbs-up."

I felt so glad.

Alan just wanted to do something good to make the world better, and he did it.

Alan believed he would make other drivers laugh. That is all, nothing deeper. But when he did that he lowered aggression and cooled tempers.

There was laughter in other cars, or maybe just a smile, but for one shining moment the world of the endless road was a better place. That is almost a miracle.

With all the anger that is on the road when someone has to get ahead of someone else to get off at the next exit and cuts in front of you and makes you hit your brakes and makes you curse, there goes Alan.

"Wooh, daddy. Read that sign."

IF YOU HURRY, YOU CAN DIE SOONER

Alan moved the mountain.

BACKHOE ACROSS CANADA

The stories that teach you the most about life usually come from the simplest beginnings. I have experienced this over and over. You do not need to go to a mountaintop to meditate or a synagogue to discuss life, although those places are fine.

Sometimes a parking lot behind McDonald's will do.

We were driving north on Boundary Road, just passing Lougheed Highway, when I said to the cameraman, "Oh, my God, I would love to do a story about him, whoever he is."

"Who?"

This is one of the rare times when I saw something before a cameraman. They are usually pointing out to me something fantastic that is right before my nose. It is good to travel through life with companions who are both observant and understanding.

"The guy in that backhoe. He looks like Santa."

"Where?"

"Going the other way."

That is sad because you can't chase down a backhoe, not one of those big ones that have wheels in the rear that come up to your shoulders, and say, "Hey, stop, stop. I want to ask you something."

And then after you get the backhoe driver to pull over he says to you:

"Here's my licence. You must be an undercover cop to pull me over and honest, this thing won't go faster than fifty klicks."

And then you tell him you want to know about his beard. Somehow you might be taking a big chance.

"Wait, he's turning," said the cameraman looking in his mirror.

"Where?"

"Into the McDonalds' drive-through."

"What?!" I shouted like my inner kid was coming out. A giant backhoe going through a drive-through?

"Stop, go, turn, hurry."

I like giving clear instructions to someone who is already turning and hurrying. A picture of an anomaly is wonderful, even if there is no story to go with it.

In fact, any picture of anything that is odd is what photographers live for.

We got into McDonald's parking lot just as the yellow steel dinosaur was pulling away from the pick-up window.

"Darn, missed it by ten seconds," I said.

Well you can't have everything. Reilly's rules are that you get what you truly want, but come on, there are limits. I haven't won the lottery. I haven't lost the twenty extra pounds that I said I wanted to lose two years ago. And we missed a funny picture.

Then the backhoe driven by Santa, who was sitting so high he might have been in a sleigh in the sky, drove past us and pulled into the waiting zone.

Oh, my heavens. We jumped out and ran over to him and said . . .

Wait. I had no idea what to say. More than ten thousand interviews in my life and I had no idea what to say to a man with a giant belly and an even bigger snow white beard whose boots were on the floor of a cab that was higher than my head and who was waiting for a delivery of something or other.

"Hello, hate to bother you. Do you come here often?"

I was hoping he didn't think I was trying to be fresh, but I didn't think he'd heard me, because his diesel was so loud.

He opened his door and shouted, "Wait minute."

He shut off his massive, noisy engine.

"What did you say?"

"I've never seen anyone drive one of these things through a drive-through."

At least that sounded honest.

"How else am I going to get my lunch?"

"Do you do this often?"

"From Thunder Bay to Prince Rupert," he said.

Oh, my heavens to Betsy. It is happening right here, right in the seat of a backhoe. Salt and pepper and Tabasco were being sprinkled onto the meal of life.

"Can you come down and talk to us?"

The giant rose from his seat and climbed down the ladder so nimbly I knew in a moment it must be Saint Nick.

"People must tell you that you look like Santa."

"All the time," he said and turned his head with a chuckle.

His other name is Ken Fast and he had driven heavy equipment for thirty-eight years, he said.

"I love this, just love it." He patted his machine. "There is nothing in the world I would rather do. Nothing. Wherever it goes," he rested his large arm on one of his huge tires, "I go."

When you find something you love you are a lucky person. And he found it in a country that he loves. He has Canadian flags flying on each side of his steel machine. "They are always there."

"Did you really drive this thing across the country?"

"How else would I get here?" he said with another chuckle.

He worked for a company that was laying optical cable across Canada and he drove every step of the way in this thing, digging a trench along the way, and when lunchtime came he went to McDonald's.

"Always McDonald's?"

"No, sometimes Burger King."

Forget the lecture on health. You do not do that to someone who looks as strong as the machine he is driving and has a very healthy laugh. Besides, it's none of my business.

"And what happens when you come up to the person at the window?"

"They usually just stare. They don't say anything. But I know it makes their day."

A young woman came out of McDonald's with a paper bag for Santa. His fries.

He thanked her and she watched without blinking as he climbed back up the ladder, like going up the chimney.

"Have a merry day," he said, and then he popped a couple of fries into his mouth hidden under the beard, started his mighty engine and drove off with a wave.

Then he stopped and stuck his head out the sliding window.

"Have a merry day and one thing more."

He fluffed up his beard.

"Ho, ho, ho," he said and waved.

Santa and his backhoe and fries.

What did it mean? I have no idea, except it is amazing to meet someone like Ken.

He gave the greatest gift of all, making others feel good by sharing his good feeling.

We did not talk about belief or dedication or values. He simply made me feel good in a way I could not explain. It was magical. He was happy and because of that I was happy.

And if happiness can make others feel good, can you imagine what would happen if we all tried a little of it? We would not have to drive a backhoe across the country or grow a beard or eat fries. But we could smile, and change the world.

THE ENDLESS GAME

Chang Poh, immigrant from Malaysia, wanted to keep his son from getting into trouble in their new home in Canada.

He had heard there were many distractions here that were not in the old country: movies, malls, kids from other neighbourhoods that the father might never meet. Some would be good, some might not be.

"You have to stay close to your children," he told me.

But how? By the time they are teenagers many kids think they have outgrown their parents. They have little or nothing in common. The kids want only to be anywhere their parents are not.

But Chang had ping pong, which he had played in Malaysia, and he had found a table tennis club in Richmond.

He went by himself and made friends and was having a good time when he realized it may be fun, but it was not being a father.

So the next day he asked his son if he would like to come with him. Dan was four years old. He was thrilled to go anywhere with his father, but especially to the big club that his father had been disappearing into.

Chang showed his son how to hold the paddle and tried to get him to hit the ball. But of course, a four-year-old cannot do that. The father was patient. He played a couple of games with some other adults. His son watched with a bottle of pop. He was still thrilled.

Several days later Chang brought his son again. He knew that half his time at the club would be spent not playing, just bouncing the ball with his son.

Then he brought him again, and again. Chang was very good at ping pong. He could have been competing with anyone at the club, basically challenging all takers, but he played with his son.

By the time Dan was an adolescent he had played thousands of games with his father.

Just as Dan became a teenager, his father went into competition and won the best over-forty tournament in the country and got a little glass trophy.

Father and son continued to play after that, three or four times a week, all at his father's request.

Dan struggled to keep up with his father. Father and son playing together, spending time together, the son, as all through history, trying to be better than the father. But even the energy of a teenager could not beat the man who was almost thirty years older.

All during his teenage years Dan and Chang played. There was no time to get into trouble. There was just sweat dripping from Dan's face as he jumped and hammered the ball back across the net at his father, who barely moved his feet.

"I use my head," Chang always said.

By the time Dan was entering his twenties, Chang went back into competition and won the best over-fifty age group in the country. He got another little glass trophy.

Now playing was just part of life. Father and son went off to the table and battled and talked and grew in admiration for each other.

Dan spent a lot of time in school, and met a pretty woman and that usually takes up all your time. But not when you father says, "Let's have a game."

By the time Dan was in his thirties and working at a good computer job and had a family with a boy the same size as he was when he started playing, his father went into competition and won the best over-sixty championship in the country. He got a little glass trophy.

"You've got to come and see my father," Dan said to me. "He has won three national championships. No one else has ever done that."

I went to the club on Steveston Highway. Dan took out the trophies for us to see. He was so proud.

Then he and his father played a game. Dan, half his father's age, was jumping and running after the ball and sweat was pouring off his eyebrows and cheeks. His father basically stood still and hit the ball back with little effort above his wrist.

Several times I saw Chang miss, and I would never say this to him, but I think he did it on purpose.

"Why do you love the game so much?" I asked Chang.

With an answer that was still heavy with the accent of his home he said, "It kept me with my son."

At the end of this year he will compete in the over-seventy tournament.

"He was my best teacher," said Dan, who is now playing with his son.

It is so much simpler than therapy or drugs or worry or gnashing of teeth or anger or yelling or drinking or excuses.

Just time, enjoyed with someone you care about. Success is guaranteed.

THE WHITE CARNATION

You know the secret that if you want something you will get it? Okay, you don't always get it, but sometimes you will get something better.

The problem with most people I have met, and that is truly most people, is they don't want anything.

Oh, they say they want to win the lottery. Or they want a new home or car or a better job. But then they go home and open a beer and watch the hockey game.

There is nothing wrong with beer. I love it. Or hockey. I love it. Or wanting to win the lottery. Impossible. Thirteen million to one odds, get real. I like the racetrack but there are only six or seven horses running, and some of them you know are just going to walk, so the odds are really just five to one, and most race fans couldn't pick a winner if their lives depended on it.

So when you say what you want in life is to win the lottery, go to a doctor and get your head screwed on right.

Remember that high school counsellor with the blue-fur-covered car a few stories ago?

"The problem with us is most of us just want things, a new house, a new car. Life is too short to put your dreams in those things. Have fun, help others, do something you love. Let that kid inside you run free." That is what he said, and believed, and out of that came a good life.

Remember the famous song from *South Pacific* that says "You've got to have a dream"?

Well you do. Because in the song, if you don't have a dream, how you going to have a dream come true?

I wanted a story, and cameraman John McCarron said he had seen someone in Discovery Park in North Burnaby taking his dog for a walk. But the dog had crippled hind feet so the man used a sling and carried the back half of the dog while the front did the walking.

Very nice.

He had seen him three days in a row while he was parked there waiting for crime to break out. That is what cameramen do, take pictures in one place until crime breaks out in another. If you want a stable, predictable job do something else.

But John loves peaceful stories. "The man with the dog. Guaranteed," he said. "He's there in the parking lot every day at 11 a.m."

10:45 and we are waiting.

11 a.m. and he is not there.

11:30. Nothing.

"But he is always here," said John.

And now we are in North Burnaby, which is a very nice place, but it is harder to find a story in North Burnaby than Main Street simply because there are fewer people.

Reilly? Really, Reilly. John knew he would see the man and his dog. Knowing should be better than believing because knowing is real while believing still has that intangible quality. On top of that I believed the man would come because John said he would.

That is a spoonful of belief along with a spoonful of knowing. Two spoonfuls, what could go wrong? That's an unbeatable dosage of belief.

But no man. No dog.

It can't always work, I think, sadly. We start to leave.

"Stop," John said. "That woman just got out of her car and picked up a feather."

"Maybe she collects them," I said. "I'll ask."

I did. It is amazing what things you can learn when you talk to people.

She said she did not want to cry, but today was the first anniversary of her mother's death and her mother always came to this park to watch the bocce players.

The woman had expected to be alone. She carried a white carnation along with the feather she had picked up. She also had the ever-present Starbucks' cup, which is usually held in the hand that is not holding the cellphone. But she had no phone, just a feather and a flower.

"Can we come with you?"

"Only if I can show you something," she said. Her name was Lauren Johnston.

She took us to a small cluster of trees just to the west of the jogging oval behind the community centre.

"My mother called this her tree family," said Lauren.

She pointed to the limbs of one tree that are wrapped around another, smaller tree.

"She said it was the mother tree holding her baby tree."

These were women you could love, both of them, mother and daughter.

"Why the feather?" I asked.

She said her sister had the belief that if you found a feather you would have a good day.

"Is today good?"

"If you weren't here I think I would have forgotten about the trees," she said. "That makes it good."

"And why the carnation?"

She said her father had given a white carnation to her mother almost every week while they were married, which was a long, long time.

When they had more money he would give her a bouquet of carnations. When they were at the bottom of the purse he gave her one.

"When she was dying in the hospital my sister and I brought white carnations. We told my mother that they were from dad, and he was waiting for her in heaven."

Then she took us to the bench where her mother sat almost every day and where she watched the bocce players.

The men playing were nearby, rolling their balls and arguing, as they have for generations, over who got the closest.

"They are probably the same men that she watched," said Lauren.

They said hello, possibly because we were there, and Lauren smiled. Whatever the reason for the hellos, that was special, she said.

"And she always drank her coffee here," she said. "That's why I brought this one."

There is nothing in this life that is more precious than the love of a family. No car or house or even lottery ticket could replace that moment when

Lauren sat on that bench and watched the bocce players and placed the white carnation down beside her.

We backed off. There are times when no one should interrupt a moment that is precious. You know those times. You have been there.

We were far enough away to be out of her world. She took a sip of coffee. And then she cried.

At that moment, Lauren made the entire experience of life precious. It was more than we believed we would find.

THE WORLD HAS A PARTY
IN SURREY

Some of us make the world better without ever holding a fishing pole or making pronouncements about belief. One of them is Elizabeth of Surrey.

I never fail to be amazed at the inventiveness of folks in British Columbia. Anvil batteries and ocean races in bathtubs and mini donuts.

But now go to the home of Elizabeth Hugi in Surrey. Each year she has her Occasional International Invitational Croquet Match and General Get Together.

She always honours a home country of one of her friends, but she doesn't tell anyone which country is the chosen land of the year.

The year I met Elizabeth it was America. Okay, I like that.

Her backyard was packed with forty, maybe fifty people, including kids. Everyone had a stars and stripes cap or scarf or apron or shirt or flag sticking out of a back pocket, all supplied by Elizabeth, who is old enough to have seen the birth and death of many nations of the world.

"Hot dogs, apple pie," she shouted to the crowd.

I went through the crowd searching for an American.

"I'm from India."

"The Philippines."

"Germany."

"Iran."

All were wearing something that was part of my heritage. The stars and stripes were on everyone, but no Americans.

"Norway."

"Sweden."

"Barbados."

"Japan."

"Trinidad."

There was a Five Cent Hot Dog Stand set up and lots of Coke and Budweiser and a pretend politician with the American flag draped over his shoulder giving a long, blustery speech.

"Where are you from?" I asked the politician.

"Uganda."

Another star-spangled banner-bedecked man was setting up the croquet game, wearing a stars and stripes cap and carrying a flag in his pocket and a picture of an American flag on his T-shirt.

"Where from?" I asked.

"England," he answered.

"But America fought a war to get away from you guys," I said.

"And Elizabeth is bringing us back together in her backyard," he said.

Elizabeth, born in BC, accepted the world as her friends and neighbours. All these people wanted to come here. Hence, it must be a good place, she said. And then Elizabeth said to each new friend and neighbour, "Come to my home and meet some other friends and neighbours."

She started her parties too many years ago to remember. Sometimes it is Indian music and curry, sometimes fish and chips, sometimes lamb, sometimes vegetarian. She has one friend from Sri Lanka who eats no meat, so on that day the plates were loaded with lentils and peppers.

The point is, by the time the croquet games end, in which the score is always misplaced, many have made new friends, friends they might not have met otherwise.

And they met them in Canada, which accepts all people. And they met them in Elizabeth's backyard, where all the people got to share and celebrate one of them.

But where's the American?

"Me," said a pretty woman in her late thirties. She was wearing a terrycloth top hat of red, white and blue and holding a hot dog.

"I was born in Oregon, but I spent my whole life in Canada so I'm really Canadian."

Aren't we all. Lucky us.

Elizabeth was wearing a stars and stripes apron. You could almost hear it singing America the Beautiful, which during the Kennedy years nearly replaced The Star-Spangled Banner as the national anthem. That was because most people knew the words better than the anthem and it was not about war. Its first stanza begins with "O beautiful for spacious skies . . ." and ends with "above the fruited plain."

I heard it singing "O beautiful for apron strings, and neighbours who can laugh at things." That seemed to fit with a group of people who turned a Surrey backyard into a nation for all.

Thank you, Elizabeth, for helping make the dream become real.

THE CYCLE OF LIFE

Just because you believe things will be good doesn't mean they will be.
Something called living and dying sometimes gets in the way.

But if you believe things will be good you change the way you see life, and
it becomes not so bad.

Even when the pain is unbearable, even when you say things will never
be good again, life and time alter that. The pain becomes bearable and life
begins again.

It happened at a baseball field in Trout Lake Park on a warm, early spring
day. I heard the sound of a ball against a bat and saw two boys about ten years
old hitting, catching, running and throwing. They were not playing a game—
it was just free-form baseball feeling free.

"How'd you get in there," I shouted through the fence because there was
no open gate.

"Climbed it," one of them said.

Now I truly like these kids. That is the way you should get onto a field.
That means you really want to be there.

I asked if we could take their picture, because with kids you shouldn't do
that without asking. I asked if there were any adults with them.

One said that his mother and father were nearby walking in the park.
They were out pushing the baby carriage.

We waited and they came and I asked the man pushing the carriage for
permission to take pictures.

He did not answer right away. He looked like he was deep in another world. Then he said we could but it was very strange that he and I should be here at this moment together.

He asked if I remembered doing a story about a boy named Conner James McCreedy?

Of course I did. I have written about him because life can sometimes be so unbearably sad that somehow you know you need to share the pain to try to humanize it and make it bearable.

Conner James McCreedy was a teenager in love when I met him in 1997. He was in this same park playing box hockey with a girl whom he had just met. His heart was pounding, his eyes were wide, and her heart and eyes were the same.

It was a lovely story of teenagers in love.

A year later I got a phone call from Conner James McCreedy's father. His son had been killed in a car crash one block from Trout Lake. He wasn't even driving.

Would I do a story about him, a memorial?

Yes. There was no other answer.

It was painful for them, but in some way, I was told by family members, it eased the hurt, even if only briefly. That was good.

Ten years later the story found its way into *The Blue Flames that Keep Us Warm*, along with stories of other teenagers who had been killed. Each tale was a search for meaning, which is all we can ever do.

"Conner James McCreedy was my brother," said the man with the baby carriage.

He pointed down at the sleeping infant.

"Meet the new Conner James McCreedy," he said.

"He looks like pictures of your brother when he was a baby," said Katie McCreedy, the new little Conner's mother.

Then the two kids who were playing ball packed up their stuff, threw the bat and gloves and ball over the fence and climbed out of the field, right next to us.

They were both nephews of the first Conner and one of them is now the big brother of the new Conner.

The new Conner opened his eyes and big brother leaned over and kissed him on the cheek.

And then they left, and life went on.

The real life stories of our families, each of us, are always among the most important things we ever have.

You don't always get what you want. That's true. You do not bring back the dead, no matter how much you want or even believe they will come through the door in a minute.

But you do get what you want, in a way. A daughter dies in a car crash. You die inside. Ten years later you have grandchildren from other daughters. A different life and joy return.

Conner dies. You cannot go on living. Ten years later, a new Conner is born. That is the way it has worked since the beginning. You don't get what you want, but then suddenly you do get something. It is not what you wanted, but it becomes what you needed, and now you want it.

YOU MET HER HOW?

At Oppenheimer Park the life flows in and out like the tide; sometimes crack and fear infest it, and sometimes flowered kimonos float above the dusty ground.

Oppenheimer Park was the centre of Japan Town before the Second World War. During the war it became a prison camp for Canadians who were Japanese.

In the 1980s and '90s it had more crack dealers than Main and Hastings. Today it is mainly a playground for those who do not play, the lost and hopeless residues of lives of drugs and abuse.

That is until the Japanese return. Sometimes they play their ancient form of croquet around the vagrants waiting for another handout. No one bothers anyone else.

But once a year in the spring the Japanese and their descendants hold their Cherry Blossom Festival in the park. There is a stage and music and sushi and grilled meats and karate and more karate and kids laughing and what can I find here that I have not done a story about before?

Whoops, there's another karate demonstration over there.

Then, in that direction off to the side of the park, there's a beautiful woman in a flowered, traditional kimono. The kimono might make a story.

"May I ask where that came from?"

"Japan," she said with a delightful Japanese accent.

And that is all she said. She was obviously Japanese from Japan. I know women in Japan are raised to be a bit more reserved than women in Canada.

"Very nice," I said.

"Thank you." She bowed.

There is a difference between wanting to do a story on a beautiful dress and being able to do it. I was not able to do this. The dress would need just a bit more substance.

But I also believed in Reilly. Of course, and here we go again. Believe you will find something, do something, get something, totally believe it, and you will find it, do it and get it.

I will find a story here. I will. And it will be something that I have never done before, at least not at this festival.

There is another karate demonstration. And there is a photographer taking pictures of it. He is Japanese and it would be interesting, I hoped, to follow a Japanese photog on the hunt for pictures in a Japanese event.

We talked. His name was Allen Ko, he spoke English more clearly than me, and he said he was searching for basically the same thing as I was, something that we didn't know we would find and then would be elated when we did.

That sounds simple—impossible, but simple.

The TV cameraman and I followed him taking pictures of the karate and kites and kids, and more karate.

"You ever get tired of taking pictures of the karate fights?" I asked.

"Never," he said. "To the Japanese that is art, and I never get tired of art."

Okay, lesson learned. Never make fun of anything that someone else has or believes in or lives by. Stick with laughing at the size of your own stomach.

He started taking pictures of the woman in the kimono whom I had tried to talk with.

"She's beautiful, but I can't get a word out of her," I said.

I can only thank the entire galaxy of heavens that I said "beautiful" and nothing else. Never, ever, ever say anything bad about anyone. That is another rule.

"That's my wife," said Allen, the photographer.

"Beautiful," I repeated.

He smiled, he nodded, he did not bow.

"Where are you from?" I asked.

"Calgary."

"And your wife is from Japan?"

The nod, and the smile.

He introduced me. She bowed.

"Can you tell me how you met?"

The smile and the laugh came before the nod, which was followed by another laugh.

This was their story, and it would be good and retold as long as they lived.

"We met in New York," he said.

That was followed by the pause, which he had practiced because it always worked.

"On the subway."

"Noooo. Really?"

"I saw her and fell in love. I talked. She bowed. We had gotten on at different stops but we got off together."

That's so nice, I thought.

Then the punchline.

"She had gotten on the wrong train," he said. "If she'd got the right one, we would never have met."

After that came many trips together. He was working in New York and she was going to school. They married and moved to Vancouver. When I met them they had been together for seven years.

When we left them we had the most beautiful picture of all: the two of them walking back into the heart of the festival side by side with their pinkies locked together. His camera was over his shoulder. Her kimono was floating like a bouquet over the dusty ball field.

He already had his work of art.

Reilly? Most people would think it is impossible to catch a fish in Trout Lake with a bent paper clip.

Oh, yeah?

OH, LORD, HE STINKS
TO HIGH HEAVEN

BC history is a story better than *CSI*. Adventurers, hangings, scandal and beer parlours gave this land its taste, from the gold miners to the Sappers, and if you don't know about them you should. They truly made this land.

A small band of soldiers, only 166 of them, patrolled a beat larger than Germany and France combined, and throw in England too, and built the roads and kept the peace. Amazing guys.

But on Canada Day in Fort Langley I learned the best part of the true history of our past. The early pioneers that we look at in paintings, with their wives and muskets, stank to high heaven.

Oh, my gosh, the smell came up like a cornered skunk. And that was from the schoolteacher who was cleaner than most.

In Fort Langley on BC Day the volunteers play their parts well. They scratch. And if they are ladies they fan their faces.

"Why are you fanning? It's not so hot."

"To keep away the smell," said a young volunteer woman who was fanning under her bonnet.

There were a few white women at the fort in 1858 when gold was discovered and the foreign Americans came to hunt for more of it. Tens of thousands of gold miners walked past the trading fort, which only dealt in the business of trading beaver pelts.

"You mean there's gold up the river? What are we doing here?"

But the employees of the Hudson's Bay Company were not allowed to hunt for gold. Their lives were basically owned by the company, which provided them with bad food, endless work, no entertainment, few days off and, to make the job even more irresistible, they were given an extreme lack of soap.

But the employees did not mind since the one thing they were not interested in was washing. The men working inside the fort stopped cleaning up in October. After that it was too cold to go down to the river and stick your head in the water.

By Christmas no one had washed for more than two months. Few changed their long johns. As it got colder they put on more layers of woollen shirts and jackets over their bodies and scratched right through them.

Toilet paper? No, it had not been invented. Eaton's did not exist so there was no catalogue to cut into pieces. Newspapers were too rare to be used for anything but reading. So they used leaves, except in winter when leaves were hard to find.

And there were no signs inside the outhouses that said employees must wash their hands before returning to work. There were no sinks, or water. Don't even try to imagine the smell.

"It was a good form of birth control," said a volunteer who was playing the part of a worker at the fort.

"What'd you say?" asked a young woman visitor who was momentarily distracted by one of her children.

"It was a good form of ..."

"That's what I thought you said," she laughed. "I'd rather go through childbirth than that."

"You mean we didn't have to wash our hands back then?" her ten-year-old son asked.

The volunteer squatted down and said: "No handwashing, no bathing, no shampoo, no tooth brushing and your mother would never tell you to wash behind your ears."

"Great," said the boy.

"But you would have lice in your hair and you would scratch your head all day and it would keep you up at night and you would have itches everywhere and by the middle of winter you might not be able to breathe when you played with a friend because he would smell worse than you."

The boy was wide-eyed and his mouth hung open. History in school was never like this.

"And in the spring your mother would take you down to the river and tell you to get out of your clothes and get in the water no matter how cold it was, and believe me, it was cold."

The boy was pulling his arms in close to his body.

"And your mother would give you the one bar of homemade soap that had lasted through the winter. It was made of lye and pig's fat."

The boy was squirming.

"You got lye when you mixed water with ashes and then stirred that into the fat, and you washed with what came out. But sometimes there was too much lye and it would burn your skin."

The boy was rubbing his arms and squeezing himself into the smallest size he had ever been.

"And back up at this fort the men would put all their winter clothes into a pile and set them on fire. They had so much grease and stink in them there was no way they could ever be washed."

The boy's eyebrows were up.

"And speaking of grease, in the spring your mother would put bear grease over your body to keep the mosquitoes from biting. Of course, the grease attracted flies but at least they only chewed on the grease, not on you."

The boy looked up at his mother who nodded, because mothers always know everything even if they don't tell you.

"Have a good day and enjoy your visit," said the volunteer.

The boy and his little brother and mother walked away, going toward the musket firing demonstration. He turned several times, looking back at the volunteer dressed in a rough, red woollen shirt and wearing a floppy hat.

The boy will retell that story a hundred times, maybe more, and each time some other kid will get excited about how we really lived. The dates, the treaties, the names may or may not come, but the bear grease will stick.

Because of that volunteer the ten-year-old boy and his friends will want to learn more about our past. And they will.

The volunteer had the belief that if he told it like it was, there was no need to tell any more.

Then he scratched under his hat and said there were a bunch of happy bugs there. What kid could forget that?

HOW TO CHANGE THE WEATHER

The rain kept coming. It is not a good day at the PNE when the rain comes. It can ruin everything.

The Pacific National Exhibition is part of everything everyone wants: mini donuts, roller coaster, cows and pigs and chickens, burgers and whales' tails. Most of it outdoors.

And Dal Richards.

But the rain kept coming. And Dal's audience had no roof, hence the audience was all of twelve, fewer than are in his band. One woman said she only comes to the PNE to hear Dal and she only comes on one day. So she sat under her umbrella on a bench far from the stage with rain falling on her shoes.

The benches are kept back because when the sun is out Dal's audience fills the grass between the stage and the benches. If there was more room, more would be there.

Dal had performed here for sixty-eight years without missing a single year. But on a rainy day it must have been tough for him to keep going, playing with almost no one listening.

But wait, I didn't notice them at first. Right in front of the stage, crouched down under a row of umbrellas and sitting on what must be very wet grass, were fans.

Except for the rain and the grass and the cold and the wind they had the best seats in the house. On the other hand there were no seats, just puddles.

"You must really like his music," I said after I'd stuck my head under an umbrella.

But I knew the reply was not going to be yes before I finished the sentence. They were all teenybopper girls.

"What music?" one said.

She had earplugs in and was listening to her iPod.

"The music up on the stage."

"That's my grandparent's music," another one said. "I don't listen to it."

Dal was playing "The Tennessee Waltz."

"But it's good, you should try."

"It's silly, and it's old," she said, emphasizing "old" in a youthfully unflattering way. It had many more "o"s than its correct spelling.

"So why are you here?"

"To hear Vanessa Hudgens," three of them yelled, as though how could I not know.

"Who?"

"Vanessa Hudgens," six of them yelled louder. "From *High School Musical*."

For a moment I could not hear the sound of, "And while they were dancing my friend stole my sweetheart away," which was coming out of large speakers right on the stage above me. The girls were loud.

Then they started singing: "We're all in this together, once we know that we are, we're all stars."

"What's that from?" I asked.

"*High School Musical*," they yelled louder and in a way that said how did I not know.

They went on with the song. Their voices were pretty, as teenage girl voices are. They were no longer loud, they were lovely.

Then I realized the music above us had stopped. I looked up and Dal, in his white dinner jacket and white hair without a hat or umbrella, had walked out to the edge of the stage in the rain and was bending over looking down.

One of his band members raced out to grab him. He was eighty-nine years old then, and quickly getting soaked.

He could have been annoyed. He could have been depressed by the rain and the lack of an audience and he could have said this singing under the stage is one rotten thing too many.

He could have told the girls to have the common decency to be quiet while he was playing. But he didn't. When the girls finished Dal started applauding. He was an audience of one.

"Beautiful," he said to them, "just beautiful." And you know he meant it. "I love your music," he added.

Then he turned around and went back to his musicians and ordered up "St. Louis Blues."

The girls stopped singing and started listening. A few of them stood and, holding their umbrellas over their heads, started dancing to Dal's music.

Dal glanced back over his wet shoulder and you could see his smile.

Rained out? Not this concert. He made the sun shine.

PNE CRIMINAL

Maybe it's the karma. Maybe it's just luck. But good things do happen. He had on a sports jacket and tie because that's the way people dressed in his day. He walked past the hamburger stand and the foot-long hot dog stand and the ice cream seller, and almost everyone else had on jeans and T-shirts and ball caps.

I thought anyone who dresses like that must have something to talk about, even if it's only why he dresses like that.

Almost everyone likes to be told they look good, so that's a good place to start.

"Excuse me, but you sure look good," I said.

He looked surprised that anyone was talking to him. Then he thanked me and said this is the way everyone dressed when they went to the fair back in his day.

His name was Ron Robinson and he had been coming here since he was eight. He was eighty-six now, "and this is the first year I'm here alone."

Sad. He walked alone past the families and the couples and we got talking about the old days.

"I got arrested here once," he said.

Wow, I thought. A PNE criminal. "What'd you do?"

"I was on the Baby Dipper, that's gone now, and I had a bottle of beer in my pocket."

A real lawbreaker on the roller coaster that was here before the present roller coaster which has been here for fifty years. This is an old-time lawbreaker.

I had seen pictures of the Baby Dipper. It was a giant baby.

"I used to know everyone here," he said. "Everyone came. You couldn't walk a couple of steps without meeting someone you knew."

That's nice, I thought, but "Please, go on with your story."

"Oh, there was nothing to it. They spotted me from the ground and stopped the ride."

"How old were you?"

"Eighteen."

Well, that is the right age to be caught drinking when you shouldn't be drinking. Younger is a problem. Older is plain stupid. Eighteen is just right to be doing wrong.

"I didn't know they could make the cars go backward, but they did."

That's pretty heavy duty, I thought, for seeing someone with a beer.

"They backed the cars right down to the starting line and there were two cops and they took me to the jail they had on the grounds."

"They don't have that any more, do they?" he said.

No, no more jail on the fairgrounds.

"They would hold everyone they arrested until they had about ten of us, then they brought us down to 312 Main to book us."

"All for a beer?"

"Stiffer rules then."

I agreed. He laughed.

"But I sure wish it was like in the old days when we always saw people we knew."

I wished that for him, too.

He was searching the crowd for a face that he knew.

"I bet I'll find someone. But first I got to get my fish and chips. I always get fish and chips."

I felt sorry for him. In this great sea of fluttering shirttails and shorts and baseball caps there was no one who dressed like Ron.

On the other hand, he was chipper. He believed he would find someone.

We talked about how the fair has changed and gotten smaller and cleaner and how they have beer tents now and gambling.

"Funny; they were the evils back then," he said.

"But no peep shows now," I said.

"You got to pretend you are moral about something," he said as we walked past a large casino that had replaced a barn where chickens and ducks used to be on show.

"But the best part of this is being with someone. That makes it fun," he said.

He kept searching, looking more at the crowd than the cotton candy.

"But I don't know any of these folks. They are all strangers."

I knew why. He looked like a stranger to them also. No one wears a jacket and creased pants to watch the Super Dogs or chew on greasy food while listening to someone trying to sell miracle mops that can do anything, including clean the floor.

"Time to eat," he said. "Fish and chips and then look at the cows and then go home."

He sounded a little like he was giving up. "There are few of us around now."

Then from behind his back, "Hey, Ron. Is that you?"

He snapped his head to the left.

"Up here, by the fish and chips."

A man and woman, she in a summer dress from a different age and he with a sports jacket. They were waving to Ron.

"You know them?" I asked. Obviously he did but I wanted to hear him say yes.

"I can't believe it," said Ron to me. "I call them Bonnie and Clyde. I've known them for years."

"Are they criminals too?" I asked.

"No, just always together."

He was smiling. But he was through telling me stories of his criminal past. He had found someone, just like in the old days.

Bonnie leaned over the railing. She was at the order window.

"We never expected to see anyone we knew here. You want us to get you some fish and chip?"

Ron said, "Yes, please." He was from the "please" age.

"What do you want to drink?" Bonnie asked him.

"Just Sprite," he said. Then he turned to me. "I'm not taking any chances."

He repeated, "It's just like in the old days." He was beaming. He had found someone, just like the old days.

How did that happen? Did he meet his friends because he wanted to or was it just luck? Well, of course it was just luck. They saw him. Or was it karma, which is the belief that good things will happen to good people? Or because he believed he would?

Or maybe it was because he was wearing a jacket that stuck out in the crowd and caught the eye of his friends?

Doesn't matter. As he left me he said, "See, you come here and you meet people. It always happens."

You can't discount the attitude.

THE SWEET SMELL OF POOP

How do you get inspired by nature and guarantee yourself a restful mini-vacation?

Well, you go to a park and walk around the trees and sit on a bench and breathe the sweet smell of freshness.

But many others had the same idea. There was no parking left in Queen Elizabeth Park. Up and down I went, driving past the little bit of nature that I should be walking in.

The tennis courts were filled. The basketball courts were filled. The mini-golf was filled. No playing, no walking, no breathing, no parking.

Wait, there's a spot. One small place I could squeeze into behind that small, red pickup. It's tight. I can make it.

Ugh, something smells here. I must have driven over some dog poop. No. Ugh, gag, as I try again to get into the spot, no, that is not dog poop on the ground that some rotten person did not pick up. That is an overwhelming stink of unbearable proportion that is making me ill.

I roll up my windows, but the smell is already in the car. The back of the truck in front of me is filled with black plastic garbage bags.

Manure? No, manure doesn't smell this bad. Of course, maybe if I am behind a truck filled with it, it would be this bad.

I would like to leave, but there is nowhere else to go. I am stuck. Leave the park or hold my breath and then come back to a car that's been sitting in the sun absorbing more stink.

I get out of my car for a second to see how bad it is. I know that sounds stupid, but when something stinks you've got to see what stinks before you get away from it.

Oh, this is much worse than I thought. I can't hold my breath because I would have had to take a breath to hold and I can't breathe in this stuff.

I trot across the street, trying to tell myself oxygen is not essential. Then I take a breath and look at the sign on the door of the truck.

"Scooby's Dog Waste Removal, from your own backyard."

There are other services like that now, but when I saw this a handful of years ago it was new. My occupation and hobby is to look for things that are new and interesting and good enough to ask about and then tell others about. This fits half the requirements. It is new and interesting, but the other half means I would have to get close to ask about it. And this I could not do.

But I am saved because there is no one to ask. He could be playing tennis or rollerblade hockey down on the concrete field. He could have gone to the toilet. How long would I have to wait? No relaxing. No fresh air. Just waiting by a pile of poop. I want to go away and breathe.

I also want to stay and learn. I am torn between my heart, which wants the story, and my nose, which at this moment is warning my feet to move or the rest of me will die.

Time does not fly in circumstances like that.

Then he came back. He had only been gone five minutes.

His name, Chris Parker. Young, good-looking, short blond hair and seemingly strong. He looked like the kind of guy who gets hired based on appearance alone even though that is never supposed to happen.

It was a one man company and yes, I could follow him as he did his work.

"Try not to drive too close behind me," he said.

We went to several locations and he got out with his shovel and a rake and plastic bag. His service was to clean backyards where owners left their dogs during the day. Dogs happy, owners happy, Chris happy.

"But how do you stand the stink?"

"You get used to it," he said, then added, "It's nothing compared to what I used to smell."

Chris's story, the same story, once again: homeless for three years.

"How?" I am looking at the guy who gets the girls and the promotions.

"The usual stuff," he said. "Drugs—cocaine, heroin, crack. If they made it I used it."

"And you wound up on the street?"

"No, the alleys. My family took me back a few times, but I always screwed up and went back to the drugs."

"And then?"

Then came the same story I, and you, have heard so many times before.

"I reached bottom. Snivelling, filthy, hurting, hurting real bad and someone said I had two choices—stop or die."

That is the dividing line. Most with Chris's kind of pain die. They hunger for the high so much they are more than willing to trade death for it.

While I was doing a series on East Hastings we met a young guy who more than wanted to show us himself shooting up crack. He demanded we watch.

"You do stories about this, you should see this," he said.

He was in front of a Chinese herbal medicine shop that had long since stopped having customers. The couple who ran the shop said they saw what he was doing all day long, every day, through their front window.

The young man was busting with bravado. He rolled up his sleeve and tied a rubber tube around his arm to make his veins stand out. He said it was getting harder to find his veins. They were collapsing under the assault of chemicals.

"I'm getting the ultimate high," he said. "This will screw with my brain. It could kill me, I don't care."

He took several small bits of crystallized cocaine, which is called crack, and put them into a syringe.

"Bet you've never seen this before," he said. "This is shooting up dry."

No, I had never seen that before. Of all the terrible ways to torture yourself just to feel a buzz for a short while, this was looking to be the worst.

He injected the needle into his arm and drew out some blood, which dissolved the hardened rocks of cocaine. Then while the needle was still in his arm, he pushed the plunger and reinjected his blood and some drug dealer's cash flow into his vein.

No wonder the veins collapse.

Almost instantly he began screaming and laughing and screaming again. He screamed that he was feeling so good, so high, that this was the best and that he didn't care about anything.

He threw his syringe like a dart and it stuck in the wooden door frame of the herbal shop. The couple inside watched the whole thing. It was a repeat performance, same show, different characters.

The shop is now closed and abandoned. The young man is dead. But he has been replaced by new actors on the same old concrete stage.

Back to Chris and his poop. He described a similar life.

But someone told him stop or die, and he listened.

"I have been clean two years, two beautiful years."

"How?" The ultimate question. Can you tell me the key that works?

"I don't know. I just wanted to."

Of course it took outside support. Of course it took biting on his finger. Of course it took incredible determination. But like all the others who did it, he wanted to.

"And I believed I could do it," he said.

There is the key. The same thing everyone talks about. The same thing that will move a mountain. He believed he could.

Then he tossed the plastic bag that was filled with poop in the back of his truck. He was heading for a poop recycling plant. There, too, was an idea for a new business that did not exist a half-dozen years ago.

"Believe me, this smell is not so bad."

As he pulled away from the curb he stuck his head out the window and said, "Watch your step."

It is an in-joke with poop collectors.

It is also just plain good advice.

THE MOST PROFITABLE FLOWER

Bev wanted her own business. She worked for the government in the tax department her entire life behind a desk and that was a good job, but it was not her job. She wanted her own business, something she could devote her life to.

For years she told her husband and others at work that someday she would have her own business and no one would tell her what time she had to get to work and no one would check sick days or question her on overtime or remind her that the tax season was extremely busy and there would be no days off during it.

"With my own business I would come and go as I wanted," she said.

That is a good dream. Many of us have it but few of us obtain it.

Bev lives in Burkeville.

Bet you a quarter you don't know where Burkeville is.

Okay, for the six of you who said "Yes," I'll be standing on the corner of Cessna and Douglas to give you your coins.

If you live near Vancouver or Richmond it's not far; this throwback to a simpler, more beautiful time exists at the edge of the airport.

Have you ever seen a Norman Rockwell painting of a small town with sweet people in it who play baseball with borrowed gloves and fish for tadpoles? That's Burkeville.

But it is not in America, which some say Norman Rockwell created. I doubt that a town like this exists anywhere in the US or anywhere in the world.

It has mostly small bungalow-sized houses with gardens in front, and in front of the gardens are drainage ditches that you need a tiny bridge to cross.

There are no sidewalks in Burkeville. There are no stores. There is no bowling alley or 7-Eleven or movie houses or drag strips or corners where teenagers hang out. But there is a creek with tadpoles.

Unless you are a teenager, it is perfect.

But if you are a teenager you only have to walk twenty minutes, oh, sure, like any teenager would do that, or drive for five, and you are in the centre of Richmond or Vancouver.

Burkeville is a small town built during the Second World War to house employees of Boeing who were working in the hangers of the South Terminal of Vancouver's airport. They were building airplanes for the war. They had to have someplace nearby to live so Boeing built the town and named it after their president, Stanley Burke. The name was chosen in a contest among Boeing employees at the airport. They were smart employees.

The town has 328 houses and no traffic lights. Once you pull off the main road there are no stop signs. On one side of town is Number Five Road, on the other is the south runway of the airport, which was the only runway for more than fifty years.

You experience Burkeville with your ears more than your eyes—children laughing, airplanes landing, frogs croaking, airplanes taking off, birds singing, airplanes revving up their engines before taking off.

"What noise?" asked Bev Sloan, who has lived there her entire life.

Like everyone in Burkeville she ignores the thrust of a million pounds of jet fuel close to the top of her head. Burkeville is beautiful, if you can forget about the 747s so near that when they are coming in their landing gear is open over your roof and you can see the pilot.

"I don't even notice the planes," said Bev.

Almost no one who doesn't know about Burkeville ever turns off Number Five road to go there. There is a grass-covered hill that keeps eyes on the road from straying onto their streets.

Before the Richmond fire department built a new station outside of Burkeville the old fire station was the kids' home base. They hung out inside the fire hall, because there was nowhere else to go.

The firemen let them in, a public relations stroke of genius, and, even more, the firemen bought pop and candy for the kids to buy from them, which saved the younger kids the long walk across busy streets to get to a corner store.

The fire department, the kids, the friendly neighbours who know each other—except for a little quiet, what more would you want?

Bev wanted her own business. Her house in Burkeville is at the end of a dead end street. As you can guess, almost no one goes into Burkeville, and of those who do even fewer go on her street.

When she retired she thought, "What do I like? Well, I like my garden."

The gardens in Burkeville are about the size of the kitchen in a house built in the 1950s—small.

Bev had been growing vegetables, which she knew she could not sell because she could not grow enough.

But flowers—everyone likes them, especially the ones that last the longest and the ones that bloom the most prolifically for most of the summer: dahlias. Plus they were her favourites.

She bought and planted some tubers. That is simple enough. She planted them in the ten foot by twenty foot back garden where she had been growing tomatoes and carrots.

The first year the dahlias multiplied. They were beautiful, but made only enough flowers to fill the vases in her tiny house.

But you know what happens to tubers. The second year she had enough to fill her plot. By the time we met her she had mountains of tubers that had gone into the ground in the spring and now had become an ocean of dahlias. Red, yellow, pink—all blowing in the wind that came off the runway and making a beautiful sight.

"So I sell them. And I have my own business."

"Do you advertise, do you stand out on the street?"

No, she puts them in vases at her front door with a sign that says: "Bouquets $3. Please leave the vase."

"Everything they say about owning your own business is true," she said while picking up an egg from her chicken that wanders through her flowers. "You have to work seven days a week. No days off."

She said she is out in the garden early, snipping and cultivating and looking, all those things that gardeners do, which are the reasons gardeners garden. And she is in her garden late, catching up on the things she did not have time to do during the day.

"That's a lot of work and you don't get paid overtime," I said.

"Doesn't matter. It's my own business."

She said she cuts about a hundred blooms a day. "The more you prune dahlias the more they grow."

Word of mouth spread, because that is what happens when there is something worthwhile coming out of the mouth.

She has half a dozen visitors a day, which keeps her busy showing them her garden and then telling them about Burkeville.

"It's a full day," she said, "and I don't get any time off until the fall."

"You work seven days a week?"

"What do you expect? It's my own business."

It was also the dream.

"It's impolite to ask, but would you tell me how much you make in a year from the sweat of your labour?"

This got the biggest smile. "About $500."

"Is it worth it?"

"Of course. It's my own business, and I'm the boss." she said. She clipped some more flowers to put in vases by the front door. It was going to be a long day of work. More clipping, more mulching, more deadheading, then a quick dinner and back to work while there was still some light.

The thunderous jets came overhead and the flowers waved, blending their colours together. She was right, what airplanes?

Very simply, what is a dream worth? Can you get what you want?

Of course. You just have to want it, and work hard enough to get it.

Does it look like what others want, or even what is generally considered sensible?

Of course not. If you measure your dreams by that, they will never be yours.

If you believe your dream will come true, will it?

Spend three dollars at Bev's front door and you will see. But please, leave the vase.

THE IMPOSSIBLE DREAM

Bang. The ground shook. The same ground they were sleeping on in a bunker covered with sandbags shook violently, again, and the eight-year-old boy with wide eyes huddled in his mother's arms.

Bang again. And again. The big US Air Force planes high above were dropping bombs on the area around the border between North and South Vietnam. More bombs were dropped in this conflict than fell from airplanes during all of World War II.

It seems impossible that one small country could take so much punishment, or that one little boy could survive it.

I met Burt Hui the day after the PNE closed for the season. He had a power drill and was taking apart the Vietnamese restaurant booth. He was whistling.

Whistle while you work and you get the world's attention.

"Hello," and all the usual stuff. "Do you work for this place?"

"Own it," he said. "I own two restaurants."

That is enough to get anyone's interest. If he owns it, why is he doing the hardscrabble work of unscrewing boards and hauling them onto the back of a truck?

"I wash dishes at night. What's the difference? Work is work."

Okay, I like him. Maybe I can learn something. He got a phone call. He spoke in Cantonese. I have been in Vancouver long enough to know Cantonese when I hear it, but he is Vietnamese.

"How did you learn that?"

"In Hong Kong," he said.

"But I thought you were Vietnamese."

"I escaped to Hong Kong."

"When?"

"During the war."

Almost no one escaped from Vietnam during the war. The massive evacuation of boat people came after the fighting had ended. During the war you could not move around, you could not get from village to village or through rice paddies without being under bombs or in someone's gun sight.

"How old were you?"

"Eight," he said.

I was thinking, that is impossible. "How?"

"It is a long story, and a scary story and I have a lot of work to do," he said. But he did not say it in a nasty or arrogant way. He spoke matter of fact. He had work to do and I was holding him back.

Then he said, because he wanted me to know who the credit belonged to, "My mother said I had to go. She told me to be strong and to believe I could make it."

"Did you believe it?"

He laughed, because he was not giving a seminar.

"I was eight years old. I did what my mother told me."

To say he survived and got to Hong Kong is to cheapen what he did. He did the impossible. With help, and sometimes without help, an eight-year-old crawled, walked, ran and sank below the rice paddies to hide from the bullets.

Think of yourself at eight. Think of a neighbour's kid who is eight, because you probably cannot remember what you were like then.

He did what his mother told him and got to Hong Kong, alone and not speaking Cantonese.

Again, try to think of yourself at eight.

He met someone who was kind. Never discount one bit of kindness to one person. That led to another person and to a bed and food and work in a kitchen and he learned a second language.

Ten years later he applied to move to Canada, just when Communist China was taking over Hong Kong. Many were coming here.

He arrived here alone, not speaking English.

Another job in a Vietnamese restaurant and he learned a third language, which is not common among immigrants who work in restaurant kitchens. They seldom have enough time off to sleep, much less go to school. But Burt did what his mother told him and believed he would learn because there was no other way out of the kitchen.

In time he brought his parents here and together they took over a going-out-of-business restaurant, which was the only business he knew. But this was a soup and sandwich place.

"What did I know of Canadian soups and sandwiches?"

"We can do what we know," said his mother.

That is no different from saying "I believe we can do better." It is not a whining that they deserve better, it is an affirmation that they will do better.

They opened a small Vietnamese restaurant offering the basics—fried rice, spring rolls and Vietnamese soups.

Now he owns the Vina Vietnamese restaurant in the West End and the one in West Vancouver.

"Bet you'll be glad when you get all this stuff done," I said looking at all the wood and metal that had to be packed up.

"Then I go to work as a waiter in one of the other restaurants," he said.

"But you're the boss."

"That doesn't mean I don't have to work. My mother told me to be strong. I have no choice."

He went back to his work and his whistling.

If his mother was on Oprah she would give the shortest answers in the interview.

"Be strong and believe you can do it. And may I take your order."

Self-help books have many titles, but the basic one is spelled: Mother.

FEEL-GOOD FOLKS

Please allow me to tell you about three people who make me feel good, and they will work on you, too.

Everyone, you and me, likes to hear our own names. You greet someone by name, and you want to hear your name back.

But then there is the "Hello . . ." followed by a mumbled silence and you know that the someone who is saying hello hasn't got a clue what your name is.

You are polite and smile and say hello and shake hands and then you move on and you feel bad because you know they don't know and, by golly, they should know because you know their name.

Carmen Louie is different. You go into the store she works in on East Hastings near Nanaimo and she will say, "Hi, Fred," or "Hello, Matilda," or "I haven't seen you for a while, Ivy, how are you?"

Try it. Go to Donald's Market, buy some carrots or potatoes and look for the smiling face at the checkout. They are all nice people who work there, but Carmen will be smiling. She is always smiling.

If it is your first time in the store she will not know your name.

"That will be six ninety-nine and excuse me, but what is your name?" she will ask.

That is very nice. No one asks for a name in a store unless they are checking on your credit rating.

Go back a week later. She will remember you, and your name. And in that moment of being remembered you will feel good. Gee, someone knows me. I must be important, or at least memorable.

Carmen remembers everyone's name. At last count she had 5,500 names on file in her head and in her notebooks.

"Hi, Betty, how are you?"

"Hi, Carol."

She waves to a woman and then says to me, "That's Carol from Chilliwack who looks like Debbie from Abbotsford."

She does this with every customer.

Adam, listed as number 2,012 in her note book: "Blond hair, nice smile."

"Hello, Matthew," she said to a passing young man wearing an Andy Capp hat.

"That's Matthew Phillips," she said to me.

He turned and came back. "That she knows my whole name blows me away."

Somehow we suspect the cap had something to do with it, but following her route would take up all my brainpower and I wanted to know more.

"*Come sta*, Isobella?"

Isobella, who speaks Italian, is being greeted in her language. What could make a person feel better? Carmen has learned enough Italian to talk with her Italian customers.

The same with Mandarin-speaking customers. And with those who talk in Cantonese or Tagalog. Can you image how all those customers feel when they pay for their bananas and bread and hear their name, with the correct accent?

Of course it is good for business, but Carmen does not own the store. She would get paid the same whether she knows you or not.

"Debbie, how are you?"

Debbie feels good.

"How did you remember me? I haven't been in here for months."

"You are unforgettable," said Carmen.

"Why do you do this?" I asked.

"Because it makes them feel good," she said.

She does not need lessons in positive thinking. She breathes it. Check her out. Buy some apples. Tell her your name. The next time you go there she will make you feel important, because you are.

And Daniel on his scooter:

"Wait, stop, turn around," I say to the cameraman as we pass a motor scooter that looks like a psychedelic visitor from the age of hippies. It has decals over its entire surface and add-ons such as stuffed dolls and little stick-on statues and flags. It is like an art car but this is not a car. It is parked at Main and Fourth.

We turn around and go back. It is gone. It cannot be gone. It was here only two minutes ago. Of course, in two minutes the universe could be gone, especially if you believe we are just a dream in the head of some schoolboy who has invented us because he is bored. And then the bell rings and class is over and he forgets about us. Poof. Gone. It is possible.

But it is not possible that a motor scooter is gone in two minutes. Well, he didn't go up Main Street because we just came down it. Go the other way.

"Turn on First," I give instructions.

The cameraman, who is much smarter than me, keeps going without turning. I am ticked off.

"He doesn't seem like a First Avenue kind of guy," is the reason.

"There he is," he says.

We pull up alongside him.

"Can you pull over?"

"You have something for my scooter?"

"No, we want a picture."

I realize if we had gone down First Avenue those words would not be spoken. I am a lucky guy. Another rule: If you demand things be done your way, get ready to live without getting the things you want.

The scooter man said he was used to people stopping him and giving him things to stick on his fenders, which had run out of room to carry anything else.

His scooter is a work of mobile art. It carries dolls and photos and toys and necklaces and happy faces and more stuffed animals under his handle bars.

"Where do you get them all?"

"I don't buy them. After I put on the first few, people began stopping me and giving me things. It sort of makes the scooter theirs," he said.

I thought I recognized him, and when he stood up and he was wearing a kilt I knew I knew him.

"Ten years ago we met," he said. "Different scooter, different kilt."

He was then a courier on a child's push scooter. One foot on the running board, the other on the ground, pushing. He was competing against a fleet of fast moving and expensive bicycles, but actually they were competing against him. On shorter trips his scooter could out manoeuvre a bicycle and he did not have to lock it up. He just picked it up when he got to an office building and carried it into the elevator.

Speed is everything in the world of couriers, and when you have a push scooter you may be slower on the street, but you are faster in the elevator lift-off. But most of all, how could you forget someone who wore a kilt in the city even in winter?

The secretaries who did the ordering for the couriers called him often.

"Are you Scottish?"

"No, I just like kilts. You feel free."

And that is what he is, free enough to do what he wants to do.

"And now, why the decals on your motor scooter? And why a motor scooter?"

He was getting older, fifty-two. He had been a courier most of his life, but it was time to take it a little easy. Instead of pushing himself around the city on his foot he opted for a 49cc engine, which is as small as an engine comes before it starts cutting grass.

And the stickers and stuffed animals?

"They make people feel good. You see them and laugh."

That is the same reason that Carmen memorizes names.

Most of us are far too conservative to even put a Canucks' sticker on our bumper. Outside of Robbie Burn's ceremonial dinners few of us would wear a kilt.

And he misses his foot-powered scooter. "It reminds me of childhood, with no licence, no gas, no parking. Now I need everything."

Daniel Deihl returns to his childhood every day with his travelling toy box, his joy, his expression, his wonderful craziness. Some might say he's just trying to get attention, but so what? Does your, or my, drive around the city in a grey car in a sea of grey cars make others feel good?

Plus, on summer weekends, wearing his kilt, he still rides his push scooter. Imagine the freedom.

———

And on Saint Patrick's Day I was hoping to get to the parade, but I missed it. Darn. If you miss the parade, what hope is there of telling folks about what happened on Saint Patrick's Day (unless you go into a bar, and that we don't do on family television).

And this is not a normal Saint Patrick's Day because it is snowing, heavily, and there will not be much of any street celebration because snowballs are not in any Irish literature.

Wait, I hear an Irish fiddle jig. It is in front of the Art Gallery. Irish people playing Irish music will do just fine.

No. If you look through the falling flakes, they are not Irish. Most of those on the small stage with their fiddles under their chins are young Chinese girls, but they sure are bouncing with a jig of Irish energy.

And standing under the falling snow about fifty people are keeping time with the music and a few of them are dancing while their hair and hats are turning white.

One man, with a cap and a scarf and holding his umbrella like a partner rather than over his head, is dancing by himself.

"Hello," etc.

"This is so wonderful, all these cultures dancing," he said with an Irish musical melody in his voice.

He was right. Around him were Native Indians, whites, blacks, East Indians and Asians, all captured by Irish music being played by Chinese girls in a storm in Canada. The leprechauns had cast a spell and everyone there became Irish.

"You came here alone?" I said to him, trying to make conversation while he continued to move his feet back and forth.

"No," he said. "Not at all. I'm Irish, you know."

Somehow he thought that explained it all.

"Who came with you?"

"My guardian angel, Kelly," he said. "My granny from the old country. Listen, I have a poem about her."

We knew he was Irish because the Irish make poetry about everything—good times, bad times and fairy godmothers.

"It's the blood that you gave me,

It's the reeling, feeling, wheeling, dancing, prancing blood that you gave me."

He danced a bit more.

"It's the blood in the veins, the veins that run with fun. Thanks, gran."

"When did you write that?"

"Just now."

His name was Michael Wicks, a retired teacher, he said.

"Your granny would be happy to hear it," I said.

He smiled. "No, my granny is happy to hear it. As I said, I am not here alone."

The music slowed and his feet did the same, sliding with the notes back and forth over the wet ground. He was right. His guardian angel was dancing with him in the snow, which he never complained about or even mentioned.

The next day I got a phone call from a woman who said that before the story came on television she had not seen Mr. Wicks since the mid-1970s. He was her teacher in grade three.

"He was the nicest man in the world. He always told us about his guardian angel and after that I believed I had one too."

But what she really liked about him was that he rode his motorcycle to school. How cool was that?

Michael Wicks, and his granny, without even trying to be positive, made the world a bit more Irish, which means they made it better.

TAKING CELLO FOR A WALK

S he did hear the music. It was going into her ears on headphones. One more block, and then there will only be thirty-five to go.

Emily turned the corner from her home and adjusted the cello in its case, which was hung by a strap over her shoulder. It was the love of her life. But you don't carry a cello thirty-six blocks unless you have more than love.

"I was born to play this," she said.

Then she quickly added, "I can't believe I said that. It sounds so corny."

She had been playing the cello, smaller versions, since before she was in kindergarten. Almost every day of her life she had gone to lessons. She had played with Yo-Yo Ma.

And now there was a bus strike and her lessons in the Vancouver Academy of Music were thirty-six blocks away. So she walked. And she did not only walk the day we saw her, but she walked five days a week carrying her love. She was just a smidge taller than it.

"It's an adrenalin rush every time I play," she said.

That is a lot of times to have adrenalin and a lot of reasons to walk. But when you want to do something you do it, and Emily Kyne wanted to play.

Think of how easy it would be not to play: the bus strike, not enough money to take a cab, you cannot carry a cello on a bike and it is thirty-six blocks away, and we have to repeat the obvious—a cello is not a violin.

And now something else that is obvious. Emily wanted to do it. She did not have to say to herself, "I will walk. I will make it. I will not drop my precious instrument."

She just set her tunes on her head and walked. An hour and a half later she was halfway across the Burrard Street Bridge and could look down at the Academy. From there she had only to finish the bridge, walk around the apartment building at the end of it, and then cut across the grass before pulling open the door and beginning playing. Nothing to it.

According to the music books, you are supposed to be rested before you start. She did this every day.

Also, according to the doctors, she would never play again after her finger was crushed in a car door accident. Someone did not see her hand on the jamb when it was slammed it shut.

After it healed she was told she would probably never again get the incredible dexterity that was needed to finger the strings.

That journey was longer than a thirty-six block walk.

"How's your finger now?"

She looked down at it wrapped around the strap that hung over her shoulder and carried her love.

"Fine, getting there," she said.

After practice she put her cello back in its case and headed home, and then to work. The bus strike lasted six weeks. She never missed a day.

On her headset?

"Backstreet Boys," she laughed. "You've got to take a break once in a while."

In her heart? Perfect sounds from a well-travelled companion of love.

She does not have to tell herself that she will get there; she knows it.

DO YOU KNOW WHAT AUTISM IS?

No, of course not. No one does, not really. If your child is autistic you know the future is miserable and your little loved one will be short-changed forever.

But what is it? The poor kid's mind just does not grasp things, ordinary things, like numbers or concepts, or what autism is.

"Do you know what autism means?" I asked Adam.

He stared at me blankly. We had been having a fun conversation about how to wash cars and how he loved getting them clean, and he loved the people he worked for and he loved the music they were playing on the radio and he loved washing cars. He also told me he took the bus from Maple Ridge to Surrey to get to his car washing job.

What? A bus ride from Maple Ridge to Surrey!? That would take half a dozen transfers. That is beyond the patience or the capacity of ninety percent of the population. But Adam did it, every day.

"I love taking the bus," he said.

Adam loves many things. In fact, Adam loves everything. No one has ever seen him not smiling.

Some autistic people are sad. Some are happy. Some are both, pretty much the way it is with ninety percent of the population.

Autism?

"No, I don't know what that is," he said.

We don't know what causes autism. There seems to be a surge of it in the last generation. It could be the air or food or medicine or, honestly, who knows? Perhaps we're just getting better at spotting the problem. In any case, autistic kids eventually become older, like Adam who is now twenty-nine.

Autism isn't like that dreadful disease schizophrenia, where you hear voices screaming at you. With autism you are just unsure of some things. There is mild autism, where you can adapt to almost an average life, and severe, where you have trouble figuring out anything.

Adam is in the middle, like the majority of autistic kids.

He has never had a girlfriend, never had a date, never been out with a bunch of friends who sneaked a beer and laughed with them and hid the adventure from his parents.

But he goes to the PNE and walks the streets and eats whales' tails and, oh heavens, there is rock and roll music over there on a stage. He is dancing, with his knapsack on his back in which are his camera and sandwiches and water and bus fare.

He is dancing in front of the stage, but on the tiny stage there are two young women with a closed circuit television camera and they call to Adam.

"Me?"

"Yes, you, come on up here."

"Me?"

The young girls do not understand someone not jumping at the chance to be on TV. With the impatience of seventeen-year-olds they say, "YES, YOU. GET UP HERE."

Adam climbs up on the stage and stands there, stiff.

"Well, dance," they say. "Dance and we'll put you on TV."

There is a monitor next to them. The camera is aimed at the call letters of a new family television station. In front of the letters is room for a few dancers.

Adam starts moving. He is grooving with the beat. He is smiling and dancing. A group of sixteen-year-old girls is watching from the ground. They jump up on the stage. They know the sweet call of television and they dance, surrounding Adam.

I do not know if they noticed at first that he was there. They were staring at the monitor while they danced.

Then one of them grabbed Adam's hand and started dancing with him. Another took his other hand. Suddenly Adam had six young, bouncing partners. The first time he had ever danced with anyone.

Then the music ended and the girls and Adam applauded themselves and I asked the girls what they thought of Adam.

"Cute," said one. "Good dancer," said another. "Yummy," said a sweet young thing with way too much makeup for a day at a country fair.

Then they jumped down and went off in search of mini donuts or teenage boys with lecherous eyes, or both.

"How was that?" I asked Adam.

"I have never been so happy in my life. That was the best thing that ever happened to me. I am so lucky."

Then he stepped down off the stage. He, like all of us eventually, was a little too old to jump off like the girls. Autism does not give you special powers.

Where does Reilly and positive thinking come into all of this?

I asked Adam after the dance what he was going to do the next day.

"I'm coming back here. I love the PNE."

And he was coming back by bus.

The escapes are not all from Main and Hastings. The wishes are not all to cure cancer or get along with your kids or succeed in your job. The belief that your life is good can happen on a bus, with a knapsack on your back and a smile on your face even if you really don't understand how vastly different you are from all those other kids and adults who have partners and cars and who do understand ordinary things that make no sense to you.

Autism is hard to understand and hard to live with. But Adam doesn't care about that. Adam loves what he is doing, whatever it is.

SHIP IN THE BOTTLE

"There's still some rum in here," I said.

Knut Hansen looked in the bottle.

"Couple of drops," he said. "We should share them."

A teaspoon for him, and the same for me. That is about perfect for a drop of rum in the afternoon. Anything more and it becomes night and you've lost the day.

"How do you get them in there?" I asked.

I asked because I had no idea how a model ship that was almost as tall as the bottle was wide and much taller than the neck, got inside, with its masts up and sails flying.

"I learned this while I was sailing on one of them," he said.

As far as we could find out, Knut was the last man in British Columbia to sail on a tall ship made of wood.

There are still training ships used by most of the navies of the world to teach their officers how it once was done. But there are no commercial tall ships still operating, and they haven't been for so long a time that almost no one remembers.

Except Knut. "We would be sixty feet up at the top of the mast and the ship was rolling in the seas and you had to hold onto the mast with all your strength to keep from getting thrown overboard."

He was remembering. He was fifteen when he left Norway aboard a sailing ship. He did all the work, all the dirty work, and ate the bad food and slept on the hard floors below the decks.

"It was the life I had dreamed of. No one in Norway was considered to be a man unless you went to sea."

He grew up high above the decks. "We had a young German fellow who was not holding on tightly enough when the ship pitched," he said. "Poor fellow, he was thrown into the sea like a rock from a sling shot. No way we could go back and look for him."

No, you could not stop the engines and lower the lifeboats when your only power was sail. By the time the sails came down the ship would be so far from the man overboard that he would be in the stomach of a shark.

And as for lifeboats, these were the old days when a life was not worth as much as a boat. No lifeboats on board. Just get a replacement for the man overboard at the next port.

In the winter nights, when sleet was coming from the blackness and you could see nothing, Knut was six storeys up the mast trying to pull up the canvas sails that weighed a ton and were slippery.

His fingers were frozen and there were no gloves that you could wear when you were up there. The melting ice went down his collar and soaked his shirt and he was frozen from the inside out.

"It was a great life," he said.

We cannot imagine.

And now I was watching him carve masts and spars out of wood and make sails out of pieces of cloth and attach them to a ship with threads that he tied into tiny knots, turning them into shipboard ladders.

"But how do you get it into the bottle?"

"Secret," he said. "If you can sail into a storm it is not a problem getting a ship into a bottle." Then he laughed.

So many people I have met laugh. It is the trait that separates them from those who suffer. They are people with the same bills, the same suffering, the same disappointments, the same tragedies and deaths and heartbreak, but they laugh. The sad don't laugh, they groan.

There is a lesson in there. I don't know which comes first, the groaning or the sadness; or the laughter or the happiness.

Knut said one of the best thing about his hobby was he had to have bottles. "And to get the bottle ready for a ship I have to empty it. Now that can be a problem." He laughed again.

He said he needed a new bottle for each new ship and each ship can take a couple of weeks to build.

"I think I'm okay. I'm ninety-six and still get my daily rum allotment."

"What?! Ninety-six! You look like you are seventy-six, and a healthy seventy-six."

"I love life. In fact, I love everything, except the things I don't like," he said.

That must be the reason. Like almost everyone else I have met who is sailing with the wind behind them, he loves being alive. That again is no secret, it is not a trick like getting the ship in the bottle. It is just a fact.

"And this is how it is done," he said.

The moment of revealing the magic is now. Do I really want to see this, or do I want to believe that a good sailor can get his ship through anything?

I want to see.

The masts are not glued onto the deck. They are laying flat down backward on the ship and their bottom ends are resting between minute strips of wood. The strips are smaller than the narrow end of a toothpick.

He puts a tiny drop of glue between the strips. The sails, the masts, the rigging is all attached but lying on the deck facing the stern. It is then small enough to sail through the neck of the bottle.

He slipped his ship in backward through the neck and anchored it onto some drops of glue waiting on the inside of the bottle. When the ship was resting on the glue he slid a piece of wire with a hook at the end through the neck.

Then he hooked the front mast and gently pulled it forward. The mast rose along with the sails and the rigging, followed by the second mast because it was tied to the first mast.

How did he plan all that?

"Easy," he said. "This is the way it's been done for a century. This is not like those things you buy with the ship in the bottle and the bottle was made to go around the ship. Those are cheaters."

And Knut did not cheat. He did not cheat on his life on the deck of a wooden ship or with his one wife for sixty years or his joy. He was the captain of his life and did not let himself drown.

And what did he get in return?

"I've had the most wonderful life anyone could hope for," he said.

He never once said his life was all based on faith or belief in himself. He simply laughed and enjoyed what he was doing.

Every time I see a ship in a bottle in an antique store I think of someone who was the captain of his soul. That line is from a famous old poem. It also says he was the "Master of his fate."

How did he rise from cabin boy to captain? There was no deep philosophy. There was nothing he told me about having a positive attitude in what you want that accounted for Knut's wonderful life. He simply had the attitude. He did not have to say it.

From where I was watching Knut slide a ship into a bottle I could see only one reason for his happiness. He laughed, and when you do that how can you be anything but happy?

HOUSE ON WEST KING EDWARD

I t is not like it was in the old days. Sadly. I used to get non-stop calls in the
newsroom saying:

"You have to see this house on West King Edward. It's all lit up for
Christmas."

And, "You have to see this house on King Edward. It's all lit up for
Halloween."

And, "You have to see this house . . . (you know where) . . . It's all lit up
for Easter."

You're getting the picture. Name a holiday and the house on West King
Edward was lit up and decorated and ready for admiration.

It was amazing. When you talk about houses with lights, this one was
glowing.

I went and found Donna, digging around in her stand-up crawl space
under the old house on West King Edward getting ready for Valentine's Day.

"I love every holiday," she said.

She had lived there all her life. Her mother and father and grandparents
had lived there. She had a picture of the house shortly after 1900 when it was
the only one on the street and the road was dirt and there were no cars, which
is not surprising since cars did not exist.

A time before cars. Amazing. Few alive now can conceive of such a time.
There was no noise, no exhaust fumes, no racing engines, no sirens, no hurrying to cross the street ahead of a traffic light. There were no traffic lights.

And that was only in the life span of this one house on West King Edward. Now the traffic screams by, noisy as an army of cylinders and tires, and the tour buses come by to see the changing of the decorations in the house.

"This was the best one," said Donna.

She showed me a note left on her front door.

Written on the paper was: "I have a group of mentally challenged adults and I drive them past your house every week in every season. Thank you for all you do."

It was signed Dianna.

"Did you ever meet her?" I asked.

"No, but I did the next best thing."

She said one Christmas with all the lights blazing on her house she put up an even bigger sign:

"Merry Christmas, Dianna, And All Your Friends."

It had spotlights shining on it.

"I hope she saw it."

Did she imply that she was doing a wonderful thing and that crowds saw it and said, "That is the most wonderful Christmas gift of all. And the person living there must be wonderful"?

Did she even try to take credit?

No. She only humbly hoped one person saw it.

Trying to make one someone happy is possibly the greatest virtue in life.

And as a result, thousands saw it, and every one of them understood and felt good.

IT'S NOT ALL MAIN AND HASTINGS. SOMETIMES IT'S JUST FUN

The only thing Mike Gair wanted for his son was something to be thankful for that his son would understand. They had their Thanksgiving turkey dinner and the family talked about how good life was and all the usual stuff, but the little boy just sat there, not wanting to eat his vegetables.

"Let's go across the street to the park," Mike said to Brandon, who was eight.

He had an idea. No cost, no stores, no boxes, no instructions or wires or things that could go wrong.

"We're going to stick race," the father said to the boy. "Go find a couple of sticks about the size of your fingers."

Brandon ran off looking. His father made him happy. But this was something different. This was a surprise and he was part of it.

He found a couple of sticks and brought them back.

"Perfect," his father said.

There is nothing more a kid wants to hear. Brandon is on the road to believing in himself.

Could you imagine if every kid was started with encouragement and compliments and if they seldom heard, "Stop, no, don't, can't, must not, should not, never do that again"?

Of course that does not apply if the kid is running toward the street.

"Now, let's go over to that stream."

The stream in Queen Elizabeth Park would not have been counted as a creek in the old days. It is so narrow you can step over it and it only runs for about thirty steps before it disappears into a miniature pond.

But if you have a stick the stream is a river wider than the Fraser and longer than forever.

"One, two, three, throw them in," said Mike.

Splash, double splash. Brandon was in the lead. Mike was catching up.

"This is called stick racing," said the father to the son.

Whoops. The swift boats got tangled in some leaves and stopped.

"I'll get it," said Brandon.

He leaned over the bank, reached down and, "Help. I'm falling."

His father grabbed his leg and pulled him back. Then his father said he would hold him and he could reach down and set them free. Brandon broke up the log jam and the race was on again and Brandon was beaming.

Suddenly, out of nowhere, Katrina was there, next to Brandon. Katrina was five.

"Can I play?"

Brandon looked at her like an intruder.

"Of course you can," said Mike. "Brandon, show her how to get a stick."

Boy and girl ran off, not far, not far enough to get anyone worried, but far enough in boy and girl's minds to feel free. They came back with a stick for Katrina.

"What is your name," because she only became Katrina at this moment.

"Are you her father?" asked Mike of the man who was standing nearby.

Alistair McColl nodded. "I was hoping we would find something to do," he said.

Katrina and Brandon ran along the creek, the stream, the river, the biggest, fastest river in the world with the fastest boats racing each other.

Whoops! Brandon slipped on the edge and slid again into the mighty Fraser.

"Boy overboard," someone called out.

Brandon pulled himself out and looked at his father and when he saw that his father was laughing Brandon started laughing. Brandon just got moved further along that road of self-confidence.

"I used to do this as a kid," said Mike. "I was hoping Brandon would learn about it."

Katrina's and Brandon's sticks both got to the end at the same time, although one of them got there first but it was hard to tell whose was whose, so really it was a tie.

"We both won," said Katrina.

"This is the greatest fun ever," said Brandon.

Then we left, because they could stay there all day and we were too old to have that much time for play. Silly us.

I did not have to ask Mike if he had found something that Brandon could be thankful for. It was the parent who should be thanked for giving to the child something that he could be thankful for, sometime in the far future when he did the same.

But Mike did not want to be thanked. He just wanted to do that and he did.

MUCH LIGHTER,
UNLESS YOU ARE SEVEN

I was so lucky to be there. The chances of me seeing it were smaller than tiny. Every fifth minute during twenty-three hours at the Variety Telethon there is a cheque presentation.

The hosts are rushed from one part of the stage to another and told only that there is a presentation. They are given a card with the names of those who are giving the money they have raised. The stage looks like a beehive on a spring day.

The hosts only have time to read the names and then they introduce the wonderful people whose names they have just read.

Each name has a story to go with the money: they raised it at bingo or at the car wash or by collecting bottles or from an auto dealership or elementary-school class.

"We are grade two students from Coast Meridian School in Richmond."

She was so cute. Seven years old with four of her classmates at her side and Kristi Gordon, the weather woman, holding the microphone in front of her.

And then she froze. Seven years old and not a word coming from her mouth or her mind. Blank. Frozen. Terrified by the big camera in her face and several smaller cameras on the shoulders of shooters who were on their knees in front of her.

Silence. The seconds took forever to pass. At seven she wanted to disappear. At seven her world was over.

"You can do it," said Kristi with the greatest of patience.

"I forget," said Claudia, who could not remember.

"You are here to donate your money to the Variety Club," said Kristi.

"We are here to donate ... I can't remember," said Claudia.

"Yes, you can," said Kristi, very lovingly and patiently.

"We are here ..." Icy, endless silence. "I can't remember," followed by a flood of tears in front of the camera, which makes everything wet and gooey because now you are on television not remembering and your cheeks are dripping.

Kristi tried to console her, but Claudia was alone with several hundred thousand people watching and her classmates standing next to her and the stage crew trying to speed things up because the telethon is like a freight train that cannot stop or even slow down. It is all timed and rehearsed and plotted and paced.

Kristi tried again to coach her. "You can do it." Silence. There is another appeal and another vignette of a child in need waiting to go on, and another countdown for a total amount also waiting. The show does go on.

Of all the times that I was in the studio, it was that moment. I could have been backstage waiting for my next appearance. I could have been talking to some of the crew. I could have, and should have, been off the stage to avoid crowding when I saw Claudia. My heart broke.

But it was time for me to stand in front of the camera and talk about the urgent need for money to ease the lives of children who have severe needs. However, like everyone else who did the formal presentations, I had a teleprompter.

I meant every word I said, as does everyone else who volunteers for that job, but I was reading. You could tell I was reading because every once in a while prompter dyslexia would hit and I would skip a line and then try to go back and say it over again, at which point I would get embarrassed because several hundred thousand people were watching and I was thinking they must be thinking that I am the dumbest person on earth. And if I was seven years old I would have cried.

I understood Claudia, at least a little bit.

When I had a break during one of the long musical concerts that give you time to watch and call with a donation I went to the outside tent for a coffee.

There was Claudia, still looking like the end of the world had come and gone and hadn't bothered to even take her with it. She was alone, with her mother, Angela Culley, and her teacher, Tammy Corness, who is in a wheelchair and was a Variety kid a handful of years ago.

Neither woman could find anything but dejection in Claudia's face.

"She practiced every day, five times a day or more," said her mother. "She knew every word. She went to bed reciting it."

"I knew she could do it," said Tammy. "She did it in class every day. She was perfect."

This was the chance for me to make something right. I could only pray for this and it was being handed to me. The little girl with red cheeks from tears running over them and red eyes from making the tears and a bottom lip that curled out from catching the tears was not happy.

I ran out of the tent and found a cameraman.

"This is big," I said to him. "This could save someone's life."

He was thinking a holdup of the charity money or someone tangled in the telephone wires.

"See that little girl," I said. "Shoot, I'll explain later."

There was no tragedy to record, just a young girl sitting at a long table trying to nibble at a cookie but not eating it and sniffing, then sniffing more.

"Does she have an incurable disease?"

"Yes," I said. "Sadness, and you are going to cure it."

We kneeled in front of Claudia.

"Do you know your lines now?" I asked.

She nodded.

"Would you like to say them to all the people watching on television?"

Her eyes widened. She stopped nibbling. She nodded very strongly.

"Just look up at that camera and say them," I said.

I held the microphone. The camera was running.

"We are grade two students from Coast Meridian School in Richmond. We raised money for Variety to help children in need. Thank you."

Who could say no to that?

Claudia wanted to say her lines. I just happened to be passing by. Maybe I could have been somewhere else, but I wasn't.

I believe it has something to do with wanting, really wanting, especially if it was both Claudia and I both doing the wanting.

At the end of the six o'clock news we ran Claudia's memorized lines. More people saw it than were watching television at eleven in the morning.

BIKE MECHANIC PHILOSOPHER

What does a philosopher look like? I know what I thought when I was in school.

He wore a scarf and carried books and looked deep in thought. Then I discovered the real world.

He was threading a chain back onto the sprocket of a bicycle. His fingers were black with grease. His nose was a little bent from a rough life and the wrinkles in his face were deeper than folds in a towel after it comes out of the closet.

"He who is really kind can never be unhappy."

That sign was on a wall just inside the rented garage where he worked on the corner of Heatley Avenue and Keefer Street. This is not a neighbourhood of independent businesses. It is a corner in transition from poverty to subsistence.

Jim Parks looks like Johnny Cash on a day when Johnny was still in prison. Rough. But, like Johnny Cash, if you have two choices you had better take the better choice or you will be banging your head against the bars forever.

Johnny Cash took the better choice and strummed his guitar and inspired millions, and Jim Parks fixed bicycles and made dozens of kids happy.

"You make a living doing this?" I asked.

"Sometimes, like this morning I did okay, but yesterday I made nothing."

Above him another sign on the wall.

"He who is really wise can never be confused."

"Do you believe that?" I asked.

"Like I believe the sun will be up tomorrow, even if there's clouds up there, and like I believe I will make a little money tomorrow even if I didn't today."

"How about that one?" I asked looking at some writing on the door frame. The writing was in Magic Marker:

"If it's not right don't do it. If it's not true don't say it."

Next to the word "right" a word was scratched out. He'd made a mistake in writing it and then fixed it. That made it right. In a way, repairing that mistake made the whole line stand out and be noticed.

"I saw that in a junkyard," Jim said. "It's all you have to know."

His shop was a one-car garage filled with nuts and bolts and pedals and bike tires and bike frames and tools.

"I didn't pay for any of this. I found everything except for the things that people gave me."

That is a good way to get a business going. But why would folks give Jim things that they could just as easily throw away or make a few dollars from in a garage sale?

He shrugged, but I knew. Jim was a nice guy and people do nice things to nice guys. He was standing near another sign:

"Be good and you don't need to worry

About making the right choice."

Standing in his rented garage was like being in philosophy class at a university. All the keys to living well were surrounding us. But in a classroom the eternal truths would be framed and credited to Plato or Socrates.

In Jim's garage they were in his handwriting.

"He who is really brave is never afraid."

"Where did you get that one?" I asked.

"Also in a junkyard. They know a lot of stuff there."

He finished putting the chain around the sprocket.

"You know, if you read that one backward it works too." Then he smiled like he had just revealed a secret.

I looked up at the sign. Don't be afraid and you will be brave. Obviously. But if you start out not being afraid you don't need to worry about how to be brave.

"This stuff is like daily maintenance," he said. "It's like brushing your teeth."

What does a philosopher look like? Bent nose, wrinkled skin, baseball cap, a sweater underneath his shirt.

"The sweater is easier to clean if you keep it covered," he said.

Greasy fingers, invisible income.

"Here comes the girl for her bike."

She was about ten years old. She did not see me or Jim. Her eyes were on the bicycle with a repaired chain that was now being polished with a clean rag.

"Is it fixed, Mr. Parks?"

"Just like new."

"My mommy said she will pay you later."

Jim handed over the bike. "Tell her it was easy. No charge."

"Thank you." It was a big thank you. It was a giant thank you.

She put her foot on a pedal and pushed off and turned around just long enough for Jim to see her smile.

"Like brushing your teeth," he said. "You got to do it every day."

REILLY'S RULES

Y ou get what you believe you will get.

You are who you want to be.

They are so simple. There are only two of them and we added the second one. And they could be reduced to one because the first is really just the second with different words and a different point of view.

Or they could be expanded to a hundred, but that is too many for a poor schmuck who only wants to improve his life to remember.

How about "Meetings are not frightening."

"Osgood, I want to see you in the morning."

Osgood is you. The I is the boss. He has told you this as you are putting on your coat at 5 p.m.

Oh goodness, dinner is going to be difficult.

"I got bad news tonight, honey. The boss wants to see me in the morning."

"Oh, you poor dear, do you know what for?"

"No, and it's making me sick."

"I made a nice dinner."

"Sorry, can't eat it."

"Johnny got an A in school."

"I don't think we can afford that school any more."

"You think it's that bad?"

"It can't be anything but something really bad, I just have that feeling."

Next morning after no sleep:

"Glad to see you, Osgood. I was wondering if you would like to join us at brunch next week. I didn't have time to ask you last night."

"Your work is outstanding and this is just a small thank you."

———✦———

Reilly's method:

"Osgood, I want to see you in the morning."

Later at home: "I got good news today, dear. The boss wants to see me. I believe something good will happen. What's for dinner?"

"Lamb. And I am so happy for you. And Johnny got an A."

"You taught him well. Let's go to bed early tonight."

"What about the meeting?"

"If he wants to fire me I'll get a better job."

———✦———

Very simple. You cannot change reality, but if you go into the meeting thinking it will be good, who is going to fire someone with a smile and a positive attitude?

And think about what you have gained; an enjoyable dinner, a chance to talk with an A student, a fine evening with a fine woman. And an early night to bed.

And if he does fire you, he is a jerk and you are now going to get a new career. I know you will, Reilly knows you will and, more importantly, you believe you will. Also, he would not tell you the night before if he was going to fire you and if you were not filled with fear you would realize that.

There is no point in worrying about what you cannot change.

This is not a new concept. Alcoholics Anonymous has used it as their mantra for four generations:

"Lord grant me the serenity to accept the things I cannot change, the courage to change the things I can and the wisdom to know the difference."

It is not rocket science. Reilly figured it out.

And don't forget to laugh. The sign above an edit room at the TV station:

"Lord grant me the serenity to accept the

Things I cannot change, the courage to change

The things I can and the wisdom to hide the bodies

Of those people I had to kill because they ticked me off."

OLD LOVE, YOUNG LOVE

This has nothing to do with believing in yourself or being who you want to be. And on the other hand it has everything to do with that.

It was Valentine's Day in Stanley Park. I had no idea what to do. No little kid was making a daisy chain for her mother. No grey-haired lady was being given chocolates by her children.

But there was a salty-haired couple, pudgy, not body beautiful types, talking to a young, beautiful couple on a rented bicycle built for two.

Maybe I can interrupt and if they don't get mad at me I can find out what they are talking about, maybe Valentine's Day.

"No, we don't really celebrate Valentine's Day in the UK," said the pudgy woman.

"We were just asking them if they could take a picture of us," said the body beautiful woman on the back of the bike. She also had an accent from England.

"You don't know each other?" I asked.

"No, but we are from towns not too far apart. Intriguing to meet," said pudgy man.

"Well, since it is the day of cupid, at least here," I said, "would you mind telling me how you each met?"

Body beautiful woman on the back of the bike said, "I fell in love with his body."

"Really?" said pudgy woman.

"We are both on the police force," BB said.

"I bet he looks better with his jacket off," said pudgy woman.

"Much," said BB and she wrapped her arms around his waist.

Mr. and Mrs. Pudgy said they met at a dance forty years ago.

"I liked his eyes," she said.

Mr. Pudgy smiled. He had probably heard that a hundred times before and smiled after every one of them.

"I bet they were married before you were born," I said to Mr. and Mrs. BB. "And they're still in love."

I was going out on the limb saying that, but they sure looked it to me. Mister and Missus BB looked a little frightened. To be in love without a slender waist and smooth skin and tight bottom and firm breasts looked to be one of those old-fashioned concepts.

"How do you do it?" asked BB on the back seat.

"He's awfully nice to me, and I try to be nice to him," said Mrs. Pudgy.

"Well, I still like my hunk," said BB on the back seat, and she rubbed his broad back.

"Me too," said Mrs. Pudgy, and she put her arms around Mr. P's arm. He looked a little uncomfortable about this public display of emotion.

"We have to get going," said the BBs. And they took off.

The Ps watched them and I heard her say to the departing double Bs, "Good luck."

Hopefully, B and B will find each other's insides before the outsides fade away. P and P did not have to tell me that they got what they wanted and that they believed in each other and in themselves. They just went on their walk, she still holding his arm.

A DATE WITH ROSE

Can you have what you want after death?

Strange question. Of course, not. After death, regardless of whether or not you believe in an afterlife, you are not here.

Unless you believe she is here, like Gerry believed.

The most touching love stories are not in the movies. Again, at the PNE I saw an old man, very old, sitting alone on a bench.

He had a hat, a jacket and still a barrel chest, even though he was ninety-two. He had a cane that he was rolling back and forth in his hand.

"Can we join you?"

"Sure," he laughed.

He had no teeth in the front. At ninety-two you learn to eat on the side of your mouth.

"You are here alone?" I asked.

He nodded. "My Rose passed away two years ago."

Sad. "How long were you married?"

"Fifty-two years."

He got married late in life. Sometimes that is good. You do not rush into marriage when the hormones are gushing. You see something deeper.

"We first came here in 1946. We came every year and saw everything."

He rolled the cane a bit. It had a brass top instead of a handle.

"During the night in the hospital the nurses kept going into her room."

He had changed subject to the one he wanted to talk about.

"One came out and said my wife had gone."

It was then that he hid his face behind one of his large hands. The sadness overcame him, the tears came out. He shook his head. It was not good to cry in public, not when you are on a date with Rose.

I noticed some tiny burned-in letters near the top of the cane.

"What is that?" I asked, trying to change the subject.

He looked down at the cane, then held it up for me to see.

"Rose."

Burned into the cane as identification long ago. His fingers wrapped around the wood and the name and squeezed, and a huge smile filled his beefy face, a smile that started more than half a century ago.

We wished him a good day and backed away, leaving him alone. Then I looked back at him sitting with his cane on the bench while the crowds passed in front of him.

I was wrong. He was not alone.

SURE YOU KNOW HIM—
NOW THE REST OF THE STORY

There is almost no one in Vancouver or BC who does not nod when they hear the name Jim Byrnes.

"Of course I know him. Great voice. And a terrific actor."

He is the handsome, rugged-faced blues singer who can be at the Yale or the Orpheum Theatre or the racetrack.

That is where Margaret Cameron saw him entertaining the crowd on a beautiful summer day

"He makes the most beautiful sound," she said.

"Did you come to hear him?" I asked.

"I didn't even know he was here," she said, "I come to the track every weekend."

"How long have you have been doing that?"

She ignored me. She was reading the racing form. Then she looked up at the tote board.

"Oh, sorry," she said. "Since I was three."

Margaret Cameron was no spring chicken, although she had plenty of spring in her step and in her attitude.

"My father was a trainer and my husband loved horses, so where else would I go?"

She was now seventy-six, and still picking them.

"But I sure love that Jim Byrnes. He sings great."

His blues was flooding over the stands and the rail and the track. Even the horses could hear him, but Margaret was standing close by his guitar and was tapping her foot while picking her horse.

"He's been on TV, you know," she said to me.

On TV? Yes, I know he has been on TV. He is a one-man acting industry. More than fifty movies and TV serials including Highlander, Da Vinci's City Hall, Stargate, Andromeda, The Outer Limits, Cold Squad and Neon Rider. And that is just a taste.

And a singer. And a volunteer. He has been on stage for the Variety Telethon and when he is there the phones ring. People like him.

"Would you like to meet him?" I ask Margaret.

I am thinking I could bring the two of them together. Jim has a kind heart, I know, and I am sure it would more than make Margaret's day.

"They're off." The words fired out with the same enthusiasm before every race making it seem like it is the first race that has ever been run in history.

"Come on number seven," shouts Margaret. "Come on, big boy."

Jim is wise enough not to play now.

"Come on," Margaret shouts. She is so excited she is jumping. People do not jump in front of slot machines or lottery terminals, not unless they have won a million dollars. Margaret has two dollars running on number seven.

"Come on, come on, come on." She's shouting. Number seven is in the lead. Jim has turned and is watching.

"He did it. He did it!"

Margaret is on top of her game. Number seven won. Racetracks are not like other forms of betting. Watching horses run is an act of participation poetry.

"Would you like to meet him now?" I ask.

Margaret is beaming from her winning. She has made a dollar on her two dollar bet.

"Meet him? Oh, no. I'm too embarrassed."

But Jim is close enough to see me trying to coax her over to his mini-platform where he has been strumming his guitar and singing. He gets down and walks over to Margaret.

I introduce her. He takes her hand, then gives her a hug. She is beaming even more. A hug in the arms is better than a horse at the finish.

While they stand there talking I am thinking about what Margaret does not know, and what most people who have watched Jim Byrnes over the years do not know.

He is from St. Louis, Missouri. He was in the US army during the Vietnam war. He fought his way through the jungles and survived. After the war he drifted into Canada playing his music.

He liked this country and stayed. He was on Vancouver Island on a wet, dark night travelling with some friends when their pickup truck broke down.

He was behind the truck pushing when a car came out of the darkness and did not see him in time and slammed into the back of the truck, with Jim caught between two grinding bumpers.

When he woke up in the hospital they told him he would have to make some adjustments to his life. They had cut off both his legs.

The chances of him ever walking again were minimal. If he did walk it would be with artificial legs, braces and crutches. Most likely he would have to get used to life in a wheelchair.

He could still sing, but he could not walk on a stage. He had wanted to act, but that was now out of the question.

Here is where believing that you can do anything you want to do no matter how unbelievable it is comes into play. Here is where the idea that you are who you want to be becomes reality. Here is where "you get what you want so long as you believe you will get it" becomes a truth.

Yes, it took unbelievable determination. Yes, it took therapy. Yes, it took pain and sweat and failure followed by more failure followed by one step on two artificial legs.

All the acting parts came after that. All the fame in singing came after that.

Jim Byrnes walked from his tiny stage at the racetrack to give Margaret Cameron a hug. He used a cane to steady himself. You would never think he had anything but possibly a sprained ankle or a sore knee.

That is all there is to it.

CURTIS'S TREE

There was another crash from behind, but this one took away a life.

Curtis Giesbrecht was driving home on Highway One near 160th Street when his car broke down. He got it to the side of the road, turned the flashers on and stood outside his car to call for help on his cellphone.

Someone did not see the flashers. When they cleared the wreckage Curtis was dead. He was twenty-one.

That happened as one century became another.

The grief was unbearable. The pain was unimaginable. The tears were endless.

Many who go through that unspeakable ache do something at the spot where their loved ones departed. There are countless crosses along roadsides. Memorials of stones with photos and teddy bears that wear out in the rain can be seen as you speed by.

Curtis's family planted a tree, a small evergreen, the kind you sometimes get in a pot for Christmas. The whole family came out a year after he was gone and dug a hole on land where you are not supposed to do that and put the tree in the ground.

They took some pictures with little cousins holding shovels and standing next to the tree, which was no taller than the kids.

For two years the tree grew undisturbed. No one told the family they would have to remove it. No one bothered them or the tree. In fact, no one besides the family knew it was there. Or at least the family thought no one knew.

Then just before Christmas of 2003 some of the family were driving by when someone shouted, "Look. Curtis's tree! It's decorated."

They stopped, well off the road, and walked back. They walked in a hurry. You do not stroll leisurely when you know something amazing is waiting for you.

There were shiny Christmas balls and garlands and stars hanging from every branch. At the top was an angel.

They all looked and shook their heads. They had not done it. A call to Curtis's mother brought her out to the highway. She parked near the other car and walked back.

Tears were falling from her eyes, once again. But this time, if there is joy to be found in death, this time there was joy.

"Who?"

"Don't know."

"Who do you guess?"

"No idea."

They called the rest of the family and then took pictures. They called friends of Curtis. No one knew, or no one said they knew, who'd done it, and no one had that hint in a voice that implied "Yes, I know, but I won't tell." Simply, no one knew.

A week after Christmas the decorations were gone.

A year later, they were back. They were a few new green and red balls along with some that had been there the year before. The garlands that had gotten torn apart by the passing wind of trucks were replaced. Someone truly cared.

They have appeared every year since then. It is on the highway westbound, just a kilometre away from the old cedar stump on the eastbound side with the maple leaf plaque on it. That was planted by an old soldier after World War I in memory of his friends who were killed.

That also was done in defiance of the law. The story of that tree is in the book, *The Blue Flames that Keep Us Warm.*

When it comes to memories, the law usually steps aside.

As for Curtis's tree, by the time I met the family and learned about it the little kids who were standing next to the tiny tree that went into the ground were much bigger. But the tree had grown even more. It was now a tree rising to the sky.

"We don't know who did it and we no longer want to find out. We just want, as always, to say thank you," said Curtis's mother.

The point of all this, besides the kindness of someone who takes no credit, is that wanting to do something, and then doing it, cannot change reality. But it can ease pain. And that is a reality of its own.

WINTER BLOOMS

We saw him standing at the end of the wooden dock at Vanier Park, behind Vancouver's Planetarium. One guy standing alone looking out at the water.

They say everyone has a story so I took that as being true and walked out to the end of the pier.

"Hello, hate to bother you," etc. "They say everyone has a great story waiting to come out. If you would like us to leave, I will not bother you or your story and I'll turn around and go."

"No way," said the man. "I just moved here from Toronto and I can't believe how beautiful and warm it is," he said.

His name was Lawrence and he said he was wandering all over the city falling in love with it.

"We still have snow, and we have cold people there," he said. "It's completely the opposite here."

We took that to mean we were getting a compliment as well as the weather.

"But look, I've got to show you this, you won't believe this. I can't." He started walking rapidly back to land and jumped off the pier onto the asphalt boat launch ramp.

"Come up here," he said.

We followed him to the top part of the ramp next to a sign that said "No Parking." At the bottom of the sign, he pointed down.

"Flowers," he said. "I don't know who planted them there, but look. Flowers in February. This is a wonderful city."

Sure enough, there was a clump of bright white and blue flowers at the bottom of the pole holding the sign saying if you park here it will be an expensive mistake.

Plus, obviously, you will be in the way of those launching their boats and in that case your car will probably get some seaweed on the windshield along with a ticket. Not everyone in Vancouver is as nice as Lawrence thought.

I was suspicious. There cannot be flowers blooming in winter, no matter how much this fellow wants to believe it, and even if they are right in front of him.

I asked a passing man who was old enough to know a flower when he saw one what he thought. He bent over and rubbed the petals.

"Flowers, definitely," he said.

"But real?"

"You want me to bend over again?"

We asked a passing woman because they are smarter than men and women know things that men do not.

She felt the flowers. "Silk," she said. "They look and feel like the real thing."

"That is the most wonderful news in the world," said the man from Toronto.

"You're not disappointed that they are not real?" I asked.

"No, this is even better," he said. "Someone did this as an act of kindness. They just wanted to make someone one else happy. You people here are wonderful."

Well, we didn't do anything. We just thought he would feel cheated because they were not real. Instead he found something good for the same reason.

We could have gotten all philosophical about how he found what he was looking for. We could have said that he had a positive attitude and that we were lucky that he moved here.

We didn't.

We just said thank you, to him.

He is the one who gave us what we wanted.

BROOM GARDEN

Everything is the biggest thing, if it happens to you. One tiny incident can be remembered forever, even if it is a one-line joke to others, so long as they laugh.

Murray Bush lives on East Georgia Street, an area that used to be an extension of Chinatown. Then it was run down with hookers and needles, and now it's being reclaimed by what used to be called yuppies, but really are just folks who see a beautiful old house that needs care and lots and lots and lots of elbow grease. Also, a lower price for the house helps.

Murray was pouring the grease from his elbows onto the floors and walls. He worked inside his house until his skin forgot what the sun felt like. He wanted flowers in his garden in the front, but it was just a patch of dirt, or mud, depending on the weather.

He said he would get to it soon, but first the ceiling had to be sanded and the baseboards had to be replaced and the floor had to be removed. It is not easy moving into an old house.

In front of his front door his patch of dirt remained a patch of dirt, or dust, again depending on the season.

He promised himself as soon as he finished the windows and the walls and the plumbing he would plant some flowers. But he only wished for that. He only wanted to do it. He only wanted it more than anything, except the gyprock, which made such a dusty mess, which he wanted even more.

He swept the white dust out of his living room and swept the front porch and his arms were aching. In a moment of exhaustion and self-deprecating humour he turned his worn out broom upside down and drove it into the dirt in his front yard.

"There. I have a garden."

Then he went inside and made tea and sat among his unending renovations and fell asleep.

When he got up in the morning he found a second broom planted next to his.

That got a laugh on his way to work, which is where yuppies have to go before they go home to a night of work.

The next morning there were two more brooms planted upside down in his dirt, and one mop.

A large smile was on his face. Something was happening although he did not know what. He left them and went to work.

The next night there was a row of dried-up, multicoloured paintbrushes planted at the base of one of the brooms, sort of spring flowers below a large bush.

Don't stop, please don't stop, he thought as he went to his day job before coming home for a night of work.

By the time I passed his home a few weeks later there were rows of old brooms and paintbrushes and a few paint rollers and a couple of whisk brooms and more mops.

"I can't believe this one," he said.

It was a broom with virtually no straw left.

"How did they use it?" he asked.

It was his neighbours, he said. He never saw one of them do it, but each night as the joke grew, more and more of them would sneak down the street where prostitutes used to prowl and under the cover of darkness would plant another brush or broom in Murray's garden.

By the time I saw it the ground was hard to see. There was a rich texture of straw and bristle and cotton and a few feather dusters blowing in the breeze.

"It's brooming beautiful," said Murray.

He planted the first broom, yes. But his neighbours wanted to make someone happy. Was there a good feeling on East Georgia? You don't have to ask.

Was the garden beautiful?

If it is not on some garden tour, the tour is shortchanging the patrons.

How did it all happen? How was one person made happy? How was an entire street made happy?

Someone wanted to do it. And someone did it.

BIRD TALES ARE THE BEST

They are the angels of the sky, angels that are real and that you can see and believe in. No person has yet been born who does not feel good when he or she hears a bird sing or sees one doing what we only dream we could do—fly.

Every bird is beyond amazing. Just ask any birdwatcher who spends a lifetime watching. Why? "They're amazing," they say.

And one of the smallest and one of the largest share the sky over Vancouver.

The eagle is the one that Americans come to Squamish to see and say, "Wow, we have never seen so many eagles. Is this part of America?"

And the hummingbird. That truly is the bird that sucks our disbelief away. It flies backward. It stops in mid-air and does not fall. It drinks nectar from flowers without landing on them. It builds its nest out of strands of abandoned spiderwebs wrapped around moss.

And in Port Coquitlam one mother hummingbird built its spiderweb and moss nest on top of the wind chime of Lynn and Fred Williams.

"I heard this chirping, but I couldn't find it. It was so tiny a sound," said Lynn.

The wind came and the metal rods moved and music flew through the air that did not have a tune or a melody. It was the music of sweet sounds.

"It sounded so sweet," said Lynn. "I looked and looked and then I looked some more. I knew it came from somewhere up by the gutter, but I couldn't find it."

The gutter ran the length of her roof, as most gutters do. And right there, over her door, was her wind chime.

"I just stood there and listened. It was so tiny, the sound," she said. "And then this hummingbird came out of nowhere. Buzzing. And flew over the top of the wind chime."

She watched the mother stop in mid-air over the top of her music maker and start to feed her children. Lynn knew what was happening. We all know instantly but mothers know even quicker.

Lynn put up a stepladder and carried a magnifying glass and there, on top of her wind chime in a spot you could lay a toonie on, was a nest. Inside, two lives that would fly to South America every year in search of flowers and then fly back to Port Coquitlam six months later to find more red blooms to feed on.

"I have never seen anything so beautiful," said Lynn.

They were the size of the tip of your pinkie, and that was after almost a week of life.

"I feel like a father," said Fred. He laughed.

Laughter is the one thing in life that makes everyone feel good. Especially new fathers.

Lynn was touching heaven.

It was the same as the couple in a condo in Metrotown who were mentioned in earlier writings. For five years a pair of chickadees found the same open sliding door on their twentieth-floor balcony and made a nest in a fig tree in their living room. They raised their children under the watch of their human grandparents.

The baby hummingbirds had the same attention. Lynn named the babies Cream and Sugar.

Why?

"Because we called the mother Honey." she said.

In two weeks they flew from the nest.

The point of this?

The smallest birds give the biggest thrills. Or in another way of saying it, life is unflippingly, unbelievably, amazing. So you had a bad day? You can go home and drink and feel miserable or go outside and look for the nest of a hummingbird.

You don't have to find it, just believe you will someday, and you will feel better.

THE TWIST
TO LOSING WEIGHT

S he was spinning a hula hoop outside what we used to call the Chinese corner store. That is what we "used" to call it but we don't any longer.

That is because the hardest-working group that ever came here, the Chinese who built British Columbia from the railways to the grocery stores, don't run the corner stores any more.

They run the economy. They fill the computer classrooms and the business classrooms. They drive the Mercedes SUVs. Most of them no longer stand behind a counter eighteen hours a day making change.

"My name is Xenis Joung," said the slightly built woman spinning the hoop.

I am so happy because we have found someone doing something that you don't see every day. She is inside her hula hoop, which is defying gravity.

I have not seen one of these for half a century. Then she stopped and went inside the store behind the footsteps of a customer to make a deal on a loaf of bread.

A Chinese woman in a Chinese corner store. Classic. Just like the old days.

Two minutes later she was back outside with her hoop.

"I'm from the Philippines," she said.

That will teach me about prejudging people.

She started spinning her hoop again. Right there, on a corner of Canada Way three blocks east of Willingdon.

For heaven's sake, how lucky can I get?

A hula hoop? I had one of those in the 1950s. Everyone had one. They were fun for a week. Then your middle got tired and you moved on to Frisbees. Just as an aside, don't let anyone tell you that an idea for getting rich has to be deep and complicated. The Wham-O company and its investors made billions off a pie plate and a hoop.

Back to Xenis.

"I cannot pronounce your name," I said.

"Call me Betty," she said.

"Are you going to do that hula hoop business again?" I asked.

"Between every customer," she said.

"Can we watch?"

It was like asking to watch a sex scene—of course we wanted to watch. Especially because there was no sex and no scene. On family television you can get the whole family to watch someone twirling a hoop of plastic and feel good about it.

"Why do you do this?" I asked while she twirled.

But it is not easy to ask someone spinning a large hoop around their middle because with each spin I had to bend away and then as the hoop went behind her back I could straighten up.

Bend back, straighten up, bend back, straighten up. We were dancing on the sidewalk.

"Because I was fat," she said.

Bend back.

"How . . ."

Straighten up.

". . . fat?"

Bend back.

She smiled.

Straighten up.

"Two hundred . . ."

Bend back.

". . . pounds."

Stop. I froze. She kept spinning with the hoop skimming by my belly, which I wished was not sticking out as far as it was.

"What did you say?" I said to someone who was slender and bending in a way that reminded me of the scene that I said earlier that we do not show on family television.

"Got to go," she said and grabbed her hoop and trotted up the stairs following a customer into her store.

"Do you know what she does?" I asked him.

"Sure, she spins her hula hoop."

"Does that surprise you?" I try to ask obvious questions because they usually get the best answers.

"No, she does it all the time."

See. The easy questions always work. And I was in heaven again, the second time in a handful of minutes.

Then when she turned her back to get something from behind the counter he added in a whisper, "You should have seen her when she started."

He held out his hands meaning big. Then he stretched them out, meaning really big.

She turned back. A little waif handing him his cigarettes. There are always ironies in life.

She said that with her second child she gained a great deal of weight and did not lose it afterward. Then she got depressed about weighing so much and gained more weight. Then she started snacking on candy bars while she was working behind the counter to make her feel better.

"I looked like a hippopotamus," she said.

"No," I said, trying to sound sympathetic.

"Yes, I know I did. My son told me."

She was selling hula hoops at the time. They were dusty. She picked up one and stepped outside and tried to spin it. It fell on the first turn.

"I could barely move my stomach."

But she picked it up and tried again, and again. The short of it is, seventy-five pounds lighter she now looks like a dancer in one of those scenes that I am not going to mention.

"I didn't want to be fat," she said. "I didn't want it very badly."

Many people say that. Many get on a scale and curse. Many swear they will give up eating, until they get hungry.

Everyone knows how to lose weight, you eat less and move more.

Then Betty added, "I believed if I did this with the hoop my son would not call me a hippo."

Everyone knows, but Betty believed she could. It does not matter what the reason was. The result was she got what she believed she would get.

Also she sells quite a few hoops now. There is nothing like honesty in advertising to increase a profit and nothing like desire and belief that you can do it, along with a hula dance, to lose weight.

THE PERFUME OF A FAMILY

Sometimes you have what you want, and you know it all your life. You just pretend you want more.

In the spring the smell is so sweet you would think you were in a candy store. But you are in Sandy's backyard in south Vancouver.

"Come out and help me," she said to her father. He was ninety-one when I met them.

He walked slowly down the back steps, the same steps he had been climbing for more than fifty years. When they moved in he could jump up the four wooden steps in one leap. Now he used a cane to go down.

"It needs some pruning," Sandy said to her father.

It did not really need pruning. You cannot prune the bottom branches on a tree that is twice the size of a house. But she knew her father wanted to touch the tree, because it was "her" tree.

But who is the "her"?

"He planted it for my mother," Sandy said, "But I always called it my tree."

She showed me some photos, black and white, crimpled edges like they used to do when the photo processor had more time.

The first picture was Sandy's mother standing near the tree, a young, vivacious woman with a pretty smile holding the top of a pencil-thin shoot that came up to her waist.

I noticed the pretty woman had a cigarette in her hand. All of the pictures of all of the women of those years showed cigarettes in their hands. Pity. I remembered the pictures of my mother with a cigarette. Pity. It was trendy, but they died so painfully.

But this was not about fashion or death, this was about life and a lilac tree.

"My father planted it for her," said Sandy, "but we had this joke that it was secretly my tree."

There were more pictures. "Here's one!" Sandy showed it to us. Sandy and the tree. She was shorter than the top of the twig. Her mother was in the background.

Sandy left home at an age when many girls leave home—she got married. "Look, here's a picture of my husband and me next to the tree," said Sandy. And her mother grew older. There's a photo of her mother in later middle age leaning up against the small tree. I could not bear to see if she was holding anything burning between her fingers. She was.

"She was your only love, wasn't she?" Sandy said to her father.

He could not hear her.

She raised her voice and repeated the words and he smiled and she rested her head on his chest and he hugged her.

In time, but too soon a time, Sandy's mother died.

"She loved this tree because he planted it for her," she said.

Then she took hold of a twig growing from the side. It was no bigger than the tree when it was planted.

"Here, would you cut this?" she asked her father.

It was a job that only he should be entrusted to do. He held his wrinkled hand next to the wrinkled bark and looked at his daughter, waiting for approval that he was going to cut the right twig.

She nodded and he snipped.

"Now it looks better," she said.

She found another twig the same size and it was cut and George looked proud that he had kept the tree in check.

Thirty-three years after Sandy left home her husband died and she returned to the home of her father and her mother's lilac.

"We still joke that it is my tree," she said. "Or at least I joke. He doesn't hear me and he just nods."

I was there in the spring when lilacs show the perfume companies how it should be done.

And when I backed away I saw Sandy and her father holding each other and looking up at the thick clusters of flowers. It was clear that they were not alone.

It was more than five years ago that I met Sandy and her dad. I still remember the perfume of their backyard. It could make you fall in love, with a family or with just being alive.

The tree continues to grow, but you really can't notice it getting bigger, just more beautiful.

The only difference now is Sandy has gotten what she said she has always wanted. She can now say that it is her tree.

But she doesn't.

"It was the tree my father planted for my mother," she said. "It is her tree."

That is what Sandy always meant to say.

THE LITTLE MOTOR THAT COULD

I n Japan Shima wanted to work on cars. He did not care about the body and fender parts, not the beauty of cars, just their souls, the motors.

"I loved the way they sounded. I loved the life in them," he said.

The more grease on his hands, the more smile on his face. He studied car mechanics in school, got a licence and a job fixing cars and he was happy.

Then he married and moved to Canada, for a better life.

He could not get a job. When you have your eyes and fingers wrapped around bolts and pistons all day you sometimes don't have the time or energy to learn another language. He thought he could pick it up after he got here.

Even without the language, he said he still believed he could get a job as a mechanic. "I will get that job," he said, to himself, in Japanese. "I will."

But there was no money coming into his home in his new country.

He walked and knocked on doors of garages and when they opened, he could not talk. He walked some more.

He passed something that was new to him, grass in front of houses. He was amazed at the number of lawns. Where he came from the gardens were tiny with no grass.

And with the lawns there were mowers cutting the grass. One day during a fruitless search for a job he passed a homeowner trying to start his mower and cursing and pulling on the cord and cursing more.

With very few words, because he had almost none, Shima pointed to the mower and then pointed to himself and bowed.

It is a universal truth that when a man can't get his mower started he will take any passing offer of help.

Shima's fingers slid over the engine. He always carried a few small tools in his pocket, the same as those in other businesses carry laptops and BlackBerries. It took only a couple of minutes and Shima had the clog in the fuel line unclogged and a valve unstuck and the mower was running.

The thanks from the homeowner were more than just enthusiastic. He offered to pay this mysterious Lone Fixer armed with a screwdriver. Shima shook his head, bowed and knew his future. It was better than a tip.

He found a beauty shop for sale. It was for sale because it was in a poor location for a beauty shop, on Nanaimo near Grandview Highway and across the street from a gas station.

Ladies did not flock there to have their hair fixed.

Shima borrowed money from friends and family and put a down payment on the shop and put up a sign that someone helped him make. It was big enough for those driving by to see: Shima's Lawn Mower Repairs. Simple.

Keep it simple and you seldom go wrong.

The first customer rolled his grass- and mud-caked dead mower into the store and past the sinks and the wallpaper with flowers. The smell of hair straighter was still in the air.

The customer looked suspicious, but by the time a mower is dead you don't care who fixes it.

Shima had it purring by the next day, and nothing is better than a good recommendation.

"Hey, I know this guy who fixes mowers in a beauty shop and he can't speak English and he's a genius."

It was almost as though the quirks, the gimmicks that make you stand out from others, were built in.

Ten years later I met Shima. His English was fluent. The flowers on the wallpaper were hidden behind shelves of lawn mower parts. In the summer he was working seven days a week because customers would not stop coming.

He never advertised.

"I cannot take anyone new," he said. "It makes me sad, but I am just too busy to take on more work."

The money was good, good enough that he could take off much of the winter and study English full-time.

"You know what's best about him?" a beefy mower owner told me. "If it's a small thing wrong he doesn't even charge you."

And what was better for Shima was that as car engines became more computerized and less the domain of old-fashioned mechanics, lawn mowers are still running the same basic ways that mechanics love.

It is true they pollute more than electric motors, which he also fixes, but when Shima is finished with a power mower it will run cleaner than when it came in.

"I believed I would fix motors," Shima said. "It is all I wanted to do."

He truly said that he believed. It was better than going home to his wife and saying he could not make it in this new country and he could not get a job and he could not speak English and everything was bad.

He believed he would fix engines. And he did.

Imagine what would happen if you tried that. You believe you can get through university. You believe you can get off welfare. You believe you can quit drinking a bottle a night. You believe you will get along with your kids. You believe you will make enough to retire.

There is nothing stopping you. Nothing stopped Shima. Just believe.

GEORGE'S RADIATOR SHOP

Cody and Wesley each have half the sign. One side says "George's Radiator Shop," and the other side says "George's Radiator Shop."

The sign hung above George's Radiator Shop one block from Douglas College in New Westminster for fifty-three years until George retired in 2004.

That is a long time to have a one-man business. It seemed even longer when I heard from George that he had not taken a day off sick for twenty-five years.

"I love my job," he said.

That is what loving what you do does for you. It keeps you healthy. You don't feel the aches and the sneezes when they do come. You go to work and you are no longer sneezing or feeling achy. Amazing medicine, loving something more than you love your complaints.

I walked into George's Radiator Shop just to ask if there is really a George, and a man with coveralls holding a radiator said with a smile—and that is the best way to get an introduction—"I'm George. I'm the only George here. In fact, I'm the only one here. What can I do for you?"

If I had a broken radiator he would have my business.

As it turned out, George was closing his shop and retiring after more than half a century in the same spot. He was seventy-three, he said, and I was thinking that was a good age to lay down the tools.

"I would love to go on, but there comes a time, you know . . ." he said without finishing whatever he was going to say.

248

I figured he was just going to say he was getting old.

George went on working while he talked. He still had a few radiators to fix before he closed the door for the last time. He put a radiator into a tank of water and looked for bubbles, the same way he has been finding leaks since he was thirteen.

He was happy when he saw a stream of air coming up from an otherwise invisible hole. He put the radiator on a band saw, cut out the leaking core and then patched it. It was heavy, dirty work on a part of the car that almost no one ever sees.

"Beautiful," he said when he'd patched it.

So what does this have to do with positive thinking and believing in what you are doing, and what does it have to do with you are who you want to be?

That's a lot of question, and the answer, I thought, was nothing.

George said he had to quit school in grade eight because his mother was supporting the family by taking in washing and he did not think it was right for him to sit in a classroom while she scrubbed.

He went to work setting pins in a bowling alley. Back then that meant you sat on a thin wooden beam between the alleys next to the pins. When the ball came and the pins went flying you jumped down off the board and pushed down on a metal bar with your foot which raised up metal pins that came up through holes at the back of the alley.

You also picked up the ball and put it back in the trough and it began its trip back to the bowlers.

And while it was rolling you grabbed the bowling pins as quickly as you could and stood them up on the metal nails in the floor, which you held up with your foot on a metal bar. The big, wooden pins in your hands had little hole in the bottoms so they would go in the same spot each time.

But before you could get them all up you heard the crashing of the pins in the alley next to the one you were working on. Those pins were flying.

You finished with the first lane and slid on your bottom over to the other lane and put the ball back in the trough and pushed down on the metal bar and put the pins on the metal nails sticking up out of the alley.

But before you could finish, the pins in the other alley were crashing and flying.

Faster, you have to work faster.

"Hey, kid, hurry up with those pins or you won't get any tip."

Those were the dreaded words because you only got ten cents a game from the bowling alley. The rest was tips and if you were not fast enough your tips would disappear.

The bowlers did not care if you had two lanes to keep going. They did not care if two bowlers rolled their balls at the same time, which would make chaos at your end of the lane.

The pins went flying and you could do nothing but hold your hands over your face and head to protect yourself from flying hardwood. Your ribs were left exposed.

And then you put the pins up, but the ball was already coming before you had a chance to get over to the other side.

Crash—behind you as you slid into the other lane.

Pins up. Crash. Up again. Crash.

Got to get to the other side. I'm so tired. Crash. Got to get to the other side again. Crash. Owww. That one hit me in the face.

All night long.

One day he passed a radiator repair shop.

"Do you have any jobs?" he asked.

"What d'you know about radiators?"

"Nothing, but I'll learn if you show me."

The sweaty, heavy, thankless work of fixing radiators was easier and more rewarding than the sweaty, heavy, thankless work of setting pins.

He has been fixing radiators ever since.

So I had met a nice guy with dirty hands. Nothing more.

Then he said the C word. His daughter had cancer, and died. George and his wife took over the care of her teenage boys, then adopted them.

Teenage boys take a lot of care, and that is why he was retiring, to give them the attention that they deserved, he said.

"I am so proud of them," he said, almost with tears.

He showed me pictures of them. He showed everyone pictures of them. His grandchildren had become his children, and they needed him.

He finished repairing the last of his radiators, and I watched him pull down the rope that closed his garage-type door for the last time. Just someone named George who somewhere near the end of his life was starting again.

What does he have to do with any of this "You are who you want to be" stuff?

He is who he wants to be: he helped his mother, he provided for his wife and helped raise a daughter, and now he was taking over her children. That is what he wanted to do.

In all the time talking to him there was not one complaint. He never said, "I have to close up so I can watch these kids." He never said that he had spent his whole life working and now, when most people think of resting or travelling, he would be taking on a couple of teenagers.

He never said anything except his life was good and he loved fixing radiators and he loved his grandsons, and each of them would get half of his sign.

It was not that he was a good guy that was wonderful to learn. It was that he was who he wanted to be and was doing what he wanted to do. He had control of himself and his life.

When he pulled the door closed he stepped out from under it and stood on the sidewalk looking up at his sign.

"I've had a good life," he said. "And it's going to get better."

George was the beneficiary of himself.

DOING WHAT COMES NATURALLY

You cannot get a winning lottery ticket just by believing you will. I know. I've tried.

The odds are still thirteen million to one and no matter what you believe you are not going to change those odds. You can say, "I believe the odds are two to thirteen million because I have two tickets."

I've tried that, but it doesn't work.

You cannot change the world or win the lottery by believing. You can only change yourself by believing, and then you can change the world.

Sunil Sanadh was helping the pastor of his church move. I suspect Sunil is religious. Why else would he be helping his pastor move?

He had just lost his job. His mortgage and insurance were due. He drained the last from his savings account: $2,000. And during the move he lost his wallet, with all the money in it.

Don't ask why he had it all in there. Most of us are not as smart as those who point out our mistakes.

He was sick. He was very sick. The mortgage was due in two days. He had no way of getting more money. This was his adopted land and there were no relatives to go to.

Rafael Tecson found the wallet. He did not have much money. He had worked in a warehouse for twelve years since coming to this country. He had a small house that needed renovations that he could not afford.

There was enough money for his renovation in the wallet. But there was also a driver's licence.

He looked up the name on the licence in the phone book and called. You can imagine the relief on the other end.

I don't know if Sunil prayed or wished or hoped his wallet would be returned. But if you have ever lost your wallet and it had cash in it you don't believe you will get it back.

But Rafael knew he would return it.

"The thought of getting new floors went through my mind, but only for a second," he said. "The money was not mine."

It is not just a matter of kindness. That goes without saying. But more than that it is the strength Rafael had in believing that he would do the right thing. He would give it back. He would do for someone else what he hoped someone else would do for him.

But as far as he knew, the owner of the wallet was rich. Why else would he carry so much money?

And as far as he knew someone with that much money must have a good job, better than working in a warehouse. And obviously anyone with a job that good would have a better house, and probably he did not need the money.

But he had none of those thoughts. He only knew he would return the money. He called Sunil. Come to the warehouse and get your wallet. Unbelievable relief.

When Sunil showed up at the warehouse he looked lost. Warehouses are big.

"Is there a Rafael here?"

"You must be the one," someone said to him. "Rafael is over there moving those boxes."

Sunil tried to give Rafael a reward in a white envelope. Rafael refused. Sunil tried harder. I was guessing there was at least $500 in that envelope, but we will never know. Rafael said no, he had a job and he learned Sunil did not.

He only asked for the thank-you card that was also in the envelope. He handed back the cash without counting it.

Rafael is who he wants to be, and who he is saved another man his mortgage and his house and his faith in people and his belief that life can be good.

You could renovate a floor with $2,000 that is not yours. And when friends ask how you got the money you either lie or tell the truth, and if you tell the truth your friends will probably never trust you again. And if you lie they will see through it and think you may have stolen the money and they will trust you even less.

But you could use the money to move a mountain. You just have to return it and believe that's the right thing. Rafael moved the mountain without ever touching it. That takes a strong person.

TALKING OVER A PIE PLATE

This has nothing to do with morality or doing the right thing. It is simply when you do something you enjoy and you believe in, you can do unbelievable things.

John MacKay was parked alone in a parking lot in North Burnaby. He is a ham radio operator. He has done this all his life. Despite computers and email he likes talking to friends around the world on his radios.

He was a radio operator in the army during World War II and had to jerry-rig his equipment every time a bullet went through it or it was dropped or spare parts were lost when bombs fell on them.

The army and a war is a good place to learn to be self sufficient. It is the creator of the famous make-do-with-what-you-got-ism.

Sixty years later John was in his car calling a friend in Japan.

"This is Victor Echo, Alpha, November." Those have been his call letters longer than PCs and Macs have been around.

Over the crackling radio came the voice of his friend from Japan.

"There he is," said John, very happy.

The radio in his car was pieced together with tape and parts that obviously did not match.

"It is just fun to do it yourself," he said.

They started talking about the weather. It was warm and sunny in Burnaby. It was night and raining in whatever part of Japan he was speaking with. It is not what is said that is important to ham operators. It is the reality that they can talk.

But John's big accomplishment was his antenna. He signed off and got out of his car. Above his roof on top of a pole attached to his door jamb was an aluminum pie plate.

"That is sending your words around the world?" I asked.

He nodded. "Some people would say this is not worth doing, but it's fun because it proves I can do it."

Holding the pie plate in the air was an old crutch.

"It is just the neatest thing in the world to make something happen," he said. "I believe I can get messages around the globe with nothing but what I have in my kitchen."

It is kind of like catching a fish. It does not prove anything, except you can do it, which proves everything.

If you can send a message with a pie plate is there really anything you can't do?

SYD THE BOWLER

S yd was having a wonderful time. He was the only man in a women's bowling league. He wasn't an official member, because you can't do that if you
are a guy, but he went to the bowling alley every Wednesday just to drive his
wife so she could join her league.

And while he was there he threw a few balls. He was not a bad bowler.
But the women loved him. When you are a woman in your seventies and
eighties, having an older guy hang around can be fun.

I met Syd at the Grandview Lanes on Commercial Drive. That is a wonderful place run by the same family that started it before World War II. The
generations change, but the alley is like home to anyone who walks in.

The first story on Syd was humorous, about a man who was ninety-six
and still bowling, and still in love with his wife.

Her name was Ray and she hugged him before each time she rolled the
ball. They had been married sixty-five years and when she walked up to the
line he looked at her like it was the first time he saw her and he was not going
to let her get away.

I learned some things about Syd then. I have told you about them before.
He'd been blind in one eye since he was twelve, when he was cleaning out a
chicken coop with lye and some of it went into his eye. It was burned out of
its socket.

So what? He got a job as a truck driver, with one eye. When he retired he
went to work as a taxi driver.

Then he lost most of the sight of his other eye. He had a disease that blocks out anything in front of his vision. He could only see things on the side.

So what? He climbed a ladder and cleaned out his gutters when he was ninety-seven. It was a two-storey house.

I did not know it, but his wife passed away later that year, just after their sixty-sixth anniversary.

The next time I heard about Syd was that his bowling friends were having a party for him for his 101st birthday.

I know other old people. I was not excited when they told me. That proves something important. Don't prejudge anyone.

"He is still living alone," said his grandson, who is getting close to retirement.

"One hundred and one and still living on his own?"

"And cooking for himself, and shovelling snow and climbing a ladder to clean his gutters."

This I have to see. The next morning I was there, in East Vancouver not too far from the PNE.

"We don't want to give out his address because if there is a home invasion he won't be able to see them well enough to fight them off."

This is one proud grandson.

Syd answered the door. He could not see a thing except the walls on either side of the door.

"Who's there?"

I told him me.

"I recognize the voice."

He was sharp. He let us in.

"I have to finish breakfast," he said.

That is finish making it, before eating it. After all, he does live alone.

Without seeing, he reached up in his kitchen cabinet and took down the oatmeal. He stretched over the top of his sink and grabbed a pot off a hook.

The oats went in and the faucet was turned on and the water poured into the pot. Salt was added. And then it went on the stove and the burner was turned on.

Remember. He is 101 years old and can't see.

Then he took out a bag of dog food and filled a dish, and put water in another dish. His dog was happy.

We made small talk about the weather. It had been snowing endlessly.

"I have to shovel again after breakfast," he said.

He turned off the heat of the stove, spooned his porridge into a bowl, offers us some, and then ate.

"Got to shovel now," he said.

He went to an inside door, opened it and walked down a steep flight.

"I made this too sharp," he says.

He built the house himself forty years ago, with one eye.

He went down the stairs backward.

"I hate doing this. It makes me seem like I can't do things."

At the bottom he reached for the old, large coal shovel that was leaning against a wall. He has been using that same shovel for fifty years. Coal shovels are good for shovelling coal. They are wide. But they are not good for snow because they grab too much and are too heavy to lift.

Syd carried the shovel outside and felt around for the snow with his foot. Overnight it had piled up to his knees in his walkway.

He shovelled, throwing the snow off to one side. He shovelled the entire walkway to the backyard.

"It was this high last week," he said holding his hand just below his waist.

"And you cleaned it yourself?"

"Of course, I'm not going to ask someone else to do it."

"I heard you clean out your gutters," I said.

"Of course, same reason."

We did not ask for a demonstration. His grandson had arrived and was waiting to take him bowling. Syd does not drive any longer. But as for the ladder and the gutters, his grandson just shook his head and smiled with that kind of smile that means you would not believe it.

"He repaired his roof last year," said his grandson, "but we had to put a stop to that. You can't be blind and a hundred years old and climbing on your roof."

Syd heard that and stopped shovelling.

"Why not?"

"'Cause you can't, grandpa."

"But I can."

"But we can't let you."

Syd drove the blade of his shovel down into the snow.

"Kids!" he said.

And then Syd was driven to his birthday party.

"I only wish Ray was still here," he said.

That was the only moment when the joy of living left his face.

The point of this? You got it. You understand it. Syd never once said he was accomplishing all this and living this way because he believed in himself. He never said "I believe I can shovel the snow." He never said "Even if I am 101 years old I believe I can make oatmeal."

He never did because he did not have to. He knew he could.

I got a call in July 2009 from one of Syd's friends. Syd again went bowling with Ray just before his 102nd birthday.

YOU CAN STILL HAVE FUN

Life of course is not all serious. Life is not only cleaning rain gutters at one hundred and one and overcoming cancer.

There are the fun things in life, too, like strikes.

The people at the Petro-Canada refinery on the Barnett Highway went on strike for improved pensions. It was the winter of '04 and it rained a lot. There was one other problem.

There were only thirty people in the local union and they had to picket seven days a week at three locations.

"Let us work this out," said the picket captain. "If each of us puts in twelve-hour days, seven days a week, we can almost put up an adequate front, unless someone wants a day off."

That is not an exact quote. It actually went more along the lines of, "What the heck are we going to do? We don't have enough people to walk the line at one location for half a week. How are we going to put up a good face?"

They walked back and forth on the road with cars zooming past and the spray from the blacktop getting thrown up in their faces. This was not a good time to walk a line.

They managed to swap off enough to get some rest, and then they were back on the line, looking like a wafer-thin protest group. There are few things worse than walking on a picket line when the next person is a hundred steps in front of you and the other one is a hundred steps behind.

Then one of the pickets had an idea. The next morning he brought a plywood cut-out of a man that had been used in a school play. He also had parts of a mannequin. And he had some plastic chairs and some coat hangers and old clothes and a hockey helmet and some hats and some more picket signs.

By the time we saw them there were six pickets on the road. Three of them were breathing. Two were sitting in plastic chairs and one was standing straight as a board. One was wearing a hockey helmet over his coat hanger head and the others had shirts and pants and coats and, most important, they had picket signs.

Jerry Pinel said, "Meet Peter the Picketer."

Peter was standing in the rain with one arm raised and a smile on his face. I had known Peter for only one minute but I was proud of him. He was putting on a brave front.

"And he never takes a bathroom break," said Jerry Dunlop, adjusting the shirt on John the quiet picketer in the plastic chair, who now was their picket leader.

"We made him the leader even though we never had a leader before. But look at him, strong, quiet and determined."

Jerry was right. No one could be stronger than someone who did not complain while water was running down his back and a coat hanger was poking him in the head. Those are the qualities of a leader.

The rain poured. The picketers kept picketing. Three of the pickets were not moving, but if you passed by in a car you saw six pickets, not three.

The third one was standing by the curb, held up by a couple of wooden poles. He was dressed in a Canucks shirt and hockey helmet. Under that were two broom sticks; one up, one across. And across his chest was a sign that said: "On Strike For Better Pension."

What more does it take to walk a line? A body, a sign and the determination to stay out in the rain.

"We love these guys," said one of the Jerrys.

"We take help from wherever we can find it."

With the extra three pickets they were able to spread out their members to get three more human pickets at another location.

It doesn't matter what you think of unions or strikes or pickets. These guys believed in themselves and they believed they would find a way to picket better, even if they did not have the moveable foot power to do minimal picketing.

You don't have to have to big ambitions like ending world hunger or pulling yourself out of the gutter of drugs and alcoholism to employ the idea that a positive attitude and a good plan will fix things. You only need the attitude and the plan, and usually the fulfilment of what you hope and wish for follows.

Imagine one other thing. Three guys have to picket an entrance to an oil refinery off the Barnett Highway. They gather in the morning in the rain. One has a bad attitude. You know him. You work with him.

"It's not going to work. Look, we only have three of us and nobody is going to notice us standing on the road and it's raining and what good are three of us going to do anyway?"

And the other guy says, "It's raining and I'm wet and I have to go to the bathroom and if I Ieave there will be only two of you and what good is that?"

And the third feels the same as the first two because bad attitudes are as contagious as good attitudes.

There you have three dummies without a single mannequin.

Now add a positive, funny thought. Add three dummies. There is joy on the picket line, which is not a usual by-product.

It wasn't an army of pickets, but it was something, and it was better than negative thought, because negative thoughts do not make a good picket line or a good anything.

In the end they won.

How?

I don't know, but the dummy power didn't hurt. It would only take one more phone call to the company than they were expecting, or one company negotiator driving by in the rain and seeing the determination, to push someone over the edge and say, "Enough. Give them what they want."

Maybe the dummies had nothing to do with it. Maybe. But the picketers believed that in numbers, even if it was only six, there was strength.

And in the end they did it. I am not promoting unions or management. I am only saying that when you put a positive spin on something, even dummies in the rain, it works. Nothing more. And nothing less.

OLD CHAIR, NEW LOVE

Once again I cannot find a story. There is nothing out there. I am riding around with John Chant, a cameraman who has had open heart surgery and laser surgery on his eyes and takes a variety of pills for his intestinal problems.

He should not be hauling around heavy equipment and chasing criminals and criminal politicians. He should be resting on a beach. But he is there driving with me and joking and saying if I fall asleep one more time he will pour his water bottle over me.

He is the one who found the most amazing story of the folks who were throwing garbage out of their expensive car and who filmed them as I confronted them, and then he kept on filming when they drove away and I threw the garbage back into their car.

A positive life is not necessarily a quiet life.

But today, as many times in the past, we cannot find anything.

Enter thoughts of Reilly.

"I believe, I believe, and again I believe we will find something."

"That's good," said John "because I bought you coffee and now it is your turn to do something."

We go up Main Street and I see a youngish fellow sitting outside his junk shop. We cannot use the word "junk shop" any longer; apparently it is demeaning.

Ten years ago Main Street between East Twentieth and Thirtieth Avenues was nothing but junk shops. Jim's father had a junk shop. He did well.

"I love junk. Junk is good. You can make a good living off junk," said Jim's father.

But times change and junk is out. The upscale people moved into Main Street and they buy antiques.

The junk shops took down their signs that said "Junk," and replaced them with signs that say: "Antiques."

"Same stuff, higher prices," said one of the junk dealers who has become an antique dealer.

But all of this we know. So what is new? Well, there's Jim sitting on one of his junk chairs on the sidewalk. Thank you, Reilly.

The sidewalk office. The office without a roof. The low cost of doing business.

We talk.

"I sit out here all summer and in there all winter," said Jim pointing inside his shop which has no room to sit.

"And why did you pick this chair?" I ask.

He smiles. He gets up and picks up the chair.

"This is truly a piece of junk. This you should not buy."

The chair wiggles. Its frame is coming apart. It has no paint on numerous parts. What a lovely story, I am thinking: the junk man on his summer chair.

"What's it worth?"

"Five dollars, but I would pay someone to take it away."

"Why do you sit on it?"

He smiles. He has experienced the truth of life. Things are not always what they seem. Things, like life, sometimes have hidden value. Things, like life, have secrets that change their worth.

"It's comfortable."

Oh, blessing story god. The whole meaning of life in one chair. Okay, maybe that is stretching it a bit, but it's only television and it is late in the day, and this, honestly, is pretty good.

See, Reilly was right again. If you believe you will find something, you will.

Thus there is before us the even more perfect story. The man who knows the unseen value of something.

John starts taking pictures of Jim in his chair. There are buses and cars passing behind him and there are pedestrians in front of him. There is a row of things that may be junk or antiques lined up in front of his shop.

"That French Provincial cabinet was worth a thousand dollars," he said.

That statement was given so that I'd know for sure that he has antiques for sale.

"But I am letting it go for seventy-five dollars."

That was said so that I'd know he has not strayed too far from his roots.

I am a happy guy.

Then a lovely young woman walks out of the store and sits next to Jim.

Darn. The moment is ruined. He is no longer a man alone in his world. The image, everything has changed.

"Do you want her in the shot?" John asks. "I don't have enough of him alone."

Darn again. What could be worse? This is as bad as a French Provincial cabinet actually selling for a thousand dollars. The magic is gone.

How do we get shots of him without her? We cannot ask her to leave. We cannot change reality, besides, that would be impolite and he is bigger than me.

But she has altered the story, which was a man alone in his outdoor office. This is unwanted change coming suddenly into a life. How do you deal with it? The old ways were good. The new ways are bad.

I had believed, as Reilly taught me, that the story would be good and now the system has failed.

"Did you meet my girlfriend?" asked Jim.

I shake my head. Girlfriend? It will never work now. A girlfriend is worse than a friend. Girlfriends don't get out of the picture. Girlfriends change everything.

"I met her in a shop like this, and I'm in love."

Love? Did he say "Love?"

Love changes everything. Love conquers everything. Love makes everything good.

"Tell us about meeting her."

It was in his uncle's store, a store just like Jim's. She (her name is Kristie) was shopping for a couch. Both Jim's uncle and his father were there. They saw her. They called Jim.

"This girl you should meet."

He came. They met. She conquered.

Now they were holding hands. Can you believe that!? Sitting next to each other on old chairs on the sidewalk on Main Street, holding hands, what could be better?

Wait. He's kissing her! That's better. On Main Street, sitting on old chairs, kissing her! Luckily John is smarter and more controlled than me and is taping this while I am simply being mesmerized.

Just for a test we ask Kristie how much did she think Jim's chair would be worth.

"That piece of junk? It almost fell apart when he sat on it yesterday. Five dollars, or give it away. But he loves it."

Bingo. A love made in a junk shop where things are sometimes worth a lot more than they seem, and have meaning deeper than at first glance.

Without those allusions to things having a deeper meaning, what does all this mean?

Simply that if you believe something is going to happen, it will happen. What happens may have nothing to do with what you think will happen. You would have to literally be God to do that, and many don't even think there is a god so there is no way you are going to put in an order for a custom-made future.

But you can believe something will happen, and if you believe it will be good that is good enough. Just give it, and yourself, a chance.

That is when you find the junk in your life becomes antiques with greater value and deeper meaning, and something you cherish.

That is not a bad return for just saying something good is going to happen, and believing it.

CLOUDS TASTE GOOD

The same kind of magical thing also happened the day before the junk-shop romance came into our lives.

The same thing meaning that you don't always get what you want, sometimes you get something better.

Same cameraman, John Chant. He has been working since early in the morning. There was a murdered woman in Lighthouse Park. He has been there. Now in the early afternoon he is working with me and trying to get his mind off bad things.

"We could do clouds," he says.

It was a cloudy day with puffs of white dotting the sky. It was not the usual Vancouver sky of a layer of grey sponge squeezing itself out over the city.

"I did clouds a few years ago," I said.

"So?"

"So we can't repeat ourselves or folks will say, 'Look at that. The guy's got no new ideas. I was telling you he would run out of stories some day.'"

"So?" repeated John. "We either do clouds again or you find something new."

I looked up. There were clouds. There is another bit of advice I gave myself long ago. Never pass a parking space or an opportunity.

"Last time we had clouds and no people," I said.

"So this time add people," said John.

How does someone get to be so bright?

He took pictures of clouds with many shapes. Then I asked the first group of women passing by: "Sorry to bother you, but what do you see in those clouds?"

All three looked up. All three stared. All three shook their heads.

"Nothing." All three said the same thing.

"Nothing?"

"Do you see something?" one asked me.

That's not fair. I'm the guy with the questions.

The next fellow passing by looked up and said he saw a man pushing a lawn mower. I was so happy.

"Where?" I asked.

"Just kidding," he said. "I don't see anything"

This is not going well. If no one sees anything then this will not work. I ask two more couples. One of them wants to know what I mean by the question.

"Do you see anything in the clouds?" I repeat.

"Is this a trick? Are you trying to advertise for something and you want us to say we see something when we don't see anything and then you will say, 'If they ate something or wore something different they would have seen this.'?"

I have that on tape. No wonder some people still think Elvis is alive and the moon landing was a hoax. They see conspiracies everywhere. Meanwhile we are getting nowhere with this super simple way of spending a day.

I need help. Try Reilly. This is silly. Reilly can't make people change. Believing that people will change their answers does not make them change their answers. They see nothing.

In truth, when I looked up I could not see anything either. It must have been a day of anonymous clouds. They were all passing by without a recognizable shape.

And worse, a clear sky was coming up behind them. And worse even than that, if anything can be worse than a clear sky when you want clouds, it was getting late.

I started doubting again, doubting that positive belief would work. After all this time I was doubting, and the doubt grew larger and stronger. In short, doubt was kicking positive thinking in the groin. Ouch.

As you see, doubt and faith in your beliefs don't fight each other only over the big things in life. This was not the same as trying to get off drugs or wondering if you can swim way out in a rough ocean to save someone's life.

This was a tiny matter of clouds. But still, it was not working, and I had believed it would. That faith was now moving into the past tense.

I call the office to tell the fellow who takes in the satellite feeds from around the world, as well as local stories that are beamed in over the air, that we might be a bit late because, "well, because I am failing. I can't find anyone who sees anything in clouds."

His name is Marco Den Ouden. He reads a lot, both highbrow libertarian stuff and comics.

"That reminds me of my all-time favourite Charlie Brown cartoon," he said. Then he went on to repeat every line in the cartoon. Lucy, Linus and Charlie Brown were lying on the ground looking up at clouds.

"Linus said he saw Saint Stephen being stoned to death. Then Lucy asked Charlie Brown what he saw, and Charlie Brown said 'Well... I was going to say I saw a duckie and a horsie, but I changed my mind.'"

Then Marco laughed. How, with sixteen million other things to remember, does someone remember a Peanuts comic, right down to the exact words? And all that while stories about bombings and political scandals are coming in on a wall of monitors in front of him?

Amazing is the human mind, I think. Then I look up at the clouds again.

Reilly! Reilly would have seen something. Charlie Brown saw something. I have this all wrong.

"Hey, that kid over there, on his bike, with his granny," I shout to John. "Got to stop him."

I start running down the bike path after a little kid.

It is not good to be seen running after a little kid. I shout, "Stop. I want to ask you something."

The kid and his granny stop, just where they were planning to stop, me having nothing to do with it.

"Can we ask him something?" I ask her.

"It depends on what, but first he really wants the ice cream I promised him."

I say this will only take a moment. We'll be done before the ice cream can melt. "Do you see things in the clouds?"

The little boy looks up. "Yes."

"What?"

"Ice cream."

"Where?"

"Right there," he points, in confusion that we don't also see it.

"Anything else?"

"A rocket ship and the letter T, upside down."

This is too good.

"How old are you?"

"Five and six-fourths," he says.

He was born to save the day. He said his name was Yui, and then he and his granny sat down and had their ice cream under the clouds.

This is so incredibly simple, a story that says adults don't see what kids see. Out of that you see that adults have lost something, a sense of wonder and fearless expression.

And one thing more. The story turned out better than the way it was planned. How did that happen? How can anything in life turn out better than you planned it?

Easy—just expect it to and have faith that it will even when it is falling apart.

And once again, if you are saying this is too much sweetness, that there are bad things that happen and just believing that things will be good doesn't work, I say yes, there are bad things. But just ask a kid to look at that same patch of sky or slice of life, and you will learn how ice cream can float in the air, which can't happen unless you believe it.

THE DAY WE ALL WON

The alarm clock rang at three a.m. It always rings at three and the huge, hard hand gropes for the button.

At seventy-six he should be sleeping as late as he wants, but George chose a career where the hours will kill you almost as quickly as the disappointments.

George Cummins is a race horse trainer. He is the guy or the gal who never rides and yet is totally responsible for getting the horse over the finish line first. Trainers are the coaches, the teachers, the brains behind the horse power.

Many at the track say the trainers count more than the horses, or the jockeys. They breathe in the smelly air that the horses breathe out. They are close enough to the powerful animals to know what a blinking eye or a wiggling ear mean.

But most of all, trainers watch a horse run and know how to encourage it to run faster. It is not through the whip. It is through knowing their stride and their strength.

Trainers tell exercise riders and jockeys when to push the horse and when to let up. They prescribe food and rest and grooming. There is no school for trainers. They learn by watching and thinking and following and trying and then starting again.

George Cummins said all of that is bunk.

"It is right here," he said pointing to the chest of an old horse. "It's the heart. It's like people. If they have the heart, they win."

George always gave full credit to the horse. He was one of the most winning trainers in the history of Hastings Park. He was there for almost fifty years. He drifted into the back stretch one day from a smaller track in the US and found his home.

"The people are nice, the scenery is good, the riders are strong and the horses, well, the horses have heart."

That was all George was interested in. He wore an Andy Capp style of hat and sort of sauntered instead of walking. He took the reins of a horse and would walk around and around the barn with it, always talking to it.

Walking a horse is the lowest job at the track. Trainers are the royalty, even looked up to by the horse owners. But George still walked horses, and talked to them. That is probably why his won so often.

"If a horse does not win I do not blame the horse. And I do not blame the jockey. And I do not blame the groom."

There are many who blame the grooms, who have the hardest jobs of all at the track. They clean the stalls and feed the horses and wash them and brush them and saddle them.

But many say, "My horse lost. It would have won if the darn groom had fed him earlier or noticed that he was not feeling well."

It does not matter what industry you are in, the bottom of the pecking order often gets the most finger pointing.

"I don't blame anyone but me," said George.

"I know if a horse has heart. My only job is to make sure he wants to show us what he has."

And that comes from love, said George. And that comes from talking, and walking, and encouraging.

The horse George was talking about was Gallant Goalie. He was ten years old, an age when most horses should be out in a field forgetting about the heart-pounding thunder of trying to be the first on a dusty track crowded with much younger opponents.

"He has heart," said George.

The story I was doing was about trainers. But the only words anyone heard in that story were that Gallant Goalie, the oldest horse running in the sixth race that night, had heart.

The story ended with George holding the reins of Gallant Goalie while walking around and around the barn, whispering things into his ear.

After the story was on the air the producers in the newsroom and the night shift reporters and editors asked if I was going to the track.

"I might stop by," I said.

"Well, here's two dollars. Put it down for me on that horse that has the heart."

"And me."

"Me too."

In all, I walked up to the betting window with a pocket full of toonies and another pocket with a list of names.

Somehow, when you do something like that you always wind up with more names than dollars. It's the same when a group orders pizza.

"To win," I said, "on Gallant Goalie."

The woman on the other side of the window had seen this before. She knew what was happening. The big pool bet. Usually everyone went away unhappy.

"He's a long shot, you know. Twenty to one."

Bad, I knew. Old horse. Staggering odds. Others had no faith in him.

"And he's got an outside position," said the woman.

That was double or triple bad. Old horse starting far from the rail where horses had to be if they were going to have a chance.

"To win," I said. "All of it."

"They're off." The loudspeaker voice shouted and seven horses broke from the gate. Gallant Goalie was left behind by six other horses, all of them closer to the inside track.

"And at the back of the pack is Gallant Goalie," said the announcer as they past the first turn.

It was a mile-and-a-half race, the longest one at the track. It is made for young, strong horses.

They disappeared in a cloud of dust on the other side of the track, all the horses in one clump fighting to be first. Boxing and hockey and football are tough sports, but a jockey's ride can be terrifying. Try holding onto a horse with just your ankles while it is going sixty kilometres an hour and other horses are almost touching you and below is a forest of pounding steel hooves and you have no seat belt.

"And Gallant Goalie is pulling out of the pack now." That is the work of the jockey and the horse and the trainer.

The announcer's voice is getting excited. Something is happening. One horse on the outside in the back is moving. The crowd is getting louder.

The announcer's voice with emotion: "Gallant Goalie is challenging. He is fifth. He is fourth."

The announcer knows this is one of those races where the unexpected is happening right in front of us. It is the reason why people go to the track, why they go to all sports, why we participate in life.

The crowd is screaming. I am screaming.

The horses are pounding down to the finish line. There is less than ten seconds to the end and Gallant Goalie is second and running like he wants to be first.

It all happens in a blur. They do not stop at the finish line. The pounding and the grunting continue until they all cross the line. But it is clear who came in first, by more than a head and a neck.

"Gallant Goalie," says the announcer followed by a cheer.

Those standing at the rail who took a chance on an old man are in love with the wisdom of making such a daring choice. They are smiling. Those who knew they should have taken a chance but didn't are shaking their heads.

The grooms come out to walk the horses back to the barns, except for Gallant Goalie. He is led back to the finish line for the traditional photo with the jockey and owners and their friends and George.

"He has heart," he told them. "You can't go wrong when you have that."

Heart, as I learned from many races at the track and many more in that race of humans, is just another way of saying they believe that they have the strength, the will, the desire, the determination, whatever it is called, to cross the finish line the best they can, and sometimes even better than others thought they could.

Horses just need someone to whisper in their ears.

In the human race we can whisper to ourselves.

LAUGHING AT THE SCREEN

He, maybe she, must be an artist. Artists do things like that, crazy things, and call it art.

We stood on the sidewalk on East First Avenue near Clark Drive, a very busy street. We were looking at someone's front garden that had two dozen televisions neatly arranged in several rows, stacked on top of each other, two high.

Facing them were several chairs.

I knocked on the door.

"Yes?"

"May I ask, why do you have televisions in your yard?"

I expect the answer, "Because it's art."

"Because I want people to think."

I know this is one of those airy-fairy reasons, because we as a people long ago stopped thinking. If we thought, we would not have closed Riverview and created Main and Hastings, and we would not have bought a new, giant television on a credit card that did not have enough room left even to pay for the groceries, and we would not have drunk a giant humongous triple mocha with whipped cream when we say we are too fat.

Thinking is out of fashion, so I know this fellow is pulling our legs.

"What do you want us to think about?" I ask.

I still think he is an artist, so I expect he is going to say, "The meaning of art."

"I hope we think about the meaning of life."

This again, I know, is never-never-land-type thinking. The meaning of life is to buy another television and car and to get a larger house and a longer vacation and to wear the right kind of sneakers and eat yogourt. I know all this because I watch television, and before the stories I do each day there are commercials telling people to do that, and then we will have a happy life.

"Do you watch your televisions?" I ask.

I expect the answer is no because they are not plugged in and you cannot watch a television that is not burning up the earth's resources to keep it going.

"Every day. I sit out here and look at them."

I know this is crazy because if a television goes blank for three seconds there are thousands of desperate phone calls to Shaw and Rogers complaining that there is nothing on and so there is nothing to do and they must DO SOMETHING to fix it immediately.

"What do you see when you look at your blank screens?" I ask.

I expect the answer will be he sees nothing because there is nothing to see, unless he is an artist who sees something in everything, although it probably will not sell because no one else sees it.

"I see the world passing by in the reflection of the screens and I think each of those cars has a person inside who could have a more wonderful life if there was less television in it and more of anything else."

I know that is beyond insane because outside of television and games on the computer there is nothing else in life. I know this because of Statistics Canada and the Neilson ratings, which say that being entertained by someone doing something on a screen in front of us takes up most of our lives. Statistics Canada is never wrong.

"What work do you do?" I ask, expecting the answer to be that he is an "artist, currently unemployed."

"I am a waiter in a restaurant while I go to school."

"To study art?" I have him this time.

"Theology," he said. "I want to help the world to be a better place." This, I thought, is better than a sermon.

Whatever church he is in I want to join. And maybe I will learn to put away prejudging others and turn off the TV, and think about something.

On the other hand, don't be silly. Without a television, how will I know what to have for dinner or which yogourt to buy or how to laugh without someone late at night telling me jokes?

And that proves my point. His televisions must be art because I do not understand them.

ROBIN AND THE BABY SEAL

Do you get what you want even if it involves someone else whom you never touch?

In short, if you wish enough and hope enough and want enough, does it work?

A baby seal appeared on English Bay, on the sand, alone. That was enough to break your heart.

"It's going to die."

"Its mother left it. We have to help."

A crowd circled around it. You could see its eyes watching, but it did not move.

"We have to do something. We have to save it."

Someone called 911 and was told to call the Aquarium. After getting the number from information, which someone did not want to do because it cost an extra seventy-five cents, the people at the Aquarium said leave it alone.

"But it's alone and it looks sick."

"Leave it alone. Its mother will come back. She has just gone off fishing," said the person at the Aquarium.

"But it has been here for hours." The voice on the beach was desperate. The seal was going to die. "It's not moving. We have to do something."

"Please, don't touch it. The Aquarium has a tank full of baby seals that have been saved from their mothers' care."

Robin showed up. She was eleven.

"I hope he's okay. Or I hope she's okay. She looks like a girl."

Robin had the face of a girl with deep concern. At eleven you can feel the fear of being alone more than at forty.

"I'm going to stay with him, or her," she said.

"How long?" I asked.

"Until his or her mother comes, or until my mother calls me."

Robin sat on a log near the seal and watched him or her. I don't know for sure what was going on in her mind, but you can guess. She was praying and wishing and hoping that his or her mother would come back.

Do you get what you want when it is outside of yourself? No, of course not. You cannot change the world.

But Robin watched as the baby lay still. The tide had gone out and there was a long way to go to get back in the water.

Robin sat on the log, wishing and hoping and praying. But you cannot change reality. You can only change yourself. I know that. The church and temple and synagogue know that. Alcoholics Anonymous knows that. Robin did not know it.

She sat and watched and waited and the sun went down. It was autumn and the sky was darkening earlier each day.

I waited, off to the side. I saw a young girl who cared. The adults had given up and left. If the Aquarium and the police were not going to do anything then there was nothing they could do. So they left.

Robin stayed. I watched as the sky grew dark and I saw a woman nearby watching Robin. She had been there for some time sitting on a bench. Several times she got up and walked to the girl and spoke with her, then went back to her bench.

I spoke to her. She was Robin's mother and she was a kind and patient mother, waiting for her child who was waiting for another mother to come back to her child. Then human mother left her bench and sat down next to her daughter on the log and put an arm around her.

But how long can you wait? There is homework to do and all those things that must be done before the day is over. But to take Robin away would break this chain of connection and she would never know if the seal's mother came back.

More minutes passed, but they seemed to take forever. The girl's mother was very good. She let her daughter stay.

And then, while the two of them were speaking, their faces looking at each other, a black head came out of the edge of the surf. Suddenly all the waiting and the patience were worth more than could be counted or imagined.

The voice from the surf made a guttural, horn-like sound that was far from sweet. The baby seal snapped his or her head around and ran to the edge of the sea. He or she did not scamper, he or she ran and dove in, and in less than a blink they both were gone.

"Robin, time to go home," said the woman.

I was close enough then to hear that.

The young girl and her mother stood up.

"Its mother came," the girl said.

"I know. I saw it too. Let's go home."

Robin and her mother walked away, together. Behind them the ocean looked empty, except for the mother and her baby.

Of course wishes and prayers and hopes don't affect anything or anyone outside of yourself. On the other hand, who knows?

YOU CAN'T CHANGE REALITY. REALLY?

I met her on Mount Seymour. I was having hot chocolate with my wife and granddaughter.

"I hate to bother you, but I have a really good story for you."

She was standing nearby.

Darn, I thought. That is the same approach I use on almost everyone. Is this how it feels? I don't want to be bothered. I don't want a good story. I am having hot chocolate with my granddaughter, who just slid down a hill with my wife on a piece of plastic that we found in the snow. It was the greatest slide ever.

"Can I talk to you for a minute?"

Darn. First of all, no one talks for a minute. Usually it is until they get everything out and then they repeat it. I just want to have the chocolate. I apologize if I sound cruel and self-important, but this one moment, while I was trying to blow on a five-year-old's hot chocolate to cool it, was forever perfect, until it ended.

"My son, Joshua, is in a wheelchair and I am running the marathon with him."

Okay, you have my attention and I apologize for being so cold and standoffish.

"I have been practicing with bags of cement in the chair."

Suddenly I feel that watching a fully healthy granddaughter slide down a snowbank has its place, and it is not the same place as a bag of concrete in a wheelchair.

Her name was Michelle and she said she would call me before the race.

But that is impossible, because for a full month before the marathon I would be off and away. That was one of the conditions of retiring and coming back on a new contract. I don't know why, but that was what the company wanted.

I returned to Vancouver two days before the marathon with jet lag. One day before the marathon I remembered the woman. My first day back at work was the day of the marathon, but as in the past I would get a cameraman who starts later in the day because the real news of the day has to be covered first.

When I got to the finish line the race was half over. There were thirty thousand people running. That is a swollen river of runners at spring runoff. The street in front of BC Place is squeaky with sweat and sneakers from curb to curb.

The runners' names were being read out by a man with a steel voice who mentions everyone. It does not matter if you arrive at the end four hours after you started, you will hear your name, and for some, actually for everyone, that is the most important part of the race.

You get recognized.

I thought of the woman and the cement but disregarded the thought. You could not find someone who was green and seven foot tall in that crowd.

"And here come Joshua and Michelle."

What!? I remember the names. I can't see, but I can hear. Above the grinding rock and roll on mega-sized speakers I heard the names Joshua and Michelle. How was that possible?

"We've got to get her," I said to cameraman Al Coen.

"Who?" he shouts.

"I don't know who. The woman with a wheelchair and a kid in it."

How? Who? Where?

I have no idea. I suspected that maybe there, in the congestion of the massive crowd on the other side of the finish line, was who we were looking for. I thought that only because there was a smaller crowd cheering someone.

We got closer and could see a woman with a carriage with a boy in it. That must be Joshua.

But he does not look happy.

After the hellos and congratulations I said, "I hate to ask, but what did Joshua get out of this?"

"He was thrilled. His class was along the side and his friends were cheering."

But Joshua did not look happy. His dog was brought to him, but no change.

Joshua has some disease that leaves him cognizant of what is around him but without the ability to speak or walk. That is sad, but again, what did he get out of that run?

What does this have to do with being positive and with having things come out the way you want?

Nothing, I thought. I could not even do the story. I started looking for something else. I cannot pretend that something wonderful has happened if it does not look that way.

Those cheering him and his mother had smiles, but Joshua's face was blank.

They were interviewed on live TV for the noon news. We watched and no happiness was on the face of Joshua.

As for Joshua, you cannot make someone happy by pushing him in a wheelchair for twenty-six miles. You cannot change reality because you train with cement and then you push yourself until you almost die while pushing your son who cannot walk.

It is wonderful what she did. But it did not seem to have an effect on Joshua.

We started to leave. There would be some other story of struggle and heroism, somewhere. I felt so bad. The mother had tried so hard.

I looked at another woman crossing the finish line while being held up by two friends who were basically dragging her across the line. I heard her name.

Maybe we could do a story about her. She doesn't have to look happy.

I turned around for one last look. This time Joshua was standing next to his carriage. His mother was holding him. His arms were out. He was trying to take a step.

Al turned on the camera faster than I had ever seen anyone turn on that machine.

She held him and he took another step, then another.

A white-haired man was on his knees two more steps away. He was holding out his arms.

Joshua took another step, then another.

"Joshua, you did it, you did it. You ran the marathon."

The words came from the man. The two bodies joined and arms wrapped around each other and tears came from the eyes of the man and Joshua's mother.

A giant, skin-stretching smile was on Joshua's face.

"You did it," said the man.

"That's his grandfather," said Michelle. "Joshua knew he would be at the end of the race. He loves his granddad."

I heard his granddad say "Joshua." It was the sound Joshua wanted to hear.

I could not talk with grandpa. He and Joshua were too close to interrupt, and grandpa was whispering things into a young, hungry ear.

"He told Josh before the race that he believed he could do it and he said he would be at the finish line waiting for him," Michelle said.

That was all it took to make an eleven-year-old boy who can do almost nothing know that something was possible. Joshua ran the marathon, for his grandpa, and at the last few steps he heard his name.

Can Joshua walk now? No. His mother was holding him for those few steps. That is as far as he can go.

Can he talk? No.

Can he believe that something wonderful happened?

Picture his face over his grandpa's shoulder and picture his mother who believed she could get him there.

They all moved the mountain.

THE CATCH OF THE DAY

Did Reilly ever catch that fish?

"I believe you get," sniff, "whatever you want," he said. Sniff.

It is all sweet and romantic to say that the great philosophy of life comes from a snot-nosed autistic ten-year-old. That gives it the aura of being mystical. Most religions and philosophies come from a single, humble human in ordinary surroundings.

But did he catch a fish? It is so easy to say everything will come out good if you believe it, but there has to be some proof.

Catching a fish with a paper clip with some gummy bread wrapped around it would be proof.

If he did not, doesn't that put the entire belief system into the field of, "That was nice to believe for a few minutes, but now let's get back to reality."

Some things you get, some you don't, and while it may have as much to do with your attitude as your paycheque, there are limits to believing that belief will make it so. Aren't there?

Getting what you want has something to do with how hard you work or how much planning you do or the weather on the day you go out to do whatever it is that you want to do. But eventually all the variables end and you either get it or you don't.

Belief that you are going to get it makes no difference. It is no different from holding onto a rabbit's foot. And if you are a rabbit missing a foot you know just how lucky those things are.

I never saw Reilly again. We got offers of fancy fishing equipment that we passed on to his foster mother by phone. But the reply was "No, thank you." Reilly said he would catch a fish his way.

I go to Trout Lake often and look at the water and watch the dogs swimming at one end and kids at the other. It is the smallest beach in the city. It has only a few spots where you can walk out on a wooden pier and put a line in the water.

I've seen other kids fishing and a few old timers. You can only fish there if you are very young or very old. I never saw Reilly again.

Maybe I missed him. Or maybe he moved on to another pond and another foster home.

But did he catch a fish? He said he would. He said he believed he would.

He had things to overcome, like no hook or float to tell him he had a nibble, or bait except for bread. He also had to overcome strange things that go on in the mind of autistic kids, like not being sure about things that most of us don't even think about, and the temper that flared up without warning that his foster mother told us about.

He also had that darn runny nose, and it is hard to concentrate on fishing when you are sniffing back nasal drippings.

I have only one thing on which to base my faith in Reilly's method: me.

Since I started getting up in the morning and saying: "This is going to be a good day," I have not had a bad day. Not one.

Okay, bad things have happened. Sometimes terrible things. But then they have gone away and good things happen. Sometimes I say I can't believe such a good thing has happened after such a bad thing. But it has.

Since I said I believed I would find something interesting to talk about, I have not missed a day.

Okay, some days have been close. Some days have been right down to the wire. Some days only strange and curious circumstances have led me to something that was right under my nose. But every day, something amazing has happened.

Since I said I believed I feel fine, I have not been sick, except for that darn day when my nose would not stop running and someone gave me a pill and fixed it.

Yes, I have sneezed and coughed and felt miserable other days. But like the people I have met who have not taken a day off from work for twenty or thirty years I feel better by my second cup of coffee and by lunch I'm as healthy as the people on TV commercials after they have taken their medicine.

It is good to feel better. It is better on the head and the stomach and the eyes. And when I say I feel good the rest of me follows and feels fine.

Since I said I would not worry when I went into a meeting because I believed it would turn out good, I have not had a moment of worry. I did not say I have not had any bad meetings.

Of course the meetings happen and they concern important things like contracts and unions and stories. And of course sometimes you hear things that you do not want to hear. But worry beforehand only hurts the stomach and if you believe the meeting will turn out good in the end, it does, or you have another meeting.

Two things I am sure about: Reilly eventually got a tissue to blow his nose. And the other, of course, is that he knows he will get a fish.

That is all there is to it. Say good things will happen. Believe what you say and watch it happen.

I watched a group of old men fishing at Como Lake in Coquitlam. They are there most summer days. Over the years their names change, but the wrinkled hands on the poles stay the same.

They are usually fancy poles with spinning reels and at the end of the line are sinkers to get their hooks out and floats to tell them when a trout has taken the bait.

But mostly they fish so they can be with others who are fishing.

"Carmine always catches something," said John, who was in the middle of three poles.

"Not true," said Carmine, who was to his left. "John gets more than me."

"No, it's Harry who is the real fishermen. But he is not here today," said Ken.

They were three races, from three countries.

"Anyone catch anything yet?" I asked.

"No," said Ken. "But we will. You know the trick, don't you?"

I thought he was going to say, "Believe and you catch one."

"The trick is to hold your tongue just right and the fish will bite."

Don't let anyone ever tell you positive thinking and belief in what you are doing has to be serious.

For the final time, like Reilly, you do not change reality. But you can change the way you see and deal with it. And then you can change everything.

And Reilly, you know as well as I and he, will get that fish.

And he will blow his nose.